STRANGE AND FASCINATING FACTS ABOUT WASHINGTON, D.C.

Fred L. Worth

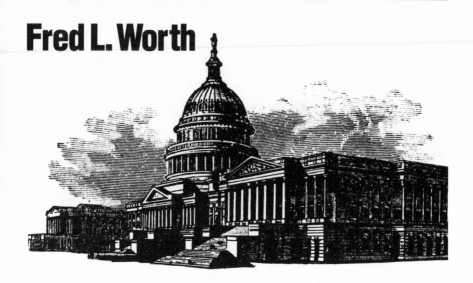

BELL BOOKS
New York

Dedicated to my uncle
BOB MERRITHEW

ACKNOWLEDGMENTS

I wish to thank my Uncle Bob, my mother, and Pam Larm for their help in making this book a reality.

Published in 1988 by Bell Publishing Company, distributed by Crown Publishers, Inc., 225 Park Avenue South, New York, New York 10003.

Printed and bound in the United States of America

Library of Congress Cataloging-in-Publication Data

Worth, Fred L.
  Strange and fascinating facts about Washington, D.C.

  1. Washington (D.C.)—Miscellanea.   I. Title.
F194.5.W67   1988   975.3   87-33672
ISBN 0-517-64113-5

h g f e d c b a

First Edition

CONTENTS

INTRODUCTION

Washington, D.C., wasn't the first capital of the United States. It was actually the tenth—after Baltimore, Philadelphia, Lancaster and then York (both in Pennsylvania), Philadelphia (again), Princeton, Annapolis, Trenton, and New York. In order to establish a new capital city that would be acceptable to both the North and the South, Congress decided to set aside 100 square miles of land in Maryland and Virginia. On December 23, 1788, the state of Maryland offered to cede an area on the Potomac River for the new Federal District. It was Paris-born Pierre Charles L'Enfant, a Revolutionary War officer, whom George Washington chose to design the Federal City, and it is his plan that the city's architects still follow in spirit today. In 1801 Congress assumed jurisdiction over the District of Columbia.

Washington is a showplace with its beautiful parks, historic buildings, numerous statues, memorials, and museums, and its vast history. It is a beautiful city, of which every American can be proud.

If you plan to visit Washington, D. C., you will want to read up on the city before you visit and, as there is so much to see, you will benefit from drawing up a plan. One hopes this book will help whet your appetite to see Washington, a city that every American should visit at least once in his or her life.

QUOTES FROM NOTABLES

"A city of Southern efficiency and Northern charm."
                                        John F. Kennedy

"A city of magnificent intentions."
                                        Charles Dickens

"A city of temporaries, a city of just-arrivals, and
only visiting, built on shifting sands of politics,
filled with people just passing through."
                                        Allen Drury

"I was delighted with the whole aspect of Washington,
light, cheerful and airy."
                                        Anthony Trollope

"The city of conversation."
                                        Henry James

"I believe there are scarcely any places in the world
more beautiful and better situated."
                                        De Graffenried

"This embryo, where Fancy sees Squares in morasses,
obelisks trees . . ."
                                        Thomas Moore

WASHINGTON'S ANNUAL EVENTS AND PRESIDENTIAL INAUGURATIONS

CALENDAR OF EVENTS

DATE	EVENT
January	
1	New Year's Day (federal holiday)
3	Congress Assembles
7	Millard Fillmore's Birthday
9	Richard M. Nixon's Birthday
Third Monday	Martin Luther King's Birthday (federal holiday)
20 (every four years)	Presidential Inauguration
29	William McKinley's Birthday
30	Franklin D. Roosevelt's Birthday
During month	Ice Show at the Capital Centre
	U.S. Army Annual Anniversary Concert
February	
1	National Freedom Day
2	Groundhog Day
6	Ronald Reagan's Birthday
9	William Henry Harrison's Birthday
12 (approximately)	Abraham Lincoln's Birthday (federal holiday)

DATE	EVENT
February	
14	Valentine's Day
22 (approximately)	George Washington's Birthday (federal holiday)
During month	Chinese New Year
	Washington International Boat Show
March	
15	Andrew Jackson's Birthday
16	James Madison's Birthday
17	St. Patrick's Day Parade (Constitution Avenue)
18	Grover Cleveland's Birthday
29	John Tyler's Birthday
During month	Easter (egg roll on White House lawn)
	Flower Show at D.C. National Armory
	Smithsonian Kite Festival (Washington Monument)
	Cherry Blossom Festival (or early April)
April	
13	Thomas Jefferson's Birthday
23	James A. Buchanan's Birthday
27	Ulysses S. Grant's Birthday
28	James Monroe's Birthday
Last Friday	Arbor Day
During month	Cherry Blossom Festival (or late March)
May	
1	May Day
8	Harry S Truman's Birthday
29	John F. Kennedy's Birthday
Second Sunday	Mother's Day
Third Saturday	Armed Forces Day
Last Monday	Memorial Day (federal holiday): Wreath-laying at Tomb of the Unknowns
Memorial Day Weekend	President's Cup Regatta
	Rodeo at the Capital Centre

DATE	EVENT
June	
21	Father's Day
During month	National Zoo Summerfest
	Outdoor Concerts, at the Jefferson Memorial, Capitol, Sylvan Theatre
	Potomac Riverfest
July	
4	Independence Day (federal holiday)
4	Calvin Coolidge's Birthday
11	John Quincy Adams's Birthday
14	Gerald Ford's Birthday
During month	Cracker Jack Old Times Baseball Classic
Wednesdays at 7 P.M.	Twilight Tattoo on the Ellipse
August	
10	Herbert Hoover's Birthday
20	Benjamin Harrison's Birthday
27	Lyndon B. Johnson's Birthday
September	
15	William Howard Taft's Birthday
First Sunday after Labor Day	Grandparent's Day
During month	Redskins open their football season
	Labor Day (federal holiday), Concert
	Rock Creek Park Day
October	
1	Jimmy (James E., Jr.) Carter's Birthday
1st Monday	Supreme Court convenes
4	Rutherford B. Hayes's Birthday
2nd Monday	Columbus Day (federal holiday)
14	Dwight D. Eisenhower's Birthday
24	United Nations Day
25	Chester A. Arthur's Birthday
27	Theodore Roosevelt's Birthday
30	John Adams's Birthday
31	Halloween
During month	International Urban Fair

DATE	EVENT
November	
2	Warren G. Harding's Birthday
2	James K. Polk's Birthday
11	Veteran's Day (federal holiday)
19	James A. Garfield's Birthday
23	Armistice Day
24	Zachary Taylor's Birthday
First Tuesday after first Monday	Election Day
Fourth Thursday	Thanksgiving Day
During month	International Horse Race at Laurel Racetrack
	Bullets Basketball season opens
December	
5	Martin Van Buren's Birthday
15	Bill of Rights Day
15	Lighting of the National Christmas Tree
17	Wright Brothers Day
21	Forefather's Day
25	Christmas Day (federal holiday)
29	Andrew Johnson's Birthday
28	Woodrow Wilson's Birthday
31	New Year's Eve
During month	Chanukah Festival
	Kwanzaa Celebration

PRESIDENTIAL INAUGURATIONS

There is no event that receives more attention in Washington than the inauguration of a new President or reelection of an incumbent. Inaugurations are celebrated with parades, the swearing in, inaugural balls, and parties, the costs of which run into millions of dollars.

January 20, every four years, is celebrated as the day of inauguration of a President, in Washington, D.C. Prior to 1937 the presidential inaugurations occurred on March 4 or, if that was a Sunday, on March 5. After 1937 the presidential inaugurations took place on January 20, to conform to the Twentieth Amendment.

The Presidential Oath

> "I do solemnly swear [or affirm] that I will faithfully execute
> the office of President of the United States, and will to the best
> of my ability, preserve, protect, and defend the Constitution of
> the United States."

- Since Andrew Jackson, all presidential inaugurations have taken place on the East Front of the Capitol, until Ronald Reagan held his inauguration on the West Front.
- On March 4, 1817, James Monroe took the oath of office on the steps of the "Brick Capitol," the city's first outdoor inaugural.
- Pierre L'Enfant, the designer of Washington, D.C., had previously designed Federal Hall, where in 1789 George Washington was sworn in as the first President of the United States.
- George Washington is the only U.S. President to have been inaugurated in two different cities, neither of which were Washington. His first inauguration took place in New York City in April 1789, and his second took place in Philadelphia in March 1793.
- George Washington needed to borrow money to attend his first inauguration.
- At George Washington's second inauguration, he spoke only 133 words, the shortest inaugural speech to date.
- Two Presidents were inaugurated in Philadelphia: George Washington and John Adams.
- On March 4, 1801, Thomas Jefferson walked from his boarding house to the Capitol for his inauguration, as the first President to be inaugurated in Washington, taking the oath in the Senate Chamber.
- The carriage built to transport Martin Van Buren to his inauguration on March 4, 1837, was constructed of timber from the dismantled ship U.S.S. *Constitution*.
- The second inauguration of James Monroe featured the first appearance of the Marine Corps Band in an official ceremony.
- Mrs. Eliza Garfield became the first woman to see her son inaugurated as President of the United States.
- Jane Pierce refused to attend her husband's inauguration, as she was in mourning over the death of their son Benjamin, who had died two months earlier in a train accident.
- William Henry Harrison, who served the shortest time as President (32 days), gave the longest inauguration speech (8,443 words), speaking for 1½ hours in a downpour. Ironically, standing in the rain contributed to his death.

- Franklin Pierce is the only President to use the word "affirm" rather than "swear" in his inauguration oath, March 4, 1853.
- It was while attending Franklin Pierce's inauguration in the bitter cold that First Lady Abigail Fillmore caught pneumonia, which led to her death later that month.
- At the time of Abraham Lincoln's inauguration, in March 1861, six Presidents were alive: besides Lincoln, there were Martin Van Buren, John Tyler, Franklin Pierce, Millard Fillmore, and James Buchanan.
- At Abraham Lincoln's second inauguration, on the Capitol steps on March 4, 1865, a photograph was taken of John Wilkes Booth standing on the balcony behind the President. Abraham Lincoln was the first President to be photographed at his inauguration.
- Outgoing President Andrew Johnson refused to ride with General Ulysses S. Grant in his inauguration parade.
- James K. Polk's inauguration, on March 4, 1845, was the first to be reported by telephone. The news of the event was sent over the wires by Samuel F. B. Morse himself.
- Calvin Coolidge's father, a notary public, administered the oath of office to his son on August 3, 1923.
- Grandstands were first constructed on Pennsylvania Avenue in 1885 for the inaugural parade of Grover Cleveland.
- Blacks first took part in an inauguration during Abraham Lincoln's first inauguration, when a battalion of black soldiers served as part of his escort.
- Lionel Hampton was the first black musician to play at a Presidential inauguration, when he performed for Harry S Truman in 1949.
- William Howard Taft weighed 332 pounds at his inauguration.
- One of the most spectacular parades was Theodore Roosevelt's 1905 Inauguration Parade with 35,000 participants, including Indians and Rough Riders.
- President Franklin D. Roosevelt was the first President to be inaugurated on January 20.

THE DISTRICT OF COLUMBIA

FACTS ABOUT THE DISTRICT OF COLUMBIA

ALSO CALLED

Washington, D.C.; Washington; the District; D.C.; the Federal City

AVERAGE MONTHLY TEMPERATURES

	High	Low
January	44	30
February	46	29
March	54	36
April	66	46
May	76	56
June	83	65
July	87	69
August	85	68
September	79	61
October	68	50
November	57	39
December	46	31

SEASONAL TEMPERATURES

	High	Low
Summer	86	67
Winter	45	29
Spring	66	56
Fall	69	50

AVERAGE YEARLY TEMPERATURE

High	Low
66	48

RAINFALL

39 inches average

SNOWFALL

17 inches average

ALTITUDE

Sea level to 420 feet

AREA

70 square miles

POPULATION (1980 CENSUS)

638,333, of which 295,417 were males and 342,916 were females

- By 1900 Washington had become the city with the largest black population in the world. Between 1950 and 1960 Washington's black population rose from 35 percent to 54 percent, becoming the first city outside Africa with a black majority. In 1960 Washington became the first major city to have a black majority. In 1980 83 percent of the workers were white, yet 70 percent of the residents of Washington were black.
- In 1950 the city reached its peak with a population of 800,000. There are over 3,000,000 people within the metropolitan area.

- Washington's population is larger than those of seven states of the Union: Alaska, Wyoming, North Dakota, South Dakota, Nevada, Delaware, and Vermont.
- For a number of years there has been a move to make Washington, D.C., a state, so that it would have its own representatives and senators. The name of the new state has been suggested to be New Columbia.

CITIZENS

Washingtonians

LIFESPAN

69.2 years is the average lifespan of a citizen, the shortest expected lifespan of any U.S. city.

PSYCHIATRISTS

Washington has more psychiatrists per capita than any other American city.

FLAG

The District introduced its own flag in 1938.

MOTTO

Justitia Omnibus ("Justice to All")

OFFICIAL TREE

Scarlet Oak

OFFICIAL FLOWER

American Beauty Rose

COST OF LIVING

Fifth most expensive city in the United States, surpassed only by Anchorage, Honolulu, Boston, and New York.

PER CAPITA INCOME

$12,039 (second only to Alaska)

TOURISTS

10 million a year, twelve for every resident

NAME ORIGIN

Named Washington after the first U.S. President, and District of Columbia in honor of Christopher Columbus.

History

The nation's capital was formed by land ceded to Congress from the states of Maryland, in 1788, and from Virginia, in 1789. Congress merged Washington and Georgetown into a territory that was to be ruled by a council of eleven men and an elected House of Delegates consisting of twenty-two men. Washington, D.C., was named the City of Washington on September 9, 1791. On December 1, 1800, it officially became the seat of government of the United States.

On May 3, 1802, it was incorporated, with the President of the United States appointing its first mayor. From 1812 to 1820, the mayor was elected by a council. From 1820 to 1871, the city's mayor was popularly elected. The city became a municipal corporation on February 21, 1871. On June 20, 1874, the territorial government of the District was abolished and replaced with a three-man commission appointed by the President. This change completely disenfranchised the citizens of the District. From 1948 to 1972, South Carolina's John McMillan chaired the House of District of Columbia Committee, ruling with an iron fist. In March 1961 the Twenty-third Amendment to the Constitution was ratified by the thirty-eighth state, Kansas, giving the residents of Washington the right to vote in national elections, as well as having three representatives to the electoral college. The citizens of Washington first voted in a national election on November 4, 1964. In 1967 the President was allowed to appoint a mayor and a nine-member council to govern the District. Congress passed a law in 1970 that allowed the District to have one delegate to the House of Representatives. Although allowed one vote on committees, the delegate cannot vote as a member of the House. The District's first delegate to Congress was black minister Walter Fauntroy.

In 1975 the Home Rule Referendum was passed, allowing the District to elect its own mayor and city council.

During the War of 1812, the British burned many of the government buildings of Washington, supposedly in retaliation for the American burning of the Canadian town of York (later to be named Toronto).

- On September 7, 1846, some of the land that had been ceded by Virginia in 1789 to form the capital was returned to the state.
- When the voters of Washington voted in the November 1968 elections for an eleven-member board of education, it was the first time in ninety-two years that Washingtonians had voted for local officials.
- Kathryn Sellers became the first female judge of a juvenile court when she was appointed in 1918 to serve on the Juvenile Court of the District of Columbia.
- President John F. Kennedy appointed the first black to serve on the three-man Board of Commissioners.
- In 1967 fifty-two-year-old housing expert Walter Washington was appointed by President Lyndon B. Johnson to serve as district commissioner (mayor). Washington became the first black mayor of a major U.S. city. In 1974 Washington became the first elected mayor of Washington.
- The District pays more taxes than does any one of eleven U.S. states.

District Building
1350 Pennsylvania Avenue, N.W.

Built in 1908, with a statue of Alexander R. "Boss" Shepherd standing outside, this is where the offices of the mayor of Washington, D.C., are located.

LAW ENFORCEMENT

There are more law enforcement officers per capita in Washington, D.C., than there are in any city within the United States, the largest concentration being in the Metropolitan Police Department, headquartered at 300 Indiana Avenue, N.W.

The following is an approximate breakdown of the city's law enforcement agencies:

5000+   municipal police officers
1100+   Capitol Police Force
850+   Executive Protection Service
500+   National Park Service officers
(including 28 saddle-horse positions)

Other law enforcement officials also operate within Washington, such as federal marshals, Secret Service agents, federal agents, and FBI agents, as well as the five law-enforcement agencies of the Treasury Department (Customs Service, Narcotics Bureau, IRS, Bureau of Alcohol, Tobacco, and Firearms, and the Secret Service).

- The White House Guards utilize German shepherds that can smell out explosives and drugs.
- Women were added to the Capitol Police Force in 1974.
- The city's first police force actually evolved from three watchmen and a sergeant, hired in 1825 to keep tourists from wandering the halls of the Capitol building at night. In 1851 the city had a total of 57 full-time police officers. Until August 6, 1861, when Congress created the Washington Metropolitan Police Force, the District had been protected by federal marshals.
- At the time of Abraham Lincoln's assassination, in 1865, it was not a federal crime to shoot a President. It was not until President William McKinley had been fatally shot in 1901 that the Secret Service was assigned to the complete and vigilant protection of the President of the United States. The Secret Service was originally created on June 23, 1860, to suppress counterfeiting of U.S. coins.
- Allan Pinkerton, who founded the first private detective agency, The Pinkertons, foiled an attempted assassination on President Abraham Lincoln's life in 1861.
- It was D.C. police officer William West who arrested President Ulysses S. Grant for speeding his horse and buggy on M Street. To stop the animal, West grabbed the reins and was dragged for half a city block. West apologized, after realizing it was the President, and wanted to let him go, but Grant insisted that he be given a ticket, ordering West to "do your duty."
- In 1979 thirty-six-year-old D.C. patrolman Ormus W. Davenport III made the national news when he underwent a sex-change operation, emerging as policewoman Bonnie Davenport.

- Some of the city's police officers drive Japanese-manufactured motorcycles.
- In 1932 Police Chief Pelham Glassford spent his own money to feed and house the World War I veterans who had marched into Washington to receive a much-needed bonus. Unfortunately, he was ordered, by President Herbert Hoover, to drive the protesters out of the city. The U.S. Army, led by General Douglas MacArthur, successfully drove the veterans out of Washington. Two of MacArthur's young officers were Major Dwight D. Eisenhower and Major George S. Patton.
- The only persons authorized to arrest the President of the United States are the sergeant at Arms of the U.S. Senate or one of his deputies.
- Policewoman Gail A. Cobb of the Washington, D.C., Police Department became the first policewoman in the United States to die in the line of duty, in September 1974.

A sample of some old laws that used to be on Washington's books include:

- If a black struck a white, a law in the District stated that the penalty was to have the black's ears chopped off. This law was overturned in 1862.
- In the city, it is against the law to punch a bull in the nose.
- It is illegal to fly a kite within Washington, D.C. (except on Kite Day).
- A city taxicab must carry a broom and a shovel.
- On May 28, 1908, the Congress passed legislation to regulate child labor within the District, in the hope that the individual states would follow their lead.
- Dueling in Washington was outlawed by an act of Congress on February 20, 1839, after New Hampshire Representative Jonathan Gilley had been killed in a duel near Anacostia Bridge.
- In 1978 a Washington, D.C., woman was found guilty of shoplifting two strawberries, and eating them, in a supermarket.

Blacks

Because many blacks had come to Washington during the Civil War as runaway slaves, free men seeking jobs, or as Union soldiers, the old black code of laws affecting them was abolished in Washington before any other American city. On January 11, 1836, James Buchanan of

Pennsylvania presented the Senate with petitions calling for the abolition of slavery in Washington, but it wasn't until September 16, 1850, that the Senate passed a bill that abolished the slave trade (33 to 19) within Washington. The next day, the House passed the bill (124 to 47). The twentieth President, Millard Fillmore, signed the bill into law, and slavery was abolished in Washington. On June 19, 1862, President Abraham Lincoln signed a law prohibiting slavery in U.S. Territories. On June 18, 1953, the U.S. Supreme Court ruled that restaurants within the District could not discriminate against the Negro. The District of Columbia has always attempted to set the example for the rest of the country when it came to laws of discrimination.

- Black surveyor Benjamin Banneker (1731–1806) assisted in mapping out Washington, beginning in 1789.
- Frederick Douglass served as a Washington councilman.
- John B. Duncan served as the first black commissioner from 1961 to 1967.
- On January 13, 1966, Robert C. Weaver, the Secretary of Housing, became the first black cabinet member.

The Columbia Historical Society
1307 New Hampshire Avenue, N.W.

Located here is a museum and library of books and maps all pertaining to the history of the District of Columbia.

OTHER WASHINGTON FACTS

- Since 1916 the Boundary Stones of the District of Columbia have been preserved by the Daughters of the American Revolution.
- Several Washington, D.C., women have won beauty contest titles:
Margaret Gorman won the Miss America title in 1921.
Venus Ramey won the Miss America title in 1944.
Stephanie Clarke won the Miss Black America title in 1970.
Twanna Kilgore won the Miss Black America title in 1976.

PREVIOUS NAMES USED FOR LOCATIONS IN WASHINGTON, D.C.

PRESENT	FORMER
Anacostia	Uniontown
Art and Industries Building	National Museum
Capitol	Congress House
Capitol Hill	Jenkins Hill
Departmental Auditorium	Inderdepartmental Auditorium
Dupont Circle	Pacific Circle
The Ellipse	White Lot
Gallaudet College	Kendall School/National Deaf Mute College
George Washington University	Columbian College
John Adams Building	Thomas Jefferson Building
Lady Bird Johnson Park	Columbia Island
Lafayette Park	President's Park
Malcolm X Park	Meridian Hill Park
Old Executive Office Building	State, War, and Navy Building
Organization of American States Building	Pan American Union
Peace Monument	Navy Monument
Reflecting Pool	The Lagoon
Theodore Roosevelt Island	My Lord's Island
Washington, D.C.	Territory of Columbia
White House	President's Palace/Executive Mansion
Willard Hotel	City Hotel

CHRONOLOGY

CHRONOLOGY OF WASHINGTON'S HISTORY

1732	Feb. 22	George Washington is born in Wakefield, Virginia.
1749		Lawrence Washington lays out the plan for Alexandria, Virginia.
1765		The Old Stone House is built.
1789	April 30	George Washington takes the oath of office as President (in New York City).
1790	July 16	The President was given the power to choose the location for the Federal City. Jenkins Hill is chosen for the site of the Capitol.
1793	April 15	Dr. William Thornton's design for the Capitol is selected.
	Sept. 18	George Washington lays the cornerstone of the Capitol.
1795	May	*Impartial Observer* and *Washington Advertiser,* Washington's first newspapers, are published.
1797		John Adams is inaugurated as President (in Philadelphia).
1798		Construction of the White House begins.
1799	Dec. 14	George Washington dies.

1800		The north wing of the Capitol is completed. Both the Senate and House move from Philadelphia. The Washington Navy Yard is built.
	June 3	President John Adams arrives in Washington, D.C.
	Nov. 17	The first session of Congress in Washington meets.
	Nov. 22	Members of both the Senate and House move into the new Capitol.
1801	May 3	Thomas Jefferson is inaugurated as the third President.
		The Supreme Court moves from Philadelphia.
		Washington is incorporated. The President appoints its first governor (mayor).
		Samuel Blodgett's *Thoughts on the Increasing Wealth and National Economy of the United States* becomes the first book published in Washington.
1809	March 4	James Madison is inaugurated as the fourth President.
1811		The new south wing of the Capitol is completed.
1814	Aug. 24	The British burn sections of Washington, including the White House.
1815	Feb. 3	A bill is passed to rebuild the federal buildings burned by the British.
	November	The Washington Canal is opened.
1817	March 4	James Monroe is inaugurated as the fifth President.
1819		The Capitol is re-occupied.
1820	May 15	Congress gives Washington, D.C., residents the right to vote.
1824	Dec. 9	Marquis de Lafayette is warmly welcomed in the House of Representatives on his first visit to the United States in forty years.
1825	March 4	John Quincy Adams is inaugurated as the sixth President.
		Architect Pierre L'Enfant dies at age 71.
1828	July 4	Construction begins on both the C&O Canal and the B&O Railroad.
1829	March 4	Andrew Jackson is inaugurated as the seventh President.

1835		The only year in history in which the United States did not have a national debt.
	Jan. 30	Andrew Jackson becomes the first President to have an assassination attempt made against him.
1837	March 4	Martin Van Buren is inaugurated as the eighth President.
1840		The B&O (Baltimore & Ohio) Railroad links the city of Washington to major rail arteries.
1841	March 4	William Henry Harrison is inaugurated as the ninth President.
	April 6	William Henry Harrison dies in office; Vice President John Tyler becomes the tenth President.
1844	Feb. 28	The Peacemaker gun on board the U.S.S. *Princeton* explodes, killing several people.
		A $25 icebox is installed in the White House.
1845	March 4	James K. Polk is inaugurated as the eleventh President.
1846		The Smithsonian Institution is founded.
		Congress passes an act that reduces the District of Columbia by one-third when Alexandria is reclaimed by the state of Virginia.
1847		A 16-foot lantern on a 75-foot pole is installed on top of the Capitol Dome.
	May 1	The cornerstone is laid for the Smithsonian Castle.
1848		Gas lighting is installed in the White House.
	July 4	The cornerstone is laid for the Washington Monument.
1849	March 4	Zachary Taylor is inaugurated as the twelfth President.
		The Petersen House is built.
1850	July 9	Zachary Taylor dies in office; Vice President Millard Fillmore becomes the thirteenth President.
1851	July 4	President Millard Fillmore lays the third cornerstone of the Capitol wearing the same Masonic apron that President Washington had worn in 1793.
		Fire destroys part of the Library of Congress.

1853	March 4	Franklin Pierce is inaugurated as the fourteenth President.
		A hot-water system is installed in the White House.
		Gas lamps are installed on Washington's main streets.
		Andrew Jackson's equestrian statue is dedicated. It is the first equestrian statue in the United States.
1857	March 4	James Buchanan is inaugurated as the fifteenth President.
	Dec. 16	First session of the House is held in the new south wing.
1859	Jan. 4	First session of the Senate is held in the new north wing.
1861	March 4	Abraham Lincoln is inaugurated as the sixteenth President.
	Aug. 6	Congress creates the Metropolitan Police Department.
1862	April 16	Slavery is outlawed in the District of Columbia.
1863	Dec. 2	The statue of *Freedom* is bolted into place atop the Capitol dome.
1864	July 2	Statuary Hall in the Capitol is established.
1865	April 5	Plumbing and steam heat are installed in the Capitol.
		The cast-iron dome of the Capitol is completed, replacing the old wood dome.
	April 14	Abraham Lincoln is shot, and Vice President Andrew Johnson becomes the seventeenth President.
	April 15	President Lincoln dies.
1869	March 4	Ulysses S. Grant is inaugurated as the eighteenth President.
		Some politicians suggest that the nation's capital be moved. New sites mentioned are St. Louis, Kansas City, Chicago, and Cincinnati.
		Howard University is opened.
1871		The Federal District is officially named the City of Washington.
1874		The first elevators are installed in the Capitol.
		Chain Bridge is built.

1874	June 2	President Ulysses S. Grant lays the cornerstone for the American Museum of Natural History.
1877	March 4	Rutherford B. Hayes is inaugurated as the nineteenth President.
		The first telephone is installed in Washington.
1878	May 10	The first telephone in the White House is installed in the Oval Office—the telephone number is "1."
1879		The first apartment house is constructed in Washington.
1881	March 4	James A. Garfield is inaugurated as the twentieth President.
		The Capitol is fireproofed.
		The first electric light is installed in Washington.
	Sept. 20	President Garfield dies in office; Vice President Chester A. Arthur becomes the twenty-first President.
1882		An elevator is installed in the White House.
1884	Dec. 6	A ceremony is held to install the capstone of the Washington Monument.
1885	March 4	Grover Cleveland is inaugurated as the twenty-second President.
1888		Washington runs its first electric streetcar.
1889	March 4	Benjamin Harrison is inaugurated as the twenty-third President.
1890		The cornerstone of the Library of Congress is laid.
1892		Electricity is installed in the White House.
1893	March 4	Grover Cleveland is inaugurated as the twenty-fourth President.
1897	March 4	William McKinley is inaugurated as the twenty-fifth President.
1900		The Capitol is completely rewired for electricity.
1901	Sept. 14	William McKinley is assassinated; Vice President Theodore Roosevelt becomes the twenty-sixth President.
1907		President Roosevelt lays the cornerstone for the Washington Cathedral.
		Union Station is completed.
1909	March 4	William Howard Taft is inaugurated as the twenty-seventh President.

1910	April 14	President Taft begins the tradition of the President throwing out the first ball of the baseball season.
1912	March 27	First Lady Helen Taft and Japan's Viscountess Chundi plant the first two cherry trees of Japan's gift to Washington.
1913	March 4	Woodrow Wilson is inaugurated as the twenty-eighth President.
1920		Arlington Memorial Amphitheater is dedicated.
1921	March 4	Warren G. Harding is inaugurated as the twenty-ninth President.
1922	April 27	The equestrian statue of General Ulysses S. Grant at the East Mall is dedicated.
1923	Aug. 3	Warren G. Harding dies in office. Vice President Calvin Coolidge becomes the thirtieth President.
1924		Key Bridge is built. The American Indians are granted American citizenship.
1929	March 4	Herbert Hoover is inaugurated as the thirty-first President. Air conditioning is installed in the Capitol.
1930		Howard Taft becomes the first President interred in Arlington National Cemetery.
1931		"The Star-Spangled Banner" is adopted as the National Anthem of the United States.
	Nov. 12	The cornerstone for the new United States Botanic Gardens is laid.
1932		The Folger Shakespeare Library opens.
1933	March 4	Franklin D. Roosevelt is inaugurated as the thirty-second President.
1935		The Supreme Court moves from the Old Senate Chamber into the new Supreme Court Building. National Archives Building is completed. The Cherry Blossom Festival is celebrated for the first time.
1936	Nov. 23	Fluorescent lighting is used commercially for the first time, introduced at a dinner to celebrate the centenary of the U.S. Patent Office.
1943		The Jefferson Memorial is dedicated.

1943	Jan.	The Pentagon office building is completed.
1945	April 12	Franklin D. Roosevelt dies in office; Vice President Harry S Truman becomes the thirty-third President.
1951		Both the Senate and House chambers are modernized.
1952		Closets are added to the White House.
1953	Jan. 20	Dwight D. Eisenhower is inaugurated as the thirty-fourth President.
1959		The Capitol building's midsection is moved outward 32.5 feet, increasing its office space by 102 rooms.
	July 4	President Eisenhower lays the cornerstone for the Capitol extension.
1960	Jan. 20	John F. Kennedy is inaugurated as the thirty-fifth President.
1962		The East Front extension of the Capitol is completed.
1963	Nov. 22	President Kennedy is assassinated; Vice President Lyndon B. Johnson becomes the thirty-sixth President.
1969	Jan. 20	Richard M. Nixon is inaugurated as the thirty-seventh President.
1972	June 17	Seven men are arrested for breaking into the Watergate complex.
1974	Aug. 9	President Nixon leaves office; Vice President Gerald Ford becomes the thirty-eighth President.
1975	May	The Old Supreme Court Chamber in the Capitol is restored to its 1860 setting, at a cost of approximately $480,000.
1977	Jan. 20	James Earl "Jimmy" Carter is inaugurated as the thirty-ninth President.
1981	Jan. 20	Ronald Reagan is inaugurated as the fortieth President.

THE CAPITOL

The Capitol of the Congress of the United States is situated on Capitoline Hill, formerly called Jenkins Hill, but more popularly known as Capitol Hill. (The original Capitoline Hill is located in Rome, Italy.) Washington's architect Pierre L'Enfant referred to it as a "pedestal waiting for a monument," and to the Capitol as "the Congress House." The Indian chief Powhatan once lived in a village located at what is today the foot of Capitol Hill.

The structure itself, which measures 751 feet long by 350 feet wide, has 540 rooms over 16½ acres of floor space, with 139 chimneys on the roof. No structure in Washington, by law, can be built higher. The Capitol was designed by a physician, Dr. William Thornton, who, in 1792, won the contest to determine the best design, as well as $500.

The location of the building's original cornerstone, laid by President George Washington on September 18, 1793, is unknown, having been lost in the remodelings and expansions. A silver plate at the cornerstone had marked the Masonic year of 5793, also the thirteenth year of American independence and the first year of Washington's second term. Congress, then made up of 32 Senators and 106 Representatives, held its first session in the new Capitol on November 17, 1800.

There are more than 670 works of art within the Capitol, including 132 portraits; 54 paintings; 102 statues; 90 reliefs; 80 busts; 137 frescoes, murals, and lunettes; 29 exterior works; and 57 miscellaneous works, including clocks, vases, and fountains.

The Capitol is connected to the congressional office buildings by an underground subway, which takes the congressmen to and from their offices in only a few minutes.

- The state capitol in Austin, Texas, is seven feet taller than that of the Capitol in Washington. It is the only state capitol that is taller.
- The Capitol has appeared on the reverse side of the fifty-dollar bill since 1929, with President Ulysses S. Grant on the front.
- Although the Capitol's original cornerstone plaque has been lost, there is another plaque commemorating that original.

Capitol Dome

This impressive dome was inspired by the world's first iron dome, at St. Isaac's Cathedral in Leningrad. The height of the Capitol dome was originally established by Congress, because that was as high as the fire department's equipment could reach.

At the top of the Capitol dome stands a 19 ½-foot-tall, 7½-ton bronze statue of *Freedom,* originally named by its sculptor, Thomas Crawford, *Freedom Triumphant.* The top of the statue stands 287 feet, 5½ inches above the ground. Thomas Crawford sculpted the statue at the Bladensburg Road Foundry with the help of slave labor.

The statue was erected on December 2, 1863, in five sections because of its great weight, and on the day of its dedication it received a 32-gun salute. At the base of the statue is inscribed "E Pluribus Unum" ("Out of Many, One"), the motto on the great seal of the United States.

- *Freedom* appeared on the front of the U.S. five-dollar notes first issued in 1861. A portrait of the first Secretary of the Treasury, Alexander Hamilton, appeared to *Freedom's* right.
- Originally *Freedom* was to have worn a folded cloth Liberty cap until Secretary of War Jefferson Davis protested, since the same cap had been worn by freed slaves in Rome.
- In the 1956 science-fiction movie *Earth Versus the Flying Saucers,* a spacecraft crashed into the building's dome.

House Chamber

This wing of the Capitol measures 139 feet long and 93 feet wide, and was first used on December 16, 1857. It is one of the largest legislative rooms in the world. Republicans sit to the Speaker's left while Democrats sit to the right. In 1912 the total membership of the House was fixed at 435. The national census, taken every ten years, adjusts the apportionment of representatives. In the ceiling are the seals of the fifty states arranged in their order of entry into the Union.

The House Mace is the symbol used by the Sergeant at Arms, to restore order. To date it has only been used on a few occasions. The Mace is 46 inches long and consists of thirteen black knobs bound with strips of silver, with an eagle sitting on a solid silver globe at the top. The Mace was adopted by the House during their first session in 1789.

The House Chamber has been the site of the following presidential inaugurations: James Madison (1809 and 1813); James Monroe (1813); John Quincy Adams (1825); Andrew Jackson (1833); Millard Fillmore (1850).

On the wall behind the rostrum, and to the right of the Speaker of the House, hangs John Vanderlyn's portrait of George Washington, while to the left hangs Ary Scheffer's portrait of the Marquis de Lafayette.

Located over the gallery doors are twenty-three marble relief portraits of the lawgivers who advanced human freedoms throughout history.

Hammurabi	Papinian	de Montfort	Pothier
Solon	Justinian I	St. Louis	Blackstone
Moses	Tribonian	Alphonso X	Mason
Gaius	Maimonides	Edward I	Napoleon I
Lycurgus	Gregory IX	Suleiman I	Jefferson
Colbert	Innocent III	Grotius	

In order to be elected to the House, one must be over the age of twenty-five, have been a citizen of the United States for at least seven years, and be a resident of the state in which one is running for office.

- The House Chamber utilizes a system of bells, as does the Senate, to call its members. The House bells are as follows:

1 Bell	Teller vote
2 Bells	Roll call
3 Bells	Call of the House
4 Bells	Adjournment
5 Bells	Recess

  A system of lights uses the same code.
- There are 50 pages assigned to the House. These young men and women range from ages fourteen to eighteen.
- On March 1, 1954, five congressmen were wounded when three Puerto Rican nationalists fired onto the House floor, wounding Michigan Republican Alvin M. Bentley, Iowa Republican Benjamin F. Jensen, Tennessee Democrat Clifford Davis, Maryland

Democrat George H. Fallon, and Alabama Democrat Kenneth A. Roberts.

- On two occasions in its history, the House of Representatives has elected the President of the United States: Thomas Jefferson in 1801, and John Quincy Adams in 1825.
- In 1868 the House impeached President Andrew Johnson, but he was found not guilty in the Senate, by just one vote.
- Former President John Quincy Adams, once a member of the House, died there on February 23, 1848.

SPEAKERS OF THE HOUSE

From April 1789, when Frederick A. C. Muhlenberg of Pennsylvania was elected as the Speaker of the House, there has been a total of forty-nine Speakers to the present Jim Wright. Portraits of the Speakers of the House can be viewed in the Speaker's lobby, located behind the House Chamber.

- Theodore Sedgwick served as the first Speaker of the House in Washington, D.C.
- Sam Rayburn of Texas served as Speaker over the longest period, more than seventeen years.
- John W. McCormack of Massachusetts served the longest continuous series of terms, with nine consecutive years.
- Thomas Pomeroy of New York served the shortest term with just one day, March 3, 1869.
- James K. Polk was the only Speaker of the House to be elected President of the United States.
- Schuyler Colfax and John Nance Garner were the only two Speakers to become Vice President.
- Speaker Robert C. Winthrop was a direct descendent of John Winthrop, the first governor of the Massachusetts Bay Colony.
- Speaker of the House William Bankhead was the father of actress Tallulah Bankhead.
- Speaker of the House Joseph G. Cannon was the first person to be featured on a cover of *Time* magazine: Vol. 1, No. 1, March 3, 1923.

Senate Chamber

The U.S. Senate met in their chamber for the first time on January 4, 1859, having moved there from the smaller Old Senate Chamber. Today,

Senators sit at the same desks as did John C. Calhoun, Daniel Webster, and Henry Clay. The majority sits on the right of the Senate's presiding officer, the Vice President, and the minority sits to the left.

The newer Senators sit in the back row. As they gain seniority they can move to desks closer to the front rostrum. Senators who retire are allowed to keep the chair in which they sat during their term or terms.

The Senate Chamber has been the site of the presidential inaugurations of both Thomas Jefferson (1801) and William Howard Taft (1909).

In order to be elected a U.S. Senator, one must be at least thirty years old, have been a citizen of the United States for at least seven years, and be a resident of the state in which one is running for office.

- There are 100 Senators, each state having two. Senators serve six-year terms.
- There are 26 pages assigned to the Senate, ranging in age from fourteen to eighteen.
- Women were not allowed on the floor of the Senate until the 1830s.
- The Senate's system of bells has different meanings from that of the House.

1 bell	Roll call
2 bells	Quorum call
3 bells	Absentee call
4 bells	Adjournment or recess
5 bells	Executive session
6 bells	Legislative session

  A system of lights uses the same code.
- Busts of the Vice Presidents can be seen in the gallery hallways. The tradition was first introduced in 1886.

Old Senate Chamber

It was in this chamber that Congress first conducted its business, beginning in 1800. Today, the room is a showcase of some of the statues given by the different states. The desk where Henry Clay sat is depicted by a mark on the floor. At this spot the whispering from a number of feet away can clearly be heard, leading to speculation that Clay could hear exactly what his opponents were saying, without their knowledge. The room was refurbished for the 1976 Bicentennial. Clio, the muse of history, is sculpted over the clock on the wall.

- In 1808 an arch collapsed in the Chamber, killing John Lenthal, the Clerk of Works.

Old Supreme Court Chamber

This semicircular room was restored under the direction of the Senate Commission on Art and Antiquities, in 1976, headed by the Architect of the Capitol, George M. White, with reproductions of the desks, chairs, and lamps used in the mid-1800s. This was the Chamber of the United States Supreme Court from 1800 until 1935, when it was moved into the new Supreme Court Building across the street from the Capitol.

Basement (the Crypt)

The basement, which had originally been planned to contain the crypt of George Washington, is now a museum for the Capitol and features a plastic model of the Capitol building.

On May 24, 1844, from the basement of the Capitol, Samuel F. B. Morse sent the world's first telegraph message, "What hath God wrought?"* to his assistant Alfred Vail at the Mount Clare Station of the B&O Railroad station, forty miles away in Baltimore. The returning question was "What is the news in Washington?" Two witnesses to the event that day were Henry Clay and Dolley Madison.

Rotunda

In the Rotunda of the Capitol are located many pieces of art, paintings, frescoes, and sculptures. In the canopy of the dome is the 4,664-square-foot fresco *The Apotheosis of George Washington,* executed by Constantino Brumidi in 1865.

A 300-foot frieze is located 58 feet above the floor with eighteen different scenes running clockwise around the Rotunda's dome. The following scenes, created by Constantino Brumidi over a period of three years, depict:

Landing of Columbus	1492
Cortez enters the Halls of Montezuma	1521
Pizarro's conquest of Peru	1533
The burial of De Soto	1542
John Smith's life saved by Pocahontas	1607
The landing of the Pilgrims	1620
William Penn making a treaty with the Indians	1682
The Plymouth Colony	1620
Governor Oglethorpe and the Indians	1732

*"What hath God wrought?" was selected by Annie Ellsworth, the daughter of the Commissioner of Patents.

The Battle of Lexington	1775
The reading of the Declaration of Independence	1776
The surrender of Cornwallis at Yorktown	1781
The death of Tecumseh	1813
General Scott entering Mexico City	1847
Discovery of gold in California	1848
The Civil War	1865
The Spanish-American War	1898
The Birth of Aviation	1903

It was while working on the scene of William Penn making a treaty with the Indians that Brumidi, one day in 1880, slipped from his ladder and hung on by his hands to the scaffolding for approximately fifteen minutes before he could be rescued. Brumidi died later that year. Filippo Costaggini, his assistant, continued his work, from 1880 to 1888, crowding the remaining scenes into a smaller space. The last three scenes were completed by Allyn Cox in 1953.

In the scene of John Smith and Pocahontas, one of the Indians has six toes, and Miles Standish has oversized feet. Brumidi also painted his own face into one of the trees out of protest, because of his salary dispute with Congress.

There are eight paintings in the Rotunda:

Baptism of Pocahontas at Jamestown, Virginia, 1613
   (Painted by John G. Chapman in 1840)
Declaration of Independence in Congress, at the Independence Hall, Philadelphia, July 4, 1776
   (Painted by John Trumbull in 1824)
Discovery of the Mississippi by De Soto, A.D. 1541
   (Painted by W. H. Powell in 1853)
Embarkation of the Pilgrims at Delft Haven, Holland, July 22, 1620
   (Painted by Robert W. Weir in 1843)
General George Washington Resigning His Commission to Congress as Commander in Chief of the Army at Annapolis, Maryland, December 23, 1783.
   (Painted by John Trumbull in 1824)
Landing of Columbus at the Island of Guanahani, West Indies, October 12, 1492
   (Painted by John Vanderlyn in 1847)
Surrender of General Burgoyne at Saratoga, New York, October 17, 1777
   (Painted by John Trumbull in 1822)

Surrender of Lord Cornwallis at Yorktown, Virginia, October 19, 1781
(Painted by John Trumbull in 1820)

- The painting of the signing of the Declaration of Independence by John Trumbull has several inaccuracies. Of the forty-seven men shown, five did not sign the document and, in addition, fourteen men who actually signed were left out.
- Trumbull's painting of the signing of the Declaration of Independence appears on the back of the U.S. two-dollar bill.

In the Rotunda stands Gutzon Burglum's statue of Abraham Lincoln. Burglum made the statue without a left ear as a symbol of Lincoln's incomplete life, cut short by assassination.

To date (1987), twenty-five people have lain in state in the Capitol's Rotunda.

Henry Clay	Speaker of the House	July 1, 1825
Abraham Lincoln	President	April 19 to 21, 1865
Thaddeus Stevens	Representative	August 13 to 14, 1868
Charles Sumner	Senator	March 13, 1874
Henry Wilson	Vice President	November 25 to 26, 1875
James A. Garfield	President	September 21 to 23, 1881
John A. Logan	Senator	December 30 to 31, 1886
William McKinley	President	September 17, 1901
Pierre L'Enfant	Architect	April 28, 1909
George Dewey	Admiral	January 20, 1917
Unknown soldier of World War I		November 9 to 11, 1921
Warren G. Harding	President	August 8, 1923
William Howard Taft	Senator	March 11, 1930
John J. Pershing	General	July 18 to 19, 1948
Robert A. Taft	Senator	August 2 to 3, 1953
Unknown Soldier of World War II		May 28 to 30, 1958
Unknown solder of Korean War		May 28 to 30, 1958
John F. Kennedy	President	November 24 to 25, 1963
Douglas MacArthur	General	April 8 to 9, 1964
Herbert C. Hoover	President	October 23 to 25, 1964
Dwight D. Eisenhower	President	March 30 to 31, 1969
Everett Dirksen	Senator	September 9 to 10, 1969

J. Edgar Hoover	FBI Director	May 3 to 4, 1972
Lyndon B. Johnson	President	January 24 to 25, 1973
Hubert H. Humphrey	Vice President	January 14 to 15, 1978

- Henry Clay, in 1852 was the first person to lie in state in the Rotunda. Abraham Lincoln was the first President.
- The only father and son to both lie in state in the Rotunda were William Howard Taft and his son Robert Taft.
- The catafalque used for the deceased Presidents laid in state was to have been used for George Washington's tomb, which was originally to have been located in the basement of the Capitol. The catafalque is on display in the basement.
- Pierre Charles L'Enfant lay in state in April 1909, 84 years after he died in 1825.
- Although there have been twenty-five people who have lain in state in the Rotunda, officially there have been only twenty-four. The Unknowns of World War II and the Korean War were laid in state together, having been counted as one person.

Statuary Hall (Old House Wing)

Located here, in the room in which the House met from 1807 until 1857, are the majority of the statues of the American Hall of Fame. These ninety-two statues of famous Americans were contributed by the states themselves to honor their favorite sons and daughters. A list follows at the end of this chapter.

INAUGURATIONS AT THE CAPITOL

Traditionally, Presidential inaugurations take place on the steps of the Capitol so that the American public can witness their newly elected President being sworn into office. The Capitol has not always been the site of swearing-in of the Presidents—some were sworn into office in the House of Representatives, some in the Senate, several in the White House, and others in different parts of the country after the death of their predecessor.

- In 1817 James Madison became the first President to be inaugurated on the East Portico. In 1841 William Henry Harrison became the second President to be inaugurated there.
- The East Portico has been used by Presidents James K. Polk, Zachary Taylor, Franklin Pierce, James Buchanan, Abraham Lincoln, Ulysses S. Grant, Rutherford B. Hayes (officially), James A.

Garfield, Grover Cleveland, Benjamin Harrison, William McKinley, Theodore Roosevelt (second term), Woodrow Wilson, Warren G. Harding, Calvin Collidge (second term), Herbert Hoover, Franklin D. Roosevelt (first three terms), Harry S Truman, and Dwight D. Eisenhower.

- John F. Kennedy was the first to use the East Front of the Capitol, which had just been renovated, followed by Lyndon B. Johnson in his first full term, Richard M. Nixon, and Jimmy Carter.
- In 1981 Ronald Reagan became the first President to be sworn in on the west side of the Capitol.

100TH CONGRESS FACTS:

Began in January 1987
House: 412 males and 23 females
Senate: 98 males and 2 females
Tallest: Tom McMillen at 6 feet, 11 inches tall
Shortest: Barbara Mikulski, 4 feet, 11 inches tall
Oldest: Claude Pepper, at eighty-six years old
Youngest: John Rowland at twenty-nine years old

HALL OF FAME STATUES

Alabama

Jabez Lamar Monroe Curry (1825–1903). Soldier, Representative, and member of the Confederate Congress. Sculpted by Dante Sodini, the 7 foot 4 inch marble statue, dedicated in 1908, is located in the Hall of Columns.

General Joseph Wheeler (1836–1906). Lawyer, Confederate soldier, and Representative. Sculpted by Berthold Nebel, this 7-foot-tall bronze statue, dedicated in 1925, is located in Statuary Hall.

Alaska

Edward Lewis "Bob" Bartlett (1904–1968). "Architect of Alaska Statehood," Secretary of Alaska, Senator, and reporter. Sculpted by Felix W. de Weldon, the 8 foot, 6 inch bronze statue, dedicated in 1971, is located in the House connecting corridor.

Arizona

John Campbell Greenway (1872–1926). Brigadier General, a member of the Rough Riders, mining engineer, and inventor of the turbo log washer. Sculpted by Gutzon Borglum, the 8-foot 2-inch bronze statue, dedicated in 1930, is located in the Statuary Hall.

Father Eusebio Francisco Kino (1645–1711). Jesuit missionary, explorer, founder of twenty-four missions, and historian. Sculpted by Suzanne Silvercruys, the 7-foot 8-inch bronze statue, dedicated in 1965, is located in the Hall of Columns.

Arkansas

Uriah M. Rose (1834–1913). Author of *Arkansas Constitution* and *Digest of Arkansas Report;* lawyer. Sculpted by Frederic W. Ruckstuhll, the 7-foot 6-inch marble statue, dedicated in 1917, is located in the Statuary Hall.

James Paul Clarke (1854–1916). Governor of Arkansas, Senator, and President pro tempore of the Senate. Sculpted by Pompeo Coppini, the 6-foot 10-inch marble statue, dedicated in 1921, is located in the Hall of Columns.

California

Thomas Starr King (1824–1864). Ordained minister; patriot. Sculpted by Haig Patigian, the 7-foot 2-inch bronze statue, dedicated in 1931, is located in the Hall of Columns.

Junípero Serra (1713–1784). Franciscan friar; founder of nine missions. Sculpted by Ettore Cadorin, the 8-foot, 9-inch bronze statue, dedicated in 1931, is located in Statuary Hall.

Colorado

Dr. Florence Rena Sabin (1871–1953). Teacher and scientist; she helped women enter the National Academy of Sciences and Johns Hopkins Medical School; faculty member of Rockefeller Institute for Medical Research; she helped to enact the Sabin Health Laws of Colorado. Sculpted by Joy Flinsch Buba, the 5-foot, 3-inch bronze statue, dedicated in 1959, is located in Statuary Hall.

Connecticut

Roger Sherman (1721–1793). Representative, Senator, and signer of the Declaration of Independence. The 7-foot 11-inch marble statue, sculpted by Chauncey B. Ives and dedicated in 1872, is located in Statuary Hall.

Jonathan Trumbull (1710–1785). Governor, aide to General Washington, and minister. Sculpted by Chauncey B. Ives, the 8-foot 1-inch marble statue, dedicated in 1872, is located in the House connecting corridor.

Delaware

Caesar Rodney (1728–1784). President of Delaware, patriot, and signer of the Declaration of Independence. Sculpted by Bryant Baker, his 7-foot 5-inch marble statue, dedicated in 1934, is located in Statuary Hall.

John Middleton Clayton (1796–1856). Senator, Representative, and Secretary of State. Sculpted by Bryant Baker, his 7-foot 6-inch marble statue, dedicated in 1934, is located in the Senate connecting corridor.

Florida

Dr. John Gorrie (1803–1855). Physician who was the first to patent mechanical refrigeration. Sculpted by Charles Adrian Pillars, the 7-foot 6-inch marble statue, dedicated in 1914, is located in Statuary Hall.

General Edmund Kirby-Smith (1824–1893). Teacher, and soldier in the War with Mexico. Sculpted by Charles Adrian Pillars, the 7-foot 5-inch bronze statue, dedicated in 1922, is located in the Hall of Columns.

Georgia

Dr. Crawford Williamson Long (1815–1878). Surgeon and humanitarian. Sculpted by John Massey Rhind, the 7-foot 2-inch marble statue, dedicated in 1926, is located in the Senate connecting corridor.

Alexander H. Stephens (1812–1883). Governor, U.S. Representative, and author of *A Constitutional View of the Late War Between the States*. Sculpted by Gutzon Borglum, the 5-foot 8-inch marble statue, dedicated in 1927, is located in Statuary Hall.

Hawaii

King Kamehameha I (1758–1819). Designed the flag that became the symbol of the state of Hawaii. Sculpted by Thomas R. Gould, the 8-foot 7-inch bronze statue, dedicated in 1969, is located in Statuary Hall.

Father Damien (1840–1889). "The Martyr of Molokai," devoted himself to the leper colony on the island. Sculpted by Marisol Escobar, the 7-foot 7-inch bronze statue, dedicated in 1969, is located in the Hall of Columns.

Idaho

George L. Shoup (1836–1904). Governor, Senator, and soldier. Sculpted by Frederick Ernest Triebel, the 7-foot 7-inch marble statue, dedicated in 1910, is located in Statuary Hall.

William Edgar Borah (1865–1940). Lawyer, Senator, "Loan Lion of Idaho." Sculpted by Bryant Baker, the 7-foot 2-inch bronze statue, dedicated in 1947, is located in the Senate connecting corridor.

Illinois

General James Shields (1810–1879). Brigadier General, Governor, and Senator. Sculpted by Leonard Wells Volk, the 7-foot 6-inch bronze statue, dedicated in 1893, is located in the Hall of Columns.

Frances E. Willard (1839–1898). Founder of World's Christian Temperance Union, educator, and journalist. Sculpted by Helen Farnsworth Mears, the 7-foot 1-inch marble statue, dedicated in 1905, is located in Statuary Hall.

Indiana

Oliver Perry Morton (1823–1877). Senator and Lieutenant Governor. Sculpted by Charles H. Niehaus, the 7-foot 6-inch marble statue, dedicated in 1900, is located in the Hall of Columns.

General Lewis "Lew" Wallace (1827–1905). Major General, Senator, author of *Ben Hur* and lawyer. Sculpted by Andrew O'Connor, the 6-foot 10-inch marble statue, dedicated in 1910, is located in Statuary Hall.

Iowa

James Harlan (1820–1899). Senator, statesman, and educator. Sculpted by Nellie V. Walker, the 8-foot 4-inch bronze statue, dedicated in 1910, is located in the Hall of Columns.

Samuel Jordan Kirkwood (1813–1894). Attorney, Senator, Secretary of the Interior, and Governor. Sculpted by Vinnie Ream, the 7-foot 4-inch bronze statue, dedicated in 1913, is located in Statuary Hall.

Kansas

John James Ingalls (1833–1900). Lieutenant Colonel, lawyer, and statesman. Sculpted by Charles H. Niehaus, the 7-foot 5-inch marble statue, dedicated in 1905, is located in Statuary Hall.

George Washington Glick (1827–1911). Governor, lawyer, and farmer. Sculpted by Charles H. Niehaus, the 7-foot 5-inch marble statue, dedicated in 1914, is located in the Hall of Columns.

Kentucky

Henry Clay (1777–1852). Secretary of State, Senator, Representative, statesman. Sculpted by Charles H. Niehaus, the 7-foot 2-inch bronze statue, dedicated in 1929, is located in Statuary Hall.

Dr. Ephraim McDowell (1771–1830). Physician who performed the first ovariotomy operation. Sculpted by Charles H. Niehaus, the 7-foot 4-inch bronze statue, dedicated in 1929, is located in the Senate connecting corridor.

Louisiana

Huey Pierce Long (1893–1935). Governor, Senator, and state railroad commissioner. Sculpted by Charles Keck, the 6-foot 8-inch bronze statue, dedicated in 1941, is located in Statuary Hall.

Edward Douglass White (1845–1921). Chief Justice, Senator, and soldier. Sculpted by Arthur Morgan, the 7-foot 1-inch bronze statue, dedicated in 1955, is located in the Senate connecting corridor.

Maine

William King (1768–1852). First Governor of Maine, and industrialist. Sculpted by Franklin Simmons, the 7-foot 5-inch marble statue, dedicated in 1878, is located in the House connecting corridor.

Hannibal Hamlin (1809–1891). Vice President, Governor, Senator, and Representative. Sculpted by Charles E. Tefft, the 6-foot 8-inch bronze statue, dedicated in 1935, is located in Statuary Hall.

Maryland

Charles Carroll of Carrollton (1737–1832). Signer of the Declaration of Independence, Senator, and patriot. Sculpted by Richard E. Brooks, the 7-foot 6-inch bronze statue, dedicated in 1903, is located in Statuary Hall.

John Hanson (1721–1783). Senator, patriot, and signer of the Articles of Confederation. Sculpted by Richard E. Brooks, the 7-foot 9-inch bronze statue, dedicated in 1903, is located in the Senate connecting corridor.

Massachusetts

Samuel Adams (1722–1803). Lieutenant Governor, Governor, and signer of the Declaration of Independence, "Father of the American Revolution." Sculpted by Anne Whitney, the 7-foot 8-inch marble statue, dedicated in 1876, is located in Statuary Hall.

John Winthrop (1588–1649). First Governor, author, lawyer, and colonizer. Sculpted by Richard S. Greenough, the 7-foot 8-inch marble statue, dedicated in 1876, is located in the Hall of Columns.

Michigan

Lewis Cass (1782–1866). Secretary of State, Brigadier General, and Governor. Sculpted by Daniel Chester French, the 7-foot 8-inch marble statue, dedicated in 1889, is located in Statuary Hall.

Zachariah Chandler (1813–1879). Senator, Secretary of Interior; helped in organizing the Republican Party. Sculpted by Charles H. Niehaus, the 7-foot 7-inch marble statue, dedicated in 1913, is located in the Hall of Columns.

Minnesota

Henry Mower Rice (1817–1894). Statesman, businessman, and Senator. Sculpted by Frederick Ernst Triebel, the 7-foot 7-inch marble statue, dedicated in 1916, is located in Statuary Hall.

Maria L. Sanford (1836–1920). First woman professor in the United States, and advocate for the education of blacks. Sculpted by Evelyn Raymond, the 6-foot 11-inch bronze statue, dedicated in 1958, is located in the Senate connecting corridor.

Mississippi

Jefferson Davis (1808–1889). Representative, Senator, and President of the Confederacy. Sculpted by Augustus Lukeman, the 7-foot 7-inch bronze statue, dedicated in 1931, is located in Statuary Hall.

James Zachariah George (1826–1897) Senator, Confederate Brigadier General, and chief justice of the state supreme court. Sculpted by Augustus Lukeman, the 7-foot 8-inch bronze statue, dedicated in 1931, is located in the Hall of Columns.

Missouri

Francis P. Blair, Jr. (1821–1875) Senator, Representative, and soldier. Sculpted by Alexander Doyle, the 7-foot 6-inch marble statue, dedicated in 1899, is located in the Hall of Columns.

Thomas Hart Benton (1782–1858). Editor of the *Missouri Inquirer,* Representative, Senator, and father-in-law of John C. Fremont. Sculpted by Alexander Doyle, the 7-foot 7-inch marble statue, dedicated in 1899, is located in Statuary Hall.

Montana

Charles Marion Russell (1864–1926). Writer, Philosopher, and humorist of the Old West, "The Cowboy Artist." Sculpted by John B. Weaver, the 7-foot 1-inch bronze statue, dedicated in 1959, is located in Statuary Hall.

Nebraska

William Jennings Bryan (1860–1925). Representative, Colonel, Secretary of State, and founder of *The Commoner* newspaper. Sculpted by Rudolph Evans, the 6-foot 7-inch bronze statue, dedicated in 1937, is located in Statuary Hall.

J. Sterling Morton (1832–1902). Secretary of Agriculture, originator of Arbor Day, leader in the early history of Nebraska. Sculpted by Rudolph Evans, the 6-foot 9-inch bronze statue, dedicated in 1937, is located in the Hall of Columns.

Nevada

Patrick Anthony McCarran (1876–1954). Senator and Chief Justice. Sculpted by Yolande Jacobson, the 7-foot 3-inch bronze statue, dedicated in 1960, is located in Statuary Hall, vestibule north.

New Hampshire

John Stark (1728–1822). Major General, fought in the French and Indian War, and leader of troops in the Battle of Bunker Hill. Sculpted by Carl Conrads, the 6-foot 5-inch marble statue, dedicated in 1894, is located in the vestibule north of the Rotunda.

Daniel Webster (1782–1852). Secretary of State, Representative, and Senator. Sculpted by Carl Conrads, the 6-foot 4-inch marble statue, dedicated in 1894, is in Statuary Hall.

New Jersey

Richard Stockton (1730–1781). Signer of the Declaration of Independence, and member of the Continental Congress. Sculpted by Henry Kirke Brown, the 6-foot 3-inch marble statue, dedicated in 1888, is located in Statuary Hall.

Philip Kearny (1814–1862). "The Perfect Soldier," Major General, fought in Algiers and in the war with Mexico. Sculpted by Henry Kirke Brown, the 6-foot 6-inch bronze statue, dedicated in 1888, is located in the Hall of Columns.

New Mexico

Dennis Chávez (1888–1962). Senator, Representative, who helped in establishing the Pan-American Highway. Sculpted by Felix de Weldon, the 7-foot 5-inch bronze statue, dedicated in 1966, is located in the vestibule north of the Rotunda.

New York

Robert Livingston (1746–1813). Secretary of Foreign Affairs, Chancellor; helped draft the Declaration of Independence, administered the first Presidential Oath of Office to George Washington. Sculpted by Erastus Dow Palmer, the 6-foot 4-inch bronze statue, dedicated in 1875, is located in Statuary Hall.

George Clinton (1739–1812) Vice President, first Governor of New York, and Brigadier General in the French and Indian War. Sculpted by Henry Kirke Brown, the 6-foot 8-inch bronze statue, dedicated in 1873, is located in the Small House Rotunda.

North Carolina

Zebulon Baird Vance (1830–1894). Governor, Senator, Representative, and colonel. Sculpted by Gutzon Borglum, the 7-foot 8-inch bronze statue, dedicated in 1916, is located in Statuary Hall.

Charles Brantley Aycock (1859–1912). Governor, educator, and U.S. district attorney. Sculpted by Charles Keck, the 7-foot 3-inch bronze statue, dedicated in 1932, is located in the Hall of Columns.

North Dakota

John Burke (1859–1937). "North Dakota's Lincoln," Governor, Senator, Chief Justice, and Treasurer of the United States. Sculpted by Avard Fairbanks, the 8-foot 6-inch bronze statue, dedicated in 1963, is located in Statuary Hall.

Ohio

James Abram Garfield (1831–1881). President of the United States, Senator, Representative. Sculpted by Charles H. Niehaus, the 7-foot 7-inch marble statue, dedicated in 1886, is located in the Rotunda.

William Allen (1803–1879). Representative, Senator, and Governor. Sculpted by Charles H. Niehaus, the 7-foot 5-inch marble statue, dedicated in 1887, is located in Statuary Hall.

Oklahoma

Sequoyah "George Guess" (1770–1845). Leader of the Cherokee Indians, who was responsible for their 86-character alphabet. Sculpted by Vinnie Ream and G. Julian Zolnay, the 7-foot 6-inch bronze statue, dedicated in 1917, is located in Statuary Hall.

Will Rogers (1879–1935). Humorist, columnist, author, goodwill ambassador, and actor. Sculpted by Jo Davidson, this 7-foot 6-inch bronze statue, dedicated in 1939, is located in the House connecting corridor.

Oregon

Reverend Jason Lee (1803–1845). Missionary and educator, who petitioned Congress to "take formal and speedy possession" of the Oregon country. Sculpted by Gifford Proctor, the 6-foot 11-inch bronze statue, dedicated in 1953, is located in Statuary Hall.

Dr. John McLoughlin (1784–1857). The "Father of Oregon"; head of the Hudson's Bay Company. Sculpted by Gifford Proctor, the 6-foot 11-inch bronze statue, dedicated in 1953, is located in the House connecting corridor.

Pennsylvania

John Peter Gabriel Muhlenberg (1746–1807). First Speaker of the House, Senator, and clergyman. Sculpted by Blanche Nevin, the 6-foot 5-inch marble statue, dedicated in 1889, is located in the Small House Rotunda.

Robert Fulton (1765–1815). Designed the first steamboat, the *Clermont;* artist, civil engineer, and inventor. Sculpted by Howard Roberts, the 5-foot 4-inch marble statue, dedicated in 1889, is located in Statuary Hall.

Rhode Island

Nathanael Greene (1742–1786). Major General, "Savior of the South"; first statue to be placed in the Statuary Hall. Sculpted by Henry Kirke Brown, the 6-foot 4-inch marble statue, dedicated in 1870, is located in the vestibule north of the Rotunda.

Roger Williams (1603–1682/83). Founder of Rhode Island, minister, colonizer. Sculpted by Franklin Simmons, the 6-foot 8-inch marble statue, dedicated in 1872, was the second statue placed in Statuary Hall.

South Carolina

John C. Calhoun (1782–1850). Vice President, Representative, Senator, and Secretary of State. Sculpted by Frederic W. Ruckstull, the 7-foot 7-inch-marble statue, dedicated in 1910, is located in Statuary Hall.

Wade Hampton (1818–1902). Governor and Lieutenant General. Sculpted by Frederic W. Ruckstull, the 7-foot 6-inch marble statue, dedicated in 1929, is located in the House connecting corridor.

South Dakota

William Henry Harrison Beadle (1838–1915). Brigadier General, educator, conservationist, statesman, and engineer. Sculpted by H. Daniel Webster, the 6-foot 4-inch bronze statue, dedicated in 1938, is located in Statuary Hall.

Joseph Ward (1838–1889). Composer of the state motto "Under God the people rule"; educator, missionary, and founder of Yankton College. Sculpted by Bruno Beghe, the 7-foot 2-inch marble statue, dedicated in 1963, is located in the Hall of Columns.

Tennessee

Andrew Jackson (1767–1845). President, Governor, Senator, and judge. Sculpted by Belle Kinney Scholz and Leopold F. Scholz, his 7-foot 6-inch bronze statue, dedicated in 1928, is located in the Rotunda.

John Sevier (1745–1815). First Governor of Tennessee, Representative, and soldier. Sculpted by Belle Kinney Scholz and Leopold F. Scholz, the 7-foot 10-inch bronze statue, dedicated in 1931, is located in Statuary Hall.

Texas

Stephen F. Austin (1793–1836). Colonizer and patriot; helped form Texas independence. Sculpted by Elisabet Ney, the 6-foot 2-inch marble statue, dedicated in 1905, is located in the Small House Rotunda.

Samuel Houston (1793–1863). Governor, Representative, Senator, and soldier. Sculpted by Elisabet Ney, the 6-foot 10-inch marble statue, dedicated in 1905, is located in Statuary Hall.

Utah

Brigham Young (1801–1877). President of the Church of Jesus Christ of Latter-day Saints, and Governor. Sculpted by Mahonri Young, the 5-foot 11-inch marble statue, dedicated in 1950, is located in Statuary Hall.

Vermont

Ethan Allen (1737–1789). Brigadier General, fighter in the French and Indian War, and author. Sculpted by Larkin G. Mead, the 8-foot 8-inch marble statue, dedicated in 1876, is located in Statuary Hall.

Jacob Collamer (1792–1865). Postmaster General, jurist, Representative, and soldier. Sculpted by Preston Powers, the 6-foot 8-inch marble statue, dedicated in 1881, is located in the Hall of Columns.

Virginia

Robert E. Lee (1807–1870). Confederate General of the Civil War, he surrendered to General Ulysses S. Grant at Appomattox. Sculpted by Edward V. Valentine, the 6-foot 6-inch bronze statue, dedicated in 1934, is located in Statuary Hall.

George Washington (1732–1799). First President of the United States, patriot, surveyor, and soldier. Sculpted by Jean Antoine Houdon, the 7-foot 6-inch bronze statue, dedicated in 1934, is located in the Rotunda.

Washington

Marcus Whitman (1802–1847). Helped in the "Great Emigration"; doctor, missionary, farmer, and pioneer. Sculpted by Avard Fairbanks, the 9-foot bronze statue, dedicated in 1953, is located in Statuary Hall.

West Virginia

John E. Kenna (1848–1893). Representative, Senator, soldier, and lawyer. Sculpted by Alexander Doyle, his 7-foot 8-inch marble statue, dedicated in 1901, is located in the Hall of Columns.

Francis H. Pierpont (1814–1899). Governor, patriot, and statesman. Sculpted by Franklin Simmons, the 7-foot 7-inch marble statue, dedicated in 1910, is located in Statuary Hall.

Wisconsin

Père Jacques Marquette (1637–1675). Pioneer explorer and French Jesuit missionary. Sculpted by Gaetano Trentanove, the 7-foot 7-inch marble statue, dedicated in 1896, is located in the House connecting corridor.

Robert Marion La Follette, Sr. (1855–1925) Governor, Representative, and district attorney. Sculpted by Jo Davidson, the 6-foot 6-inch marble statue, dedicated in 1929, is located in Statuary Hall.

Wyoming

Esther Hobart Morris (1813/14–1902). Judge, and leader of women's suffrage in Wyoming. Sculpted by Avard Fairbanks, the 8-foot bronze statue, dedicated in 1960, is located in the Statuary Hall vestibule north.

THE WHITE HOUSE

The White House

1600 Pennsylvania Avenue, N.W.

Sometimes referred to as the "President's Palace," the "President's House," or the "Executive Mansion," the White House is the oldest public building in Washington. President Harry S Truman liked to call it "the great white jail on Pennsylvania Avenue." Theodore Roosevelt affectionately referred to the White House as "a bully pulpit!" William Howard Taft referred to it as "the loneliest place in the world." Calvin Coolidge once remarked, "Nobody lives in the White House, they just come and go." The house has also been called "a great stone house, big enough for two emperors, one pope and the grand lama in the bargain."

Its 132 rooms, 28 working fireplaces, and 20 baths and showers are situated in a building that is both a home and an office. Two million visitors a year (approximately 5,000 tickets are given out each visiting day) walk through but a small portion of the 86,184 square feet of the White House, which is situated on an 18-acre park across the street from Lafayette Park on the north side and across the street from the Ellipse on the south.

The exterior of the White House is constructed of Virginia Aquia Creek sandstone. The West Wing is the working part of the White House. The East Wing was added in 1902 and enlarged in 1934.

The cornerstone for the building was laid on October 13, 1792, on the

300th anniversary of Christopher Columbus's discovery of America. James Hoban, the White House architect, had copied the design for the building from that of the Duke of Leinster's House on Kidare Street in Dublin, Ireland, and won the "best design" competition held for the President's new home. One of the persons who submitted a design for the mansion in 1792 was signed A.Z. The design was rejected, but it wasn't until later that it was revealed that A.Z. was actually Thomas Jefferson.

The White House's first residents were President John Adams and First Lady Abigail Adams, who moved in on November 1, 1800, from their previous home in Philadelphia. Upon moving in, they found out that only six of the thirty rooms had been plastered.

On August 24, 1814, the White House was one of the buildings burned by the invading British. It was rebuilt and ready for occupancy in December 1817, when President James Monroe moved in.

Five years later, in 1824, the South Portico was constructed and, in 1829, the North Portico and entrance were added.

The White House has the only zip code within the United States that ends in a double-0: 20500.

State Dining Room (Open to the public)

This room has a 140-guest seating capacity for luncheon or dinner banquets. It is the second largest room in the White House. Over the fireplace President John Adams wrote the words, "I pray heaven to bestow the best of blessings on this house and all that shall hereafter inhabit it. May none but honest and wise men ever rule under this roof." He had written the line in a letter to his wife on November 2, 1800, the day after they had moved into the White House.

The Red Room (Open to the public)

"The President's Antechamber" was once called Dolley Madison's "Yellow Drawing Room." On March 3, 1877, in a secret ceremony, Rutherford B. Hayes was sworn into office as President by Chief Justice Morrison Waite. It was the only time that a President has been sworn into office within the walls of the White House.

The Blue Room (Open to the public)

This oval room is where the White House Christmas tree is usually put on display. It was named the Blue Room because of the blue upholstery with which President Martin Van Buren decorated the furniture in 1833.

It was here, on June 2, 1886, that 49-year-old President Grover

Cleveland married 21-year-old Frances Folsom, who would become the youngest First Lady in U.S. history.

The Blue Room was where First Lady Bess Truman noticed the chandeliers shake every time someone walked across the room, leading to the discovery that the building was very much in need of renovation.

The Green Room (Open to the public)

This room, which connects the East and the Blue rooms, has been used as a parlor since James Madison lived there, and was originally known as the Card Room. The Green Room is identical in size and shape to the Red Room. James and Elizabeth Monroe used green silks to decorate the room. After the death of Willie, the son of Abraham and Mary Lincoln, his body was prepared for burial in the Green Room, after which the First Lady never again entered the room.

The East Room (Open to the public)

Called the "Public Audience Room," this is the largest room on the first floor. It became famous as the room in which First Lady Abigail Adams hung her clothing to dry and where President Theodore Roosevelt's children often rollerskated. In 1803 the ceiling of the East Room collapsed, due to a leaking roof.

Four Presidents' daughters have been married in the East Room: Nellie Grant, the daughter of Ulysses S. Grant; Alice Roosevelt, the daughter of Theodore Roosevelt; Jessie Wilson, the daughter of Woodrow Wilson; and Lynda Bird Johnson, the daughter of Lyndon B. Johnson.

The funeral services for six Presidents have been held in the East Room: William Henry Harrison in 1841, Zachary Taylor in 1850, Abraham Lincoln in 1865, Warren G. Harding in 1923, Franklin D. Roosevelt in 1945, and John F. Kennedy in 1963.

The East Room has been seen many times by the public as the location of the majority of the presidential press conferences. It is also where the Garfields' son Irving liked to ride his bicycle.

OTHER ROOMS

V.I.P. tours usually include four additional rooms on the ground floor:

The Diplomatic Reception Room

This ground-floor oval room has the presidential seal inlaid in marble. The room is the setting of many social functions. On the walls hang portraits of the White House hostesses. It was this room in which President Franklin D. Roosevelt gave his famous "fireside chats" on the radio.

The Library

There are 2,800 volumes here, as well as the busts of Abraham Lincoln and William Henry Harrison placed in the room's two windows. Around the fireplace, scenes depicting the "Life of the Presidents" are shown in tile.

The Vermeil Room

Also called the Gold Room.

The China Room

Originally called the Presidential Collection Room, this room contains a seven-foot-tall painting of Mrs. Grace Coolidge. In the center of the room is an old-fashioned settee, upholstered in red to harmonize with the dress worn by Grace Coolidge in her portrait. The room has built-in cupboards to show off the White House china collection, started by First Lady Caroline Harrison.

ROOMS NOT OPEN TO THE PUBLIC

The Map Room: Used by President Franklin D. Roosevelt during World War II as the situation room.

The Lincoln Bedroom: Included here is a reproduction of the rocking chair in which President Abraham Lincoln sat in his box at Ford's Theatre. A hologram shows his Gettysburg Address.

The Lincoln Sitting Room
The Treaty Room
The Yellow Oval Room
The President's Dining Room
The Oval Office
The Family Dining Room

It was in the White House basement that First Lady Edith Bolling Wilson learned to ride a bicycle.

White House Additions

ITEM	PRESIDENT	YEAR
Piano	John Adams	1800
Furnishings	James Monroe	1817
Billiard table	John Quincy Adams	1826
Plumbing	Andrew Jackson	1833
Furnace	Martin Van Buren	1838
Gas lighting	James K. Polk	1848
Icebox	James K. Polk	1849
Library	Millard Fillmore	1850
Kitchen stove	Millard Fillmore	1851
Central heating	Franklin Pierce	1853
Greenhouse	James Buchanan	1858
Hot-air heating	Ullysses S. Grant	1874
Bathtub	Rutherford B. Hayes	1878
Telephone	Rutherford B. Hayes	1878
Elevator	James Garfield	1882
Electricity	Benjamin Harrison	1890
Electric Lights	Benjamin Harrison	1892
West Wing	Theodore Roosevelt	1902
Oval Office	William Howard Taft	1909
Air conditioning	Herbert Hoover	1931
Fire alarm system	Franklin D. Roosevelt	1936
Swimming pool	Franklin D. Roosevelt	1937
Second-story porch	Harry S Truman	1948
Motion-picture room	Dwight D. Eisenhower	1954
Central vacuum-cleaning system	Dwight D. Eisenhower	1954
Hot Line (with Moscow)*	John F. Kennedy	1963
Tape recorder (Oval Office)	Richard M. Nixon	1971
Dolby stereo in movie room	Ronald Reagan	1980

WHITE HOUSE STRUCTURAL CHANGES

In 1902, during Theodore Roosevelt's administration, the White House underwent structural changes, including interior renovation. The State Room was enlarged, an office complex was added to the west terraces, the main staircase was removed, and the east terrace was rebuilt.

*On June 5, 1967, President Lyndon Johnson became the first President to use the Hot Line to Moscow.

- In 1920 the executive office building was enlarged.
- In 1927 the third story and the roof were remodeled.
- In 1946 a balcony was constructed off the second floor.

Between 1948 and 1952, while the Trumans lived at Blair House, the White House was gutted, except for the exterior walls, and completely rebuilt. Walls and floors were built with modern reinforcement. Rooms were added so that at the completion of the renovation, the White House contained 132 rooms with 20 showers, where formerly it had had 62 rooms and 14 baths. Four new elevators were added. The restoration was completed on March 27, 1952, and the Trumans moved back into the brand-new White House.

The White House Grounds
The first White House Easter Egg Roll was held on April 12, 1877; prior to that, it had been held on the Capitol grounds, since its introduction in 1810.

President Jimmy Carter witnessed, on the White House lawn, the signing of the peace treaty between Egypt and Israel after their thirty years of hostilities.

- On July 14, 1911, Harry N. Atwood piloted a Moth, the first airplane to land on the White House lawn, where President William Taft awarded him with a gold medal.
- On April 22, 1931, James G. Ray landed an autogyro on the White House lawn.

The Rose Garden
Created by First Lady Jacqueline Kennedy, the garden was where Tricia Nixon married Ed Cox on June 12, 1971. It was renamed the Jacqueline Kennedy Garden by First Lady Lady Bird Johnson.

STAFF

- One of the White House staff members was Pam Powell, the daughter of actor Dick Powell and actress June Allyson.
- One of President Franklin Roosevelt's cooks was named Jimmy Carter.
- Dr. Janet C. Travell became the first female White House physician when she was appointed by President John F. Kennedy in 1961.
- First Lady Caroline Harrison forbade any of the staff to wear

uniforms, while William Howard Taft's wife ordered that no bald-headed waiters or butlers could serve in the White House dining room.

- Irwin "Ike" Hoover served as the first chief usher of the White House, from 1891 to 1933. He authored the book *Forty-Two Years in the White House.* He served in the White House while Herbert Hoover was President.
- White House maid Lillian Rogers Parks authored the 1961 book *My Thirty Years Backstairs at the White House,* which was made into the TV mini-series *Backstairs at the White House,* with Leslie Uggams portraying Lillian Parks.

VISITORS

- In 1979 John Paul II became the first Pope to visit the White House.
- During Franklin D. Roosevelt's term he hosted George IV and Queen Elizabeth of Britain, who spent a night in the White House. The President served the royal couple American frankfurters. When the Trumans hosted the Queen, First Lady Bess Truman served them baked ham.

SECURITY

The White House is protected by the White House guards.

- While President Andrew Jackson lived in the White House, a man entered by mistake only to leave hurriedly after learning where he was. A drunk once wandered into the White House and fell asleep on a couch while President Martin Van Buren slept upstairs.
- On February 17, 1974, a stolen U.S. Army helicopter was shot down over the White House lawn. It had been piloted by a twenty-year-old Army mechanic who was not charged with the theft and damage of Army property, but was charged with unlawful entry onto the White House grounds.
- It was President Richard Nixon who attempted to outfit the White House guards in brand new uniforms, a change that lasted only a few weeks.

FACTS ABOUT THE WHITE HOUSE

- Although it was George Washington himself who both selected the site of the White House and laid its cornerstone, he was the only President who never lived there.
- The first presidential mansion was located at 1 Cherry Street in New York City, where President George Washington and First Lady Martha Washington resided from April 23, 1789, to February 23, 1790.
- It wasn't until 1902 that the White House was officially known by that name, by an act of Congress. President Theodore Roosevelt is credited as first referring to it officially by that name, also including its name on official White House stationery.
- On the back of the U.S. twenty-dollar bill, an illustration of the White House can be seen. When President Harry Truman had the second-story balcony added onto the south porch, engravers in July 1948 had to add the balcony and two chimneys, along with more trees, to the new 1934C series of the bill.
- Thomas Jefferson's grandson James Madison Randolph was the first child to be born in the White House. Born in 1806, he was named for President James Madison. Esther Cleveland was the first President's child to be born in the White House, September 9, 1893.
- Singer Pearl Bailey holds the distinction of having been the only person ever to dance with Egyptian President Anwar Sadat at a White House reception.
- Thomas Jefferson, an amateur inventor, set up revolving circular shelves in some of the White House cabinets, introducing the "lazy Susan."
- President James K. Polk gave the first Thanksgiving dinner held in the White House.

THE SUPREME COURT

The Supreme Court building, designed by Cass Gilbert and constructed in 1935, is located on the site of the Old Capitol Prison. The motto on the building reads "Equal Justice Under Law," attributed to the building's architect Cass Gilbert. Prior to the construction of the building, the Supreme Court met in the Capitol for 135 years, in what is now referred to as the Old Supreme Court Chamber. The area directly in front of the building is called Judiciary Square. The front of the building is decorated with a double row of eight Corinthian columns of Vermont marble, giving the building its dignified appearance.

When Cass Gilbert designed the 60-foot-long front pediment of the building called "Equal Justice Under Law," four living persons were included in the figures. They were Elihu Root (former Secretary of State), Cass Gilbert (architect), Charles Evans Hughes (Chief Justice), and Robert Aitken (sculptor). Also included on the pediment are figures of Chief Justices John Marshall and William Howard Taft. Two 45-ton human figures stand at the building's steps facing the Capitol, called the *Authority of Law* (male) and the *Contemplation of Justice* (female). The two marble statues were designed by Cass Gilbert and sculpted by James Earle Frazer. *Contemplation of Justice* holds a book in one hand and a small statue of Justice in the other; *Authority of Law* holds a sword.

The pediment on the building's east facade, also designed by Cass Gilbert, features the figures of such great thinkers as Moses, Confucius, and the Athenian lawgiver, Solon. Herman A. MacNeil sculpted the figures on this pediment, on which is inscribed "Justice the Guardian of Liberty."

The 3,000-pound bronze front doors of the Supreme Court Building, called the *Evolution of Justice,* were designed by Cass Gilbert and sculpted by John Donnelly, and were installed in 1935. The two 17-foot-high doors feature four scenes on each door panel. The right door shows the Magna Carta, the Westminster Statute, Lord Coke and James I, and John Marshall. On the left panel is shown the Shield of Achilles, Praetor's Edict, Julian and the Scholar, and the Justinian Code.

The Supreme Court Chamber measures 82 feet by 91 feet with a height of 44 feet from floor to ceiling. The room, which is surprisingly small, allows for the seating of only 188 members of the public. On the bench, each justice has a button on his desk in case of a medical emergency. Spittoons, snuffboxes, and ten-inch-long white goose-quill pens are still on display. Traditionally, attorneys take one of the goose-quill pens with them as a souvenir of their day in the supreme court of the land, concluding their limited time of a thirty-minute argument before the court. The Supreme Court bench is no longer a long, straight bench, but is now winged, with the Chief Justice sitting in the middle. Within the building, two self-supporting cantilevered marble spiral staircases ascend five stories. The only other two places in the world with such staircases are the Paris Opera House and the Vatican.

The first Monday in October is the opening day of the annual court term and is considered to be the beginning of Washington's social season. From October to June, the Court meets on Monday, Tuesday, and Wednesday from 10 A.M. to 12 noon and then from 1 P.M. to 3 P.M. for approximately two weeks of each month through April. During the months of May and June, the Court convenes at 10 A.M. to deliver its opinions. Of the over 4,000 cases submitted to the Supreme Court each year, only about 160 (4 percent) are chosen to be heard. The Supreme Court chooses only those cases they deem important. The Supreme Court oversees ninety-two U.S. district courts and eleven U.S. courts of appeal.

When the court convenes the crier announces: "The honorable, the Chief Justice and the Associate Justices of the Supreme Court of the United States!" "Oyez! Oyez, Oyez! [Hear ye! Hear ye, Hear ye!] All persons having business before the Honorable, the Supreme Court of the United States, are admonished to draw near and give their attention, for the Court is now sitting. God save the United States and this honorable Court!"

A half million visitors a year come to see where the law of the land is upheld or ruled unconstitutional. On the second and third floors, there is a library; on the ground floor, there is a small museum administered by the Supreme Court Historical Society that features busts of the Chief Justices and portraits of the associate justices. A short movie on the Court can also be viewed. There stands a statue of John Marshall at the end of the Main Hall.

When court is not in session, visitors can sit in on courtroom lectures, which are given at announced times during the day. In 1977 the Supreme Court Building was declared a National Landmark.

The first session of the Supreme Court took place on February 1, 1790, at the Royal Exchange Building on New York City's Broad Street. John Jay was the first Chief Justice. The five associate justices were John Rutledge, William Cushing, Robert Harrison, James Wilson, and John Blair. All the members had been chosen by President George Washington.

Justices are appointed by the President of the United States and confirmed by the Senate. They can be impeached only for misconduct.

SUPREME COURT FACTS

- In 1895 the U.S. Supreme Court ruled that the federal income tax was unconstitutional; however, a later Court reversed that decision.
- Prior to sitting on the bench, the Supreme Court justices give one another a traditional handshake called the Conference Handshake.
- New justices appointed by the President are sworn in with a Bible dating back to 1818, the oldest Bible still used by the federal government.
- In 1893 the Supreme Court declared that the tomato is a vegetable and not a fruit. Not a major decision, but one that helps to answer a popular trivia question.
- Atheist Madelyn Murray O'Hare, who took her case to the Supreme Court on November 6, 1967, became the very first guest on TV's "Donahue" show, where she talked about her case.

Supreme Court Chief Justices

Following are the people who have served as the Chief Justice of the Supreme Court from 1789 to the present.

John Jay	1789 to 1795
John Rutledge	1795
Oliver Ellsworth	1796 to 1800
John Marshall	1801 to 1835
Roger B. Taney	1836 to 1864
Salmon P. Chase	1864 to 1873
Morrison R. Waite	1874 to 1888
Melville W. Fuller	1888 to 1910
Edward D. White	1910 to 1921
William H. Taft	1921 to 1930
Charles E. Hughes	1930 to 1941
Harlan F. Stone	1941 to 1946
Fred M. Vinson	1946 to 1953
Earl Warren	1953 to 1969
Warren E. Burger	1969 to 1986
William H. Rehnquist	1986 to present

FACTS ABOUT SUPREME COURT FIGURES

- The first Chief Justice, John Jay, resigned his position in order to become Governor of New York.
- Charles Vernon Bush became the first black Supreme Court page.
- Chief Justice Roger Brook Taney swore into office more U.S. Presidents than any other judge. The Presidents were:

  Martin Van Buren in 1837
  William Henry Harrison in 1841
  John C. Tyler in 1841
  James K. Polk in 1845
  Zachary Taylor in 1849
  Millard Fillmore in 1850
  Franklin Pierce in 1853
  James Buchanan in 1857
  Abraham Lincoln in 1861

- Charles Evans Hughes (1862–1948) is the only Supreme Court justice to run for president of the United States, when he ran against Woodrow Wilson in 1916.
- William Howard Taft is the only person to have served as both President and as Chief Justice. He was instrumental in the construction of the Supreme Court building.

- In the funeral procession of Chief Justice John Marshall, the Liberty Bell cracked while it was being rung in his honor.
- William O. Douglas sat on the Supreme Court longer than any other person (36 years). He became the youngest justice at age forty.
- Chief Justice Salmon P. Chase never attended law school. His portrait appears on the ten-thousand-dollar bill.
- Although never a Chief Justice, Oliver Wendell Holmes is known as the Magnificent Yankee.
- Justice Byron White was an All-American football player as well as a Rhodes Scholar.
- Justice Louis D. Brandeis became the first Jew to sit on the Supreme Court when he was appointed in 1916.
- Justice Thurgood Marshall was the first black to sit on the Supreme Court. He was appointed by President Lyndon Johnson in 1967.
- Justice Sandra Day O'Connor is the first woman to sit on the Supreme Court, appointed in 1981. She and Chief Justice William Rehnquist were in the same graduating class at Stanford, in 1952.
- Howard Taft was selected as Chief Justice of the Supreme Court after having served as President of the United States. He enjoyed his years as the Chief Justice more than those as President. It was Taft who pushed for the construction of the Supreme Court building.
- Over half the Chief Justices never attended law school. John Marshall, for example, had only two months of legal training.
- Fifteen justices were born outside the United States.
- Supreme Court Justice James Wilson, a signer of the Declaration of Independence, was arrested for nonpayment of debts.
- President Franklin D. Roosevelt, who served longer than any other President, selected the most justices (eight).
- Chief Justice Edward White served in the Confederate Army during the Civil War.
- The Father of Justice Oliver Wendell Holmes, Jr., invented the stereoscope, the first device to show 3-D photos, in 1861.
- Many of the justices have been portrayed in movies: Edward White was portrayed by Joseph L. Greene in the 1944 movie *Wilson*, Earl Warren was portrayed by John Houseman in the 1980 TV movie *Gideon's Trumpet*, and Oliver Wendell Holmes was portrayed by Louis Calhern in the 1950 movie *The Magnificent Yankee*.

Brick Capitol

The present site of the Supreme Court is where the Brick Capitol once stood. The brick building was built in just six months on the site of Tunnicliffe's Tavern. It served as the home for the U.S. Congress from December 1815 to December 1817, while the Capitol was being repaired after the British had burned it. On March 4, 1817, James Monroe took the oath of office on the Brick Capitol's steps, the city's first outdoor inauguration. During the Civil War, the building was used as a prison.

After the burning of Washington by the British in August 1814, the members of Congress meeting in the Brick Capitol agreed by just nine votes not to move the nation's capital out of Washington and back to Philadelphia, which many believed to be a safer location.

GOVERNMENT DEPARTMENTS AND BUILDINGS

The primary function of the District of Columbia is administration of the federal government. The number of federal employees has greatly increased since 1800 when only 130 people were employed:

1800	130 employees
1865	7,000 employees
1901	28,000 employees
1940	140,000 employees
1980	400,000+ employees

U.S. CABINETS

Departments	Established	First Secretary
Department of State	January 10, 1781	Thomas Jefferson
Department of the Treasury	September 2, 1789	Alexander Hamilton
Department of the Interior	May 3, 1849	Thomas Ewing
Department of Agriculture	May 15, 1862	Norman J. Colman
Department of Justice	June 22, 1870	Edmund Randolph
Department of Commerce	March 4, 1913	William Redfield

Department of Labor	March 4, 1913	William B. Wilson
Department of Defense	September 18, 1947	James Forrestal
Department of Transportation	October 15, 1966	Alan S. Boyd
Department of Energy	August 4, 1977	James R. Schlesinger
Department of Education	October 17, 1979	Shirley Hufstedler
Department of Health and Human Services	May 5, 1980	Patricia Harris

Past Departments

The War Department existed from 1789 to 1947.
The Department of Commerce and Labor existed from 1903 to 1913.
The Department of Health, Education, and Welfare existed from 1953 to 1979.

THE FEDERAL TRIANGLE

This site of twelve government buildings is formed by Pennsylvania Avenue, Constitution Avenue, and 15th Street. Most of these buildings, were planned by the McMillan Commission and completed in 1938. The board was commissioned by the Secretary of the Treasury Andrew Mellon. Each building was designed by a different architect, using the same overall style of design, and all built to the same height.

The twelve buildings are:

National Archives
Labor-Interstate Commerce Corporation
U.S. Information Center
Federal Trade Commission
Farm Credit Building
Department of Justice
Internal Revenue Service
Apex Building
Post Office
District Building
Commerce Building
Old Post Office

CONGRESSIONAL OFFICE BUILDINGS

There are five congressional office buildings located near the Capitol Building with an underground railway connecting the offices with the Capitol.

Russell Senate Office Building

This office building for Senators was named for Richard Russell of Georgia.

Dirksen Senate Office Building

This office building for Senators was named for Everett Dirksen of Illinois.

Cannon House Office Building

This office building, constructed in 1908, for Representatives was named for Speaker of the House Joseph Cannon.

Longworth House Office Building

This office building, constructed in 1933, was named for Nicholas Longworth of Ohio.

Rayburn House Office Building

This $86 million office building, constructed in 1965, was named for Speaker of the House Sam Rayburn of Texas. The building, which has 169 offices, features nine hearing rooms, a gymnasium, and a swimming pool.

DEPARTMENT OF AGRICULTURE

Established by President Abraham Lincoln on May 15, 1862, this department, located at 14th Street and Independence Avenue, S.W., employs 120,000 people. Construction began in 1905 by the firm of Ranking, Kellogg, and Crane. The first building erected under the McMillan Commission plan, it was finally completed in 1930. Since its creation in 1862 the department has been headed by a commissioner, and it was also decided to have a cabinet member head the department. Norman J. Colman was the department's first secretary, appointed by the President on February 13, 1889.

- The first father and son to occupy the same cabinet position were Henry C. Wallace and his son Henry A. Wallace. Henry C. Wallace had served as Secretary of Agriculture under both Presidents Warren Harding and Calvin Coolidge, while his son served as Secretary of Agriculture under President Franklin D. Roosevelt.

- The Department of Agriculture, like all other government agencies, spends money for unusual projects. They once spent $113,000 in order to find out if mothers generally prefer children's clothing that needs no ironing.
- J. Sterling Morton, who had served as the Secretary of Agriculture, was the originator of Arbor Day.
- In 1986 a 24-hour hot line for around-the-clock computer service was established, free to companies and organizations wanting information from the department.

DEPARTMENT OF COMMERCE

This building at 14th Street and Constitution Avenue, named the Herbert C. Hoover Building and completed in 1932, is the tallest office building in Washington. The building has 3,311 rooms, 5,200 windows, 8 miles of corridors and 32 elevators, and covers approximately eight acres. In the basement is the National Aquarium, the oldest aquarium in the United States, established in 1874. Its 60 tanks feature sharks, octopus, electric eels, snapping turtles, and over 2,000 species of North American fish life. In the building's lobby is the Census Clock, which tabulates the increases and decreases in our society since 1926. The present model was installed in 1966. Also located there is a seismograph to record earthquake activity. In room 1905, as well as in the basement, are bookstores. Room 1905 is run by the Government Printing Office, while the one in the basement sells books and pamphlets relating to aquatic life, as well as souvenirs.

The Department of Commerce was established on March 4, 1913, by an act of Congress. William Cox, the previous head of the Department of Commerce and Labor, served as its first secretary.

The Bureau of Standards is a division of the Department of Commerce. Their Cesium Atoms Clock will gain or lose only one second in 300 years.

- Assistant Secretary of Commerce Clarence M. Young (under Presidents Herbert Hoover and Franklin D. Roosevelt) was married to film actress Lois Moran, who had been F. Scott Fitzgerald's inspiration for his character of Rosemary in his novel *Tender Is the Night*.

- On February 27, 1922, Secretary of Commerce Herbert Clark conducted the first national radio conference in history.
- President Harry S Truman appointed Allen Varley Astin, the father of actor John Astin, as director of the National Bureau of Standards.

DEPARTMENT OF DEFENSE (DOD)

The Department of Defense was founded on September 17, 1947, with James Vincent Forrestal as its first head. The department is located in the Pentagon, which was named for the huge building's five-sided design, its five stories, and its five separate concentric corridors. The building, which was officially opened on January 15, 1943, has 150 staircases, 19 escalators, 4,200 clocks, and 683 water fountains.

The Pentagon consists of 3.7 million square feet, with 17½ miles of corridors that allow a person to travel from one office to any other office within six minutes or less. It has humorously been suggested that no spy would enter the Pentagon for fear that he wouldn't be able to find his way out. The Pentagon was completed in January 1943, after 16 months of construction. Like the Lincoln Memorial, the Pentagon was constructed on reclaimed swampland near the Potomac River. The building's foundations rest on 41,492 concrete piles.

Each one of the rings is lettered from A to E, with A being closest to the building's center. Room 2-D-9-42 could be located by proceeding to the second floor, ring D, corridor 9, and room 42.

In the building's Hall of Heroes is a complete listing of all the men and women who have won the Congressional Medal of Honor.

The building, which for years was claimed as the biggest office building in the world, is now second to New York City's World Trade Center. Yet today the Pentagon is considered too small to house the needs of the employees of the Defense Department.

Other facts about the Pentagon are: rest rooms (280); windows (7,748), parking spaces (67 acres). Some 200,000 telephone calls are made from the Pentagon each day.

- On the very first Peace March in Washington, 647 people were arrested when a huge crowd encircled the Pentagon in an attempt to levitate it.
- The Pentagon was the recipient of Senator William Proxmire's Golden Fleece Award after the Defense Department had spent $3,000 on a six-month test to see whether umbrellas detracted from the appearance of military officers.

- The Department of Defense, with its huge budget, has produced a dozen films over the last twelve years to teach American soldiers and sailors how to brush their teeth.
- Near the site of the Pentagon, President Theodore Roosevelt established a "poison farm" in 1904, where fields of opium, marijuana, and other drug-producing plants were grown so that the United States wouldn't have to import them.
- In a 1987 survey, approximately 45 percent of the automobiles parked in the Pentagon parking lot were foreign made, the majority in Japan.

DEPARTMENT OF HEALTH AND HUMAN SERVICES (HHS)

Hubert H. Humphrey Building

This building, at Independence Avenue and 3rd Street, S.W., was designed by Marcel Brever and completed in 1976. The Department of Health and Human Services, nicknamed "The People's Department," previously called the Department of Health, Education, and Welfare, was created on April 11, 1953, by President Dwight D. Eisenhower. The department's first secretary was Oveta Culp Hobby, a Texas lawyer, newpaper woman, and the first director of the WACs.

HHS operates the Social Security Administration, the Family Support Administration, Human Development Services, the Public Health Service, and the Health Care Financing Administration.

On the building's second floor is the Voice of America, run by the U.S. Information Agency, which broadcasts approximately 1,000 hours of information, in 42 languages, each week. The network utilizes 110 transmitters (76 overseas and 34 in North America).

- HHS accounts for 35 percent of the entire Federal budget, greater than the expenditures of all fifty state governments combined. The HHS budget is the fourth largest in the world, surpassed only by those of the United States itself, the Soviet Union, and Japan.
- The department was a recipient of one of Senator William Proxmire's Golden Fleece Awards after it spent $21,592 of the taxpayers' money to teach college students how to watch television.
- In the early 1950s, prior to becoming an actor, Telly Savalas hosted a talk show on the Voice of America, on which he interviewed celebrities.

DEPARTMENT OF HOUSING AND URBAN DEVELOPMENT (HUD)

Designed by Hungarian architect Marcel Breuer, the massive ten-story building at 7th Street and D Street, S.W., was completed in 1968, the first federal office building to be constructed of precast concrete. The construction utilized a double-Y layout, which Breuer had introduced in 1958 in his design of the NATO headquarters building in Paris. President Lyndon Johnson appointed Robert C. Weaver as the department's first secretary, in January 1966.

- When Robert C. Weaver was chosen as the first secretary of HUD, on January 13, 1966, by President Lyndon Johnson, he became the first black to serve in a cabinet-level position.
- When Patricia Harris was chosen to serve as the secretary of HUD in 1977, she became the first black female cabinet member.

DEPARTMENT OF JUSTICE

This massive eight-story building, completed in 1934 at a cost of $10 million, is located in the Federal Triangle at 10th Street and Pennsylvania Avenue, N.W. There is underground parking for 150 vehicles. The mosaics used in the building were the first ever made of American material, having been precast in Rosslyn, Virginia. Each entrance features doors twenty feet high. The building is filled with WPA artwork: murals, reliefs, paintings, statues, and sculptures.

Until the FBI moved into their own office building on Pennsylvania Avenue, they were also located in this building. The Department of Justice is headed by the Attorney General, with the U.S. attorneys and federal marshals carrying out a part of the department's law enforcement.

- The salary of the first Attorney General was $1,500 a year.
- For a time the Department of Justice's library was housed in the old Corcoran Art Gallery on 17th Street and Pennsylvania Avenue.
- Robert Kennedy served as Attorney General while his brother, John F. Kennedy, was President.
- Steve Troth, as associate attorney general (the number-three man in the criminal division), was once a member of the 1960s folk group The Highwaymen, which charted the number-one hit song "Michael" and the number-thirteen hit song "Cotton Fields," both in 1961. The popular trio had been formed at Connecticut's Wesleyan University.

- President Ulysses S. Grant had five Attorney Generals, more than any other President.
- President Richard Nixon's Attorney General, John Mitchell, was Lt. John F. Kennedy's commanding officer in the Solomon Islands during World War II.

Federal Bureau of Investigation

Dedicated in 1975, this modern yellow building on Pennsylvania Avenue between 9th and 10th Streets, N.W., was named the J. Edgar Hoover Building after its former chief of forty-eight years (he served as Assistant Director from 1921 to 1924 and as Director from 1924 to 1972 under eight Presidents), who is honored with a special display including the desk he had used. Before moving to this new structure, the FBI had been located in the Department of Justice building, which can still be seen in many old movies.

The FBI's computerized fingerprint files are made available to every law enforcement agency in the United States, free of charge. The Automatic Fingerprint Reader can analyze, sort, and identify a fingerprint in a matter of seconds. There are approximately 170,000,000 fingerprints in the Criminal File and the Civil File.

Forensic science laboratories are also located in the building, each handling a different area of criminology. One laboratory studies and identifies paints, another materials, and another blood types. Several of these laboratories are shown during the FBI tours.

Collections and files are kept on hundreds of makes of typewriters. The bureau's collection of firearms, most of which were confiscated during arrests or raids, is extremely impressive and would be the envy of any gun collector.

The photos and identities of the latest FBI's Ten Most Wanted Criminals is prominently displayed for anyone visiting the building. Twice, visitors have identified criminals from these photos during the tours. In both cases it led to the arrest of the wanted men.

A range for target practice and testing of weapons is a highlight for tourists. Live ammunition from machine guns is fired by agents, who are separated from the tours by bullet-proof glass.

- The firing range used by the FBI agents is located less than a mile from the White House.
- There is only one known photograph of FBI chief J. Edgar Hoover

kissing a member of the opposite sex. The photo shows him kissing young actress Shirley Temple.

- When J. Edgar Hoover died in 1972, he became the first civil servant ever to lie in state in Washington.
- On July 29, 1935, the FBI founded the first police training school.
- J. Edgar Hoover wasn't the first Director of the FBI, but he served under Presidents Harding, Coolidge, Hoover, Roosevelt, Truman, Eisenhower, Kennedy, Johnson, and Nixon.

DEPARTMENT OF LABOR

Frances Perkins Building

The Department of Labor was founded in 1913 after the split of the Department of Commerce and Labor. William B. Wilson was chosen by President Woodrow Wilson to serve as its first secretary. In 1933 President Franklin D. Roosevelt appointed Frances Perkins* to be the Secretary of Labor, the first female to hold a government cabinet post. She was instrumental in the passing of the Social Security Act of 1935 and the Fair Labor Standards Act of 1938. The present building was named in her honor.

DEPARTMENT OF THE INTERIOR

On March 3, 1849, President Zachary Taylor appointed Thomas Ewing to serve as the first Secretary of the Interior. This building at 18th Street and C Street, N.W., features a museum founded in 1937 by Secretary of the Interior Harold L. Ickes. Displays of the history of the National Park Service and wildlife preservation can be seen. Indian artifacts, such as arrows, headdresses, pottery, and baskets, are also on display, as is a mounted Heath Hen bird, which became extinct in 1932. There is also a geological display by the Bureau of Mines.

- Secretary of the Interior Stewart L. Udall authored the best-selling environmental book, *The Quiet Crisis,* in 1963.

DEPARTMENT OF THE TREASURY

Bureau of Engraving and Printing

Located south of the Mall, this old brick building at 301 14th Street, S.W., is where the Treasury Department prints 59 billion dollars each

*Frances Perkins wrote the book *My Years with Franklin D. Roosevelt.*

year, in paper currency, treasury bonds, food stamps, and public debt securities. In addition, 34 billion postage stamps are printed there each year. This government facility, which employs 2,300 workers, is the third most popular visitor's site in Washington.

The existence of the Bureau dates back to August 29, 1862, when only two men and four women were employed in a single room of the Treasury Building. Their job was to print the Treasury seal and the Register of the Treasury and the Treasurer on one-dollar and two-dollar notes that had been printed by private companies under contract to the U.S. government.

Today visitors enter on 14th Street and exit on 15th Street. There is generally a long line for this tour, but tours depart every twenty-five minutes, with approximately 5,000 people going through the facility each day.

Toward the end of the tour there is a counterfeit money exhibit in which tourists can try to identify the real and the counterfeit bills.

- Each of the printing presses in the plant cost $500,000.
- A dollar bill's life expectancy is only 18 months.
- The portraits currently appearing on the various denominations of paper currency were adopted in 1928, when the size of the notes were reduced from 7.42 by 3.13 inches to their present smaller size of 6.14 by 2.61 inches.
- American paper currency is actually made up of 75 percent cotton and 25 percent linen.
- Only the front of a dollar bill is considered money and has any value to it.
- The portrait of George Washington by Gilbert Stuart that appears on both the one-dollar bill and on the one-cent stamp can be seen on display at the National Portrait Gallery in Washington.
- The two-dollar bill was the only popular U.S. currency that the German government did not counterfeit during World War II.
- The first U.S. postage stamp was issued in the United States in 1847. The Bureau printed their first stamp in 1894.
- U.S. paper currency of $500 and higher denominations were discontinued in 1969, except for the $100,000 bills, which are only used in transactions between government agencies.
- By law, no portrait of a living person can appear on a U.S. postage stamp, yet there have been two exceptions. One of the flag raisers at Iwo Jima was still alive when the famous scene was printed on a stamp and John F. Kennedy, Jr., can be seen on another stamp, watching his father's funeral parade.

- In 1861 Lucy Holcombe Pickens became the first American woman to appear on currency, the Confederate $100 bill.
- Martha Washington was the first woman to appear on U.S. currency (one-dollar bill) in 1886 and on a U.S. postage stamp (8 cents) issued on December 6, 1902.

Internal Revenue Service

The IRS, located at 1111 Constitution Avenue, N.W., has an annual budget of $4 billion, and collects over 90 percent of the federal tax revenues. In 1787 the Constitutional Convention gave Congress the power to levy excise taxes and, in emergency situations, direct taxes. This was the beginning of a series of acts that would eventually lead to the establishment of the Office of the Commissioner of Internal Revenue, on July 1, 1862. In 1913 the Sixteenth Amendment to the Constitution authorized Congress to levy taxes on the incomes of individuals and corporations. In 1952 the Bureau of Internal Revenue became the Internal Revenue Service. There are approximately 4,500 employees of the IRS working in Washington, out of its total work force of 85,000.

- The very first income tax in American history was levied on August 5, 1862, to raise money for the Civil War. Any income above $800 was taxed at 3 percent.

Treasury Building

Designed by Robert Mills, a former student of the Washington architects James Hoban and Benjamin Latrobe, the four-story building at Pennsylvania Avenue and 15th Street, N.W., was constructed between 1842 and 1869. The four units of the structure join at right angles, forming a large rectangle. The building's controversial location blocks the uninterrupted view of the Capitol from the White House down Pennsylvania Avenue that architect Pierre L'Enfant had envisioned. In 1833 the previous Treasury Building had been completely destroyed by an arsonist's fire. The Treasury Building, which is the oldest "department" building in Washington, features statues of Alexander Hamilton and Albert Gallatin, two of the Secretaries of the Treasury.

- The Department of Treasury has a number of enforcement agencies under its jurisdiction, including the Bureau of Engraving and Printing, IRS, Bureau of the Mint, U.S. Secret Service, U.S. Customs, and the Bureau of Alcohol, Tobacco, and Firearms.
- President Andrew Jackson became so impatient with the commissioners who couldn't decide where to construct the Treasury

Building that Jackson stuck his cane in the ground, ordering that the building be constructed on the spot: "Here, right here is where I want its cornerstone laid." Unfortunately, he was standing on a spot that would obstruct the view on Pennsylvania Avenue from the White House to the Capitol. Some believe that Jackson intentionally blocked the White House view of the Capitol so that he wouldn't feel the frustration of Congress when he looked out of his east windows.

- By law, Secretaries of the Treasury are forbidden to purchase government savings bonds. The law was enacted in order to prevent officials in government from speculating on the bonds that they regulated.
- Between 1912 and 1918, it was the job of the Treasury Department to wash, dry, and iron dirty money.
- During the 1833 blaze that destroyed the Treasury Building, one of the many Washingtonians on the bucket brigade assisting in throwing water on the fire was President John Quincy Adams.
- The Treasury Building can be seen on the reverse side of a U.S. ten-dollar bill. The automobile in the forefront is a 1926 Hupmobile.
- Secretary of the Treasury William Gibbs McAdoo married Eleanor Wilson, the daughter of President Woodrow Wilson.
- Ulysses S. Grant's inaugural ball was held in the north wing of the Treasury Building. It turned into a melee when tickets for five times as many people as the building could comfortably accommodate were sold.
- A tunnel was built connecting the White House with the Treasury Building, so that in case of a nuclear attack the President and his family could use the basement of the building as a bomb shelter. The tunnel is no longer in use.
- Actress Patricia Priest, who played Marilyn Munster on the 1964–66 TV series "The Munsters," is the daughter of Ivy Baker Priest, the former Secretary of the Treasury.
- The signature of the Secretary of the Treasury is on all U.S. paper currency.

DEPARTMENT OF TRANSPORTATION (DOT)
Nassif Building
This building, at 7th Street between D and E Streets, S.W., was constructed in 1969 on designs by Edward Durell Stone, with the same

marble used in the John F. Kennedy Center. The Nassif Building is not owned by the federal government but was built privately and is leased by the DOT.

Some of the agencies under the Department of Transportation are U.S. Coast Guard, Federal Aviation Administration, Federal Highway Administration, Maritime Administration, and National Highway Traffic Safety Administration.

FEDERAL RESERVE

The Federal Reserve, on Constitution Avenue, was established on December 23, 1913. The "Fed," which has only 1,500 employees, administers as well as formulates policy for the credit and monetary affairs of the United States. Visitors should contact Room 2234 to make an appointment for a tour.

- Each working day the Federal Reserve Bank destroys $6 million in worn-out U.S. currency.
- There are twelve federal reserve banks throughout the United States. Missouri is the only state that has two of them. Their initials on U.S. currency are:

A	Boston	E	Richmond	I	Minneapolis
B	New York	F	Atlanta	J	Kansas City
C	Philadelphia	G	Chicago	K	Dallas
D	Cleveland	H	St. Louis	L	San Francisco

GOVERNMENT PRINTING OFFICE (GPO)

This red brick building at 710 North Capitol and H Streets, N.W., built in 1901, is one of the world's largest printing plants, utilizing forty-one offset presses and thirty letterpresses. Built in the Romanesque Revival style, the building occupies a 33-acre site, with over 5,000 government employees. Ten freight-car loads of paper are used every working day. Each year the GPO publishes 1.4 billion volumes, with the *Congressional Record* and *Federal Register* being the highest priority. Annually Congress spends close to $100 million on the printing of bills for proposed laws, as well as for government documents.

The Government Printing Office was created by an act of Congress on June 23, 1860. The printing plant of Joseph T. Crowell in Washington was purchased by the government on February 19, 1861. John Dougherty

Deprees served as the first Superintendent, having been appointed by President Abraham Lincoln.

A GPO bookstore with 300 titles in stock and 17,000 additional catalogued titles can be found in every major city within the United States. Any books ordered from the bookstore will be shipped to any location within the United States free of charge. A bookstore is also located within the building, its front entrance on North Capitol Avenue.

- Since it was first printed in 1914, *Infant Care,* at 17,000,000 copies, has been the GPO's best-selling book.
- Mr. Public Printer is the official title of the head of the Government Printing Office.
- The GPO receives the daily session records of Congress until midnight, after which they are printed as the *Congressional Record,* with 27,000 copies produced by 8 A.M. the following morning.
- The Current Public Printer, Ralph E. Kennickell, Jr., at forty-one years old, is the youngest of the twenty-one Public Printers.

NATIONAL ARCHIVES

In the rotunda of the National Archives building on Constitution Avenue, between 7th and 9th Streets, N.W., kept under guard, are the Nation's most sacred documents—the Constitution, the Declaration of Independence, and the Bill of Rights. These treasures are housed in a special display case that, in the event of nuclear attack, will slide safely into an underground vault. An integrated burglar alarm system helps to protect against theft of the documents.

The Constitution Avenue entrance to the Archives building features bronze doors, each weighing six and a half tons.

- The National Archives has enough records to fill 150,000 four-drawer filing cabinets.
- The two bronze doors at the Archives entrance are the largest bronze doors in the world.
- The National Archives was built on the site of the Center Market.

POST OFFICE DEPARTMENT
City Post Office (Main Post Office)

This building, on Massachusetts Avenue at North Capitol Street, N. E., designed by Daniel H. Burnham, was constructed of white

Italian marble with a base of granite. It was completed in 1914 and remodeled in 1933. Built at a price of $7 million, it was designed to complement and harmonize with Burnham's other structure, Union Station, which is situated just across the street.

The inscriptions chiseled in marble that are displayed over both the west and east entrances were composed by Charles W. Eliot, the president of Harvard University.

WEST PORTAL
Messenger of Sympathy and Love
Servant of Parted Friends
Consoler of the Lonely
Bond of the Scattered Family
Enlarger of the Common Life

EAST PORTAL
Carrier of News and Knowledge
Instrument of Trade and Industry
Promoter of Mutual Acquaintance
Of Peace and Good Will
Among Men and Nations

The inscription on the West Portal was edited by President Woodrow Wilson.

The City Post Office should not be confused with the Old Post Office, which is located in the Federal Triangle.

- On July 26, 1775, Benjamin Franklin was appointed as the first Postmaster General under the Continental Congress.
- Abraham Lincoln served as the postmaster of New Salem, Illinois.
- It was President George Washington who sent the first airmail letter in the history of the United States. The letter, which introduced baloonist Jean Pierre Blanchard as a guest of the United States, was carried by Blanchard in his balloon from Washington to Gloucester County, New Jersey, a flight of 46 miles.
- U.S. Senators receive approximately 3 million letters each month from their constituents.
- The House of Representatives receives approximately 7½ million letters each month from their constituents.
- During President Grover Cleveland's administration, the Post Office deleted the letter "h" from the name of Pittsburgh, Pennsylvania, because they thought it was unnecessary to the pronunciation of the city's name.

- The Post Office Department in Washington first introduced the Dead Letter Office, in 1825.

Old Post Office

During the War of 1812 the Old Post Office, which also housed the Patent Office, was the only government building that the British did not burn, thanks to the pleas of the Superintendent of Patents, Dr. William Thornton. Appealing to a British officer, he said, "Are you Englishmen or Goths and Vandals? This is the Patent Office, the depository of the inventive genius of America, in which the whole civilized world is concerned. Would you destroy it?"

It was here that Congress convened after the British burned the Capitol. Conducting the business of the country there for a short time, Congress soon moved into a structure called the Brick Capitol. The Old Post Office was destroyed by fire on the night of December 15, 1836, and was later rebuilt.

The Old Post Office's Observatory Tower of the Pavilion gives a wonderful vantage point for viewing the downtown area. The recently renovated building now contains restaurants and many small stores. It is the oldest of the buildings in the Federal Triangle.

- The Old Post Office is home to the Congress Bells, which are rung at the opening and closing of Congress.
- A scene from D. W. Griffith's 1914 silent film *Birth of a Nation* is set in the Washington Patent Office, which was turned into a Civil War hospital for wounded Confederate soldiers.

DEPARTMENT OF STATE

Established on January 10, 1781, this was the first of the thirteen cabinet departments, with Thomas Jefferson serving as its first Secretary. On the eighth floor of the building, at 2201 C. Street, N. W., is a display of American antiques.

- Secretary of State Philander Knox (1909–1913) once stated that "There's just not enough work to do to occupy the Secretary's entire day."
- Secretary of State Dean Acheson won the Pulitzer Prize in history in 1970 for his book, *Present at the Creation*.
- Secretary of State Cordell Hull won the Nobel Peace Prize in 1945.
- Secretary of State Henry Kissinger and North Vietnam Politburo member Le Duc Tho were awarded the Nobel Peace Prize in 1973.

CHESAPEAKE & OHIO CANAL

The C & O Canal begins in Georgetown, and runs 22 miles northwest to Seneca, paralleling the Potomac River. It was restored in 1938 and is now operated by the National Park Service.

The C & O Canal once linked Georgetown with Cumberland, Maryland, a distance of over 184 miles, with 74 locks and an average traveling time of ten days upstream and three days downstream. The chief cargo carried into Georgetown by the mule-pulled barges was much needed coal. Steam vessels, which were much faster than barges, had to be banned on the canal because their wake caused serious damage along the canal's banks.

Construction began on the C & O Canal on July 4, 1828, in Georgetown when President John Quincy Adams turned over the first shovelful of earth. Ironically, on the very same day in Baltimore Charles Carroll, the last surviving signer of the Declaration of Independence, turned over the first shovelful of dirt to begin the construction of what eventually would be the canal's downfall—the Baltimore and Ohio Railroad.

In 1938, after many years of disuse, the canal, which had last been used commercially in 1924, was turned over to the U.S. government. Today, during the summer, spring, and fall, the Park Service offers two different canal boat rides, each with a boat pulled by a set of mules at approximately four miles per hour. The 90-foot-long *Georgetown* leaves the Foundry Mall, at 1055 Thomas Jefferson Street, N.W., and proceeds along the canal just past Key Bridge, then returns to the mall. The *Canal Clipper* leaves Great Falls Tavern in Great Falls, Maryland, and proceeds along the C & O Canal to a point at the end of MacArthur Boulevard, at Exit 41 of the George Washington Parkway.

The Great Falls Tavern, which was constructed in 1830, is now home to both a museum and a visitor's center. There is a Chesapeake and Ohio Canal Park located at 11710 MacArthur Boulevard in Potomac, Maryland.

- One of the investors in the canal was George Washington, who put up $10,000 in the Potowmack Canal Company.
- Two names that were originally considered for the C & O Canal were Union Canal and Potomac Canal.
- In the tradition of great erroneous statements of history, the *Intelligencer* newspaper said that railroads would be a costly experiment and would never become the transport system that could compete with a canal.

A second canal, the Washington Canal, traversed Washington, D.C., during the 1800s. Built by Irish laborers, the canal ran just below the White House, dividing the Mall from Pennsylvania Avenue, and was opened in November 1815. Years of neglect in which sewage, mosquitoes, and dead animals accumulated in the canal resulted in a dangerously polluted environment, so in 1872 the canal was filled in and Constitution Avenue was paved over it. The only reminder of the canal is an old house in which one of the lock keepers lived.

CEMETERIES

ARLINGTON NATIONAL CEMETERY

Of the 490 acres of land on which Arlington is situated, 210 acres were once owned by Robert E. Lee. He chose to become the commander of the Confederate Army, turning down an offer to command the Union Army. He was then stripped of his citizenship; his house and surrounding land were confiscated by the government. The Union, in an act of defiance, turned the grounds into a cemetery for Union soldiers that would fall to Lee's soldiers during the Civil War. To further punish Robert E. Lee, Quartermaster General Montgomery Meigs made the house and surrounding garden unlivable, so that Lee could never return to the mansion. He had the bones of over 2,000 Union soldiers who were killed at Bull Run buried next to the house and a large monument built where Mrs. Lee's rose garden had been. Ironically, the first man to be buried in Arlington, in May 1864, was a Confederate soldier who had been a patient at one of the many hospitals in Washington. The first Union soldier buried was Private William Christman on May 13, 1864. The first unknown soldiers buried at Arlington have grave markers located just behind the grave of Private Christman.

Buried in Arlington are thousands of American military veterans and their family members. In addition there are forty-four non-Americans buried in Arlington, including Ignace Jan Paderewski, the concert pianist

who became the Prime Minister of Poland from 1919 to 1921. Just a few
of the thousands of people buried at Arlington are:

John Foster Dulles	Politician	1888–1959
Omar Bradley	General	1893–1981
William Jennings Bryan	Politician	1860–1925
John J. Pershing	General	1860–1948
Pierre L'Enfant	Architect	1754–1825
Philip Sheridan	General	1831–1888
Robert Todd Lincoln	Politician	1843–1926
Virgil Grissom	Astronaut	1926–1967
Jonathan Wainwright	General	1883–1953
Audie Murphy	Soldier and Actor	1924–1971
Abner Doubleday	Soldier	1819–1893
Richard E. Byrd	Explorer	1888–1953
Joe Louis	Boxer	1914–1981
Francis Gary Powers	U-2 pilot	1829–1977
Thomas Selfridge	Soldier	1836–1924
Ignace Jan Paderewski	Musician/Politician	1860–1941

The graves of George Washington Parke Custis and his wife, Mary, are
located in Arlington. Explorer Robert E. Peary's grave has a large globe
of the world as its marker.

In addition to the 185,000 graves, there are a number of memorials,
such as the Confederate Memorial and the Tomb of the Unknowns, as
well as numerous memorials to great Americans. Medal of Honor win-
ners have letters in gold with a design of the medal itself on their
gravestones. The gravestones of Confederate soldiers have a pyramid on
the top, designed so no one could sit on them. Two thousand soldiers
killed at Bull Run are buried in the Civil War section.

Only two U.S. Presidents are buried in Arlington National Cemetery:
Willliam Howard Taft in 1930 and John F. Kennedy in 1963.

John F. Kennedy's Grave

An eternal flame fueled by gas marks the location of the grave of
President John F. Kennedy. To the left of JFK's grave is the grave of his
son Patrick Bouvier Kennedy, August 7, 1963–August 9, 1963. To the
right of JFK's grave is the grave of his unnamed daughter who was
stillborn on August 23, 1956. To the far left, about 100 feet away, is the
grave of his brother Robert Francis Kennedy, with a simple white cross as
its marker.

Confederate Memorial

The 32-foot-high bronze Confederate Memorial, sculpted by Moses Ezekiel in 1914, is located at Jackson Circle. When the monument was dedicated in 1914, President Woodrow Wilson spoke to approximately 3,000 veterans of the Civil War, both Confederate and Union soldiers. The inscription on the monument reads, "Not for fame or reward, not for peace, or for rank, not turned by ambition or goaded by necessity."

Tomb of the Unknown

(Formerly the Tomb of the Unknown Soldier)

This memorial is a fifty-ton block of white marble dedicated to the unknown American soldiers of World War I, designed by Lorimer Rich and sculpted by Thomas Hudson Jones. On Memorial Day in 1958, two additions were added to the memorial, for the unknown soldiers from World War II (1941–1945) and the Korean War (1950–1953). Officially, there are no unknown soldiers from the Vietnam War.

Nearby is a 4,000-seat amphitheater designed by Carriere and Hastings, constructed in 1920, which houses a trophy room featuring the statue of *Victory* by Augustus Saint-Gaudens. The amphitheater also features a small museum that tells the history of the unknown soldiers.

CHANGING OF THE GUARDS

Every hour during the day a ceremony is held in which the single guard is relieved from his vigilance by a new guard. The sergeant in charge first inspects the relieving soldier's rifle, uniform, and appearance. Upon passing the traditional inspection, the new sentinel will spend one hour (two hours at night) marching in front of the tomb. He marches by forty-two times, each march consisting of twenty-seven steps of 30 inches each. The guard's bayoneted rifle is always placed on the shoulder farthest away from the tombs. The sentinel will warn anyone who attempts to enter the restricted area around the tomb. All the U.S. Army soldiers who guard the tomb are volunteers of the Old Guard, from the First Battle Group of the Third Infantry Regiment. Each soldier must be highly recommended by their superior officers.

At times a visiting dignitary will place a wreath at the Tomb of the Unknown, after which they are saluted by cannonfire.

Arlington House

Robert E. Lee's house is now a museum overlooking the cemetery and Washington from the west, often referred to as the best view of Washington. When George Washington Custis owned the estate, he called it Arlington House. During the Civil War, the soldiers assigned to guard the house called it the Lee Mansion. From 1955 to 1972, the house was officially called the Custis-Lee Mansion. Today the Robert E. Lee Memorial is once again referred to as Arlington House. Arlington House was the site of the first official Memorial Day service in the United States, on May 30, 1868.

Originally, the house had been the home of George Washington Parke Custis (1781–1857), the grandson of First Lady Martha Washington by her first husband. In 1804 Custis married Mary Lee Fitzhugh and they moved into the newly constructed house. In 1831 their daughter Mary Ann Randolph married Robert E. Lee, the son of "Light Horse Harry" Lee (1756–1818), the man who eulogized his friend George Washington as "First in war, first in peace, and first in the hearts of his countrymen." The house then became the home of that great soldier, Robert E. Lee, whose citizenship was finally restored by Congress on July 22, 1975. In 1925 the house, which until then had served only as a living quarters for the cemetery staff, was restored by the National Park Service.

Other Memorials

- The pyramid-shaped Tampa monument was erected to the 192 officers and men who went down on the Coast Guard cutter *Tampa* during World War I.
- The white marble Army and Navy Nurses Memorial overlooks the graves of hundreds of nurses who died serving their country.
- In 1922 the Argonne Cross was erected to commemorate the more than 5,000 U.S. servicemen killed during World War I who are buried at Arlington. The Argonne Cross was erected by the American Legion.
- Near Arlington House is a memorial to the unknown dead of the Civil War.
- Other memorials at Arlington include the Canadian Memorial Cross, The Rough Riders Memorial, the U.S.S. *Forestal* Monument, the Chaplain's Memorial, and the U.S.S. *Submarine F4* Memorial.

- The Temple of Fame, dedicated to George Washington and eleven Union generals, was built in 1866 where the original rose garden of Arlington House was located. The memorial was torn down by the National Park Service in 1966 in order to restore the rose garden.

ARLINGTON CEMETERY FACTS

- The grave of Washington architect Pierre Charles L'Enfant was transferred to Arlington in 1902 from the foot of a tree at the Green Hill Mansion.
- The white mast from the battleship U.S.S. *Maine,* which was sunk in Havana harbor on February 15, 1898, is located on the grounds as a memorial to those 229 Americans who lost their lives when the ship was sunk.
- The cremated remains of the seven crew members of the space shuttle *Challenger,* which exploded just 73 seconds after takeoff in January 1986, were buried in a small grave in May 1987 in a secret ceremony. Near their grave are the graves of the three Americans who were killed in 1980 in the unsuccessful attempt to rescue the American hostages held in Iran.
- Many guides of cemetery tours erroneously credit Abner Doubleday as the inventor of baseball, even though today there is proof that he was not the game's creator.

MARINE CORPS WAR MEMORIAL

Located next to Arlington Cemetery is the only U.S. national monument that was inspired by a photograph: the Pulitzer Prize-winning photo by Joe Rosenthal of the raising of the American flag on Mt. Suribachi on Iwo Jima, February 23, 1945. Iwo Jima was one of the U.S. Marine Corps' bloodiest battles, with 5,550 killed and 17,000 wounded. The statue, which measures 32 feet high with a flagpole 60 feet high, was designed by Felix W. de Weldon and dedicated in 1954. At the base of the monument is the inscription of a quotation by Fleet Admiral Chester W. Nimitz, "Uncommon Valor was a Common Virtue." The flag on the memorial is raised and lowered ceremonially each day.

- A few years ago, Representative Charles S. Joelson was extremely upset when he discovered that souvenir statues of the soldiers raising the flag at Iwo Jima being sold at the memorial were manufactured in Japan.

The Netherlands Carillon

Located on the grounds of the Marine memorial is this 127-foot-high gift of the Netherlands to the United States. The steel tower consists of forty-nine stationary bells, with the smallest weighing 41.8 pounds and the largest 12,654 pounds. The bells chime each afternoon, except on Sundays, at exactly 3:45. The bells were presented to the people of the United States in a ceremony on April 4, 1952. The completed carillon was dedicated on May 5, 1960, on the fifteenth anniversary of the liberation of the Netherlands during World War II.

BATTLEGROUND NATIONAL CEMETERY

This is the smallest national cemetery in the United States. Buried here are forty-one Union soldiers who were killed at the Battle of Fort Stevens while defending Washington on July 12, 1864, during the Civil War. The cemetery is located at 6625 Georgia Avenue, N.W.

CONGRESSIONAL CEMETERY

Buried here, at 1801 E Street, S.E., on thirty acres located on the north bank of the Anacosta River, is almost every congressman who died in office from 1807 until 1876. After that year, Arlington National Cemetery became the primary burial place for congressmen. By the time the cemetery was closed, a Vice President, several Chief Justices of the Supreme Court, the first five Mayors of Washington, nineteen Senators, and forty-two Representatives found their final resting place in the cemetery.

Some of the celebrities buried here are:

John Philip Sousa	Composer and band leader	1854–1932
Mathew Brady	Civil War photographer	1823–1896
J. Edgar Hoover	Chief of the FBI	1895–1972
Henry Clay	Senator	1777–1852
Elbridge Gerry	Vice President	1744–1814
Joseph Gales	Publisher	1786–1860
Adelaide Johnson	Sculptor	1859–1955
Anne Royall	Journalist	1769–1854
Robert Mills	Architect	1781–1955
Push-ma-ta-ha	Choctaw chief	?–1824

FBI chief J. Edgar Hoover was born, and died, in Washington, D.C. John Philip Sousa, who had also been born in Washington, D.C., died in Reading, Pennsylvania. Vice President Elbridge Gerry, who died in 1814, was a signer of the Declaration of Independence. First Lady Dolley Madison's son John Payne Todd, by her first marriage, rests here. Theoderic Bland of Virginia, who is buried here, was the first congressman to die, passing away on June 1, 1790. Marion Kahlert, a ten-year-old girl who became the first victim of an automobile accident in Washington, in 1904, is buried here.

A mass grave beneath a 20-foot marble shaft is the resting place of twenty-one women who were killed in the explosion of the Washington Arsenal in 1864.

GLENWOOD CEMETERY

This 38-acre cemetery at 2219 Lincoln Road, N.E., which was dedicated in 1954, originally stretched over 90 acres until 52 of its acres were sold to Trinity College to create part of their campus.

People buried here include Alexander Gardner, photographer (1821–1882), and Emanuel Leutze, painter (1816–1868).

Benjamin C. Grenup, the first recorded fireman to die in Washington, is also buried here. Emanuel Leutze painted the 1851 masterpiece *Washington Crossing the Delaware*.

HOUSE OF THE TEMPLE

Buried here, at 1733 16th Street, N.W., is poet Albert Pike (1809–1891).

IVY HILL CEMETERY

Werner von Braun (1912–1977), the German-born scientist who led the United States into the development of rockets, is buried here. The cemetery is located at 2823 King Street, Alexandria, Virginia.

MOUNT OLIVET CEMETERY

This 75-acre cemetery on Bladenburg Road was purchased in 1858 by the Catholic Church from the Fenwick Farms, after which the remains of all the Catholics buried in the city were moved to Mount Olivet in order to comply with an 1852 city ordinance prohibiting burials within the city limits.

People buried here:

Constantino Brumidi	Painter of the Capitol Rotunda	(1805–1880)
James Hoban	Designer of the White House	(1726–1831)
Mary Surratt	Convicted for complicity in the assassination of President Abraham Lincoln	(1820–1865)

Mary Surratt, who is buried in grave 12F, Lot 31, has a gravestone marked simply, "Mrs. Surratt."

MOUNT VERNON

Mount Vernon, in Virginia, was the home estate of George Washington and his family after 1674, when John Washington, his great-grandfather, had it constructed. George Washington was entombed in the family vault in 1799, although it had originally been planned to have him buried in the basement of the Capitol.

MOUNT ZION CEMETERY

This is one of the oldest historical sites in Washington. It was the cemetery for Mt. Zion United Methodist Church, the first Negro church in Washington. The cemetery also contains the graves of German mercenary soldiers who died when Washington was captured by the British in August 1814.

OAK HILL CEMETERY

This 25-acre cemetery, at 30th and R streets, situated on four plateaus, was founded in 1848 by William Wilson Corcoran, who presented it to the city. Its Gothic Revival chapel was designed and built in 1850 by James Renwick.

Buried at Oak Hill Cemetery are:

Edward D. White	Supreme Court Justice	1845–1921
Dean Acheson	Secretary of State	1893–1971
John A. Joyce	Poet	1842–1915
Edwin M. Stanton	Secretary of War	1814–1869
James G. Blaine	Secretary of State	1830–1893
John Howard Payne	Poet	1791–1852
Joseph Henry	Secretary of the Smithsonian	1797–1878

- John Howard Payne was the composer of the song "Home, Sweet Home." He died in Tunisia and his body was brought back to Washington in 1883.
- Joseph Henry, physicist and inventor, served as the first secretary of the Smithsonian Institution in 1846.
- The very first person to be buried at Oak Hill Cemetery was George Corbin Washington's daughter Eleanor, who was laid to rest on April 13, 1849.

PRESBYTERIAN MEETING HOUSE

This Alexandria cemetery, at 312 S. Fairfax Street, was established in 1774 by John Carlyle. It contains the remains of many patriots who died during the Revolutionary War. Buried here is the Unknown Veteran of the Revolutionary War.

ROCK CREEK CEMETERY

Washington's oldest cemetery, at St. Paul's Episcopal Church, features the statue of *Grief* by Augustus Saint-Gaudens. The statue is located at the Adams Memorial, the grave of Henry Adams and his wife, Clover. Its setting was designed by architect Stanford White. The Adams Monument was originally dedicated as a memorial to Mrs. Henry Adams. St. Paul's, built in 1771, is the oldest church in Washington. In 1921 the original building was rebuilt after being destroyed in a fire.

Buried here are:

Henry Adams	Minister to Britain	(1838–1918)
Harlan Fiske Stone	Chief Justice	(1872–1946)
John Marshal Harlan	Justice	(1833–1911)
Alexander Shepherd	Mayor of Washington	

Alexander Shepherd was the second, and last, territorial governor of the District of Columbia.

- First Lady Eleanor Roosevelt often sat in front of the statue of *Grief*, in order to help her to put her problems aside.

ST. MARY'S CHURCH

F. Scott Fitzgerald (1896–1940) and his wife Zelda Fitzgerald (1900–1948) are buried here. The cemetery is on Vier Mill Road, Rockville, Maryland.

SOLDIERS HOME NATIONAL CEMETERY

The Soldiers Home and adjoining Memorial Gateway Cemetery at Rock Creek Road and Upshur Street, N.W., was founded by an act of Congress in 1851, at the suggestion of General Winfield Scott and Major Robert Anderson.

WASHINGTON NATIONAL CATHEDRAL

Cathedral of St. Peter and St. Paul, commonly called the Washington Cathedral sits on the 400-foot-high Mt. St. Alban, higher ground than either the Washington Monument or the Capitol Building. It is located at Massachusetts and Wisconsin avenues.

Buried here are:

George Dewey	Admiral	(1837–1917)
Helen Keller	Author	(1880–1968)
Annie Sullivan	Teacher	(1866–1936)
Cordell Hull	Secretary of State	(1871–1955)
Woodrow Wilson	President	(1856–1924)

Other Burial Places

- Charles Julius Guiteau, the man who assassinated President James Garfield in 1881, was buried at the Old Washington Jail and Asylum at 19th Street and Independence Avenue, S.W. He was hanged in Washington on June 30, 1882.
- James Smithson, benefactor of the Smithsonian, is buried in a tomb at the entrance to the Smithsonian's Castle. Although he never

visited the United States, his body was moved to the Smithsonian Institution from an Italian cemetery.

People Who Have Died in Washington, D.C.

George Clinton	Vice President	April 20, 1812
Gerry Elbridge	Vice President	November 23, 1814
Push-ma-ta-ha	Indian chief	December 24, 1824
John C. Calvin	Politician	May 31, 1850
Henry Clay	Senator	June 29, 1852
Roger B. Taney	Chief Justice	October 12, 1864
Abraham Lincoln	President	April 15, 1865
James Garfield	President	September 19, 1881
Emanuel Leutze	Artist	July 18, 1868
Edwin Stanton	Secretary of War	December 24, 1869
Albert Pike	Poet	April 2, 1891
George Bancroft	Historian	January 17, 1891
Frederick Douglass	Orator	February 20, 1895
Walter Reed	Bacteriologist	November 23, 1902
Robert Perry	Explorer	February 20, 1920
Woodrow Wilson	President	February 3, 1924
William Howard Taft	President	March 8, 1930
Charles Curtis	Vice President	February 8, 1936
John J. Pershing	General	July 15, 1948
George C. Marshall	General	October 16, 1959
Douglas MacArthur	General	April 5, 1964
John L. Lewis	Labor leader	June 11, 1969
Vince Lombardi	Football coach	September 3, 1970
J. Edgar Hoover	FBI chief	May 2, 1972
Earl Warren	Justice	July 9, 1974
Mamie Eisenhower	First Lady	November 1, 1979
William O. Douglas	Justice	January 19, 1980

General George C. Marshall is the only general to have won the Nobel Prize (Peace Prize, 1953).

CHURCHES

"Washington is a city of churches, and even Brooklyn, which has for a long time assumed this title, does not now number as many churches in proportion to the population," wrote Stilson Hutchins and Joseph Moore in 1885.

There are 446 Protestant, 23 Roman Catholic, 10 Jewish, and 23 other places of worship in Washington, D.C., with 1,200 churches of 70 denominations in and around Washington.

The Most Popular Houses of Worship of Washington

NAME	YEAR ESTABLISHED	ARCHITECTS/DESIGNERS
Adas Israel Synagogue (old)	1876	
All Souls Unitarian Church	1921	Coolidge and Shattuck
Asbury Methodist Church		
Calvary Baptist Church		Adolph Cluss
Capitol Hill Presbyterian Church		
St. Sophia's Cathedral	1956	Archie Protopappas
Christ Church	1805	H. Latrobe
Christ Church of Alexandria	1773	James Wren
Christ Church of Washington	1885	Henry Laws

NAME	YEAR ESTABLISHED	ARCHITECTS/DESIGNERS
Christ Church of Washington	1967	Milton J. Prassas, McArthur Jollay
Church of St. Stephen and the Incarnation	1928	Northrop Dudley
Church of the Annunciation		Philip Hubert Frohman
Church of the Ascension and St. Agnes		Charles Carson and Thomas Dixon
Church of the Epiphany		
Church of the Holy City	1895	H. Langford Warren
Ebenezer United Methodist Church		
First Baptist Church	1955	Harold E. Wagoner
First Church of Christ Scientist		
First Congregational Church		
Foundry United Methodist Church	1904	Appleton P. Clark
Fourth Church of Christ Scientist	1929	Howard L. Cheney
Franciscan Monastery	1899	
Friends Meeting of Washington	1930	Walter Price
Georgetown Lutheran Church		
Grace Episcopal Church	1866	
Grace Evangelical and Reform Church		
Holy Trinity Catholic Church	1851	Francis Stanton
Islamic Center and Mosque	1949	
Luther Place Memorial Church	1870	Judson York
Metropolitan A.M.E. Church	1881	Samuel T. Morsell
Metro Memorial Methodist Church		
Mt. Vernon Place United Methodist Church	1917	Sauginet and Straats

Name	Year Established	Architects/Designers
Mt. Zion United Methodist Church		
National Baptist Memorial Church		
National City Christian Church	1930	John Russell Pope
National Presbyterian Church		
National Shrine of the Immaculate Conception	1926	Maginnis and Walsh
New York Avenue Presbyterian Church	1860	
Our Lady of Victory Church		Donald Johnson & Harold B.
Saints Constantine and Helen Greek Orthodox Church	1953	Milton J. Prassas
St. John's Church–Georgetown	1804	Dr. William Thornton
St. John's Episcopal Church	1816	Benjamin H. Latrobe
St. Mary's Catholic Church		
St. Mary's Episcopal Church	1887	James Renwick
St. Matthew's Cathedral	1899	Heins and La Farge
St. Nicholas Cathedral	1963	Alexander Neratov
St. Patrick's Roman Catholic Church	1884	
St. Paul's Rock Creek Church		Philip Hubert Frohman
St. Stephen's Catholic Church	1865	Donald Johnson and Harold L. Boutin
St. Thomas Apostle Catholic Church	1891	Donald Johnson and Harold Boutin
Sixth Church of Christ	1962	Chatelain and Gauger
Third Church of Christ Scientist	1972	I. M. Pei
Unification Church	1933	Young and Hansen
Washington National Cathedral	1907	George F. Bodley and Henry Vaughan

Name	Year Established	Architects/Designers
Washington Hebrew Congregation	1954	F. Wallace Dixon
Wesley Methodist Church		Philip Hubert Frohman
Western Presbyterian Church		

All Souls Unitarian Church
16th Street and Harvard Street, N.W.

This church was built in 1924 by the architectural firm of Coolidge and Shattuck at the cost of almost $1 million. The building is a replica of London's Church of St. Martin's in the Field, built on Trafalgar Square by James Gibbs. Three U.S. Presidents have worshipped at All Souls Church: John Quincy Adams, Millard Fillmore, and William Howard Taft. President William Howard Taft was interred at All Souls Church in 1930, before he was buried at Arlington National Cemetery.

• Note that there are no religious icons in the church's interior.

Apostolic Delegation Church
3339 Massachusetts Avenue, N.W.

This Catholic Church was constructed in 1938 from designs by Frederick Vernon Murphy. The church is the home of the apostolic delegate, who represents the Pope in the United States.

Calvary Baptist
8th Street and H Street, N.W.

Built in the 1860s by Adolph Cluss.

Christ Church of Washington
Massachusetts Avenue at Idaho Avenue, N.W.

Completed in 1967, the church was designed by its pastor, Reverend McArthur Jollay.

Christ Church (Washington Parish)
620 G. Street, S.E.

Built in 1806 by Benjamin Latrobe, this church is considered to be the oldest church building in Washington.

- Presidents Thomas Jefferson, James Madison, and James Monroe worshipped at Christ Church. Another member of the congregation was attorney Francis Scott Key.

Christ Church (Alexandria)
Cameron Street and Columbus Street

Built between 1767 and 1773, the church was designed by James Wren, a descendant of famed British architect Sir Christopher Wren.

The church features a crystal chandelier and a silver-plated communion rail. The pews feature silver plaques identifying their previous owners.

On the National Day of Prayer in January 1942, President Franklin D. Roosevelt and British Prime Minister Winston Churchill worshipped here together.

- President George Washington worshipped here at pew 46. He also purchased pew 60 for 36 pounds, 10 shillings. General Robert E. Lee also was a member of the church's congregation, being confirmed there in 1853.
- President Ronald Reagan and the First Lady attended services at Christ Church on February 21, 1982, on the eve of the 250th anniversary of George Washington's birthday. This was the first church service attended by the Reagans since June 14, 1981.

Church of the Ascension and St. Agnes (Episcopal)
Massachusetts Avenue and 12th Street, N.W.

This Victorian Gothic structure was built in 1875 from designs by architects Thomas Dixon and Charles Carson on land dedicated by W. W. Corcoran. Its interior features cast-iron columns and walnut pews. This is the only church named for St. Agnes that has a relic of the patron saint.

First Baptist Church
1326 O Street, N.W.

The original church was designed by W. Bruce Gray and built in 1890 with a campanile tower 140 feet high. From 1953 to 1955, a new First Baptist Church was built on the site, designed by Harold E. Wagoner.

Presidents Harry S Truman and Jimmy Carter attended the First Baptist Church when they lived in the White House. Truman often walked several blocks from the Executive Mansion to the church. He worshipped in the original structure, while Carter worshipped in the newer building.

- President Jimmy Carter conducted Sunday school classes at the First Baptist Church on several occasions while President.

First Congregational Church

10th Street and G Street, N.W.

During one Thanksgiving Day service at this church, President Calvin Coolidge just missed being hit by falling plaster from the ceiling.

Foundry United Methodist Church

1500 16th Street, N.W.

This unusually named church was established in 1814 by Henry Foxall, owner of an iron-ore foundry in Georgetown.

- At the Christmas service in 1941, President Franklin D. Roosevelt and British Prime Minister Winston Churchill prayed in adjoining pews.

Franciscan Monastery

1400 Quincy Street, N.E.

At this monastery are several religious reproductions, including the catacombs of Rome, the Grotto of Lourdes, the Grotto of Bethlehem, and the Altar of Calvary.

Friends Meeting of Washington

211 Florida Avenue, N.W.

The building, completed in 1930, was designed by Walter H. Price, reflecting the simple tastes of the Quaker religion.

President Herbert Hoover worshipped here when he lived in the White House. Although Richard Nixon also was a Quaker, he and First Lady Pat Nixon did not elect to worship there.

- The family upon whom Jessamyn West based her popular novel *Friendly Persuasion* were the ancestors of Richard M. Nixon.

Grace Evangelical and Reform Church

15th Street and O Street, N.W.

President Theodore Roosevelt, who laid this church's cornerstone, attended services here from 1901 to 1909. The church now has a collection of Roosevelt's memorabilia.

- Although President Theodore Roosevelt attended services at Grace Evangelical and Reform Church, his wife and family attended St. John's Episcopal Church.

Islamic Center and Mosque
2551 Massachusetts Avenue, N.W.

This house of worship was constructed by fifteen Moslem countries after World War II. The cornerstone was laid on January 11, 1949. The mosque's first director was Dr. Mahmoud Hoballah.

- Muslims are the third largest religious group in the United States, following Christians and Jews.
- This Islamic mosque is the only mosque in the United States to have air conditioning.

Metropolitan African Methodist Episcopal Church
1518 M Street, N.W.

The A.M.E. is the oldest black religious denomination in the United States. The national cathedral of African Methodism, with its eighteen stained glass windows, was constructed from 1854 to 1881, by both free blacks and slaves, from the design by Samuel T. Morsell. The church, which was the religious temple for many of Washington's poorer citizens, has a pew dedicated to Frederick Douglass and another pew dedicated to Paul Laurence Dunbar. In 1895 Frederick Douglass's funeral was held in the church. Many members of the congregation were instrumental in helping slaves escape via the underground railway.

- The walls that enclose the first floor are two feet thick.
- Several American Presidents have spoken from the church's pulpit, including William Howard Taft and Jimmy Carter.
- First Lady Eleanor Roosevelt also spoke from the church's pulpit.

Mt. Vernon Place United Methodist Church
900 Massachusetts Avenue, N.W.

This religious house features the largest Protestant congregation in Washington, D.C.

National City Christian Church
14th Street and Massachusetts Avenue, N.W. at Thomas Circle

Designed by John Russell Pope and dedicated in 1930.

- Two Presidents, James A. Garfield and Lyndon B. Johnson, have been among the church's congregation.

National Conference of Catholic Bishops
1312 Massachusetts Avenue, N.W.

Designed by architect Frederick V. Murphy.

- When the 22-foot-tall statue of Christ, sculpted by Eugene Kormendi, was dedicated in 1949, it became the first statue of Jesus ever erected in Washington. The funds for the statue were raised by Bishop John F. Noll of Fort Wayne, Indiana.

National Shrine of the Immaculate Conception
4th Street and Michigan Avenue, N.E.

This is the largest Roman Catholic church in the United States, and the seventh-largest church in the world. Built in 1926, this huge church, 459 feet long, 157 feet wide, and 329 feet high, includes a Memorial Hall, a Founder's Chapel, and a Lourdes Chapel. The dome itself measures 108 feet in diameter and is 237 feet high. The outside of the shrine was completed in 1959 when a $1 million, 56-bell carillon was installed.

The National Shrine of the Immaculate Conception, which is also called the Crypt Church, has thirty-two chapels, and was built with funds contributed by every Catholic church parish in the United States.

- The only person buried in the church is Bishop Thomas Shahan, one-time rector of Catholic University.
- The National Shrine of the Immaculate Conception, which has been called "the greatest church edifice in the western hemisphere and one of the most magnificent basilicas in the world," is considered by others to be the ugliest Catholic church in the United States.

Old Adas Israel Synagogue
3rd Street and G Street, N.W.

Although no longer used as a house of worship, the building has been restored to its appearance when President Ulysses S. Grant dedicated it in 1876. It was the first building constructed in Washington especially to be a synagogue.

The building has since been a Greek Orthodox Church (Saint Sophia) and a Church of God, as well as a warehouse. The building was moved from its original location at 6th Street and G Street when the Metro subway was built. It is also the home of the Lillian and Albert Small Jewish Museum.

The present-day Adas Israel Synagogue is located at Connecticut Avenue and Porter Street.

- When Ulysses S. Grant attended the dedication ceremonies in 1876, he became the first U.S. President to attend a Jewish house of worship.

- Singer Al Jolson's father, Chazan Yoelson, was a rabbi, who lived in Washington, D.C., having emigrated from Russia in 1886. His two sons, Al and Harry, grew up in Washington.

St. Albans Church
Wisconsin Avenue and Cathedral Place

Built in 1852, this was the first free church in the diocese of Washington.

St. John's Episcopal Church
16th Street and H Street, N.W., Lafayette Square

Located across the street from the White House, this place of worship was designed by Benjamin H. Latrobe and built in 1816. In 1883 its interior was constructed from designs by James Renwick. Latrobe served as the church's first organist.

St. John's is called "the Church of the Presidents." It is believed that every President since James Madison has worshipped there at some time, because it is so close to the White House. First Lady Dolley Madison was baptized at St. John's, and President Gerald Ford attended a private service there just prior to announcing a pardon for former President Richard Nixon.

During the War of 1812, the patriots captured a 1,000-pound British cannon, which was melted down and recast into a bell. In order to celebrate the Japanese surrender, ending World War II in 1945, the bell was rung so often that the bellrope broke.

- Some of the church's parishioners have been Presidents James Madison, James Monroe, Martin Van Buren, William Henry Harrison, John Tyler, Zachary Taylor, Franklin Pierce, and Chester A. Arthur. Abraham Lincoln and Franklin D. Roosevelt also attended services there.
- The church's pew 54 was originally rented by James Madison and has been occupied by ten Presidents in all.
- In August 1842 the Parish House, next door to the church, served as the residence of Lord Ashburton, the British Minister. It was here that the United States and Canada signed the treaty establishing the borders between the two countries, with Daniel Webster representing the United States.
- President Chester A. Arthur dedicated a stained-glass window in the memory of his wife, Ellen, who had sung contralto in the choir.

- While living in the White House, President William McKinley often turned his chair so that he could view the spire of St. John's from his office window.

St. Matthew's Cathedral
1725 Rhode Island Avenue, N.W.

Built from 1893 to 1899 on plans by Grant La Farge, this church is today the seat of Washington's Catholic archbishop. The cathedral was named for St. Matthew as well as in honor of Father William Matthew, the first native Marylander to be ordained a priest.

St. Matthew's is often remembered as the church where President John F. Kennedy and his family attended Catholic services, as well as where Kennedy's funeral mass was celebrated.

- The first contributor of funds used in the building of St. Matthews was Father William Matthew.

St. Nicholas Cathedral (Russian Orthodox)
3500 Massachusetts Avenue, N.W.

Built in 1963 as both the Russian Orthodox church and a national war memorial shrine of the Orthodox church in the United States, the church was modeled by Alexander Neratov after St. Dimitri's, which was built in Vladimir, Russia, in 1195.

St. Patrick's Roman Catholic Church
619 10th Street, N.W.

This church was completed in 1806. An organ was installed in 1810.

St. Sophia's Cathedral (Greek Orthodox)
Massachusetts Avenue and 36th Street, N.W.

Built in 1956 by architect Archie Protopappas, this is the largest Greek Orthodox church in the United States.

- President Dwight D. Eisenhower and First Lady Mamie laid the cathedral's cornerstone in 1956.

Washington National Cathedral
(Cathedral Church of St. Peter and St. Paul)
Wisconsin Avenue and Massachusetts Avenue, N.W.

The cornerstone of this 80 percent completed church was laid in 1907. It is the sixth-largest religious structure in the world. The church was granted the charter to establish the Protestant Episcopal Cathedral

Foundation in 1893. George F. Bodley and Henry Vaughan were the original architects in 1907, with the addition of Philip H. Frohman in 1920.

Church services were first held in the cathedral in 1912. The cathedral features many beautiful and unusual stained-glass windows and several chapels, including the Children's Chapel, St. John's Chapel, St. Mary's Chapel, and the Bethlehem Chapel. The cathedral is the seat of two bishops: the presiding bishop of the Episcopal Church of the United States, and the Bishop of the Diocese of Washington.

Located on top of Mount St. Albans, the cathedral features the Gloria in Excelsis Tower with its 53-bell carillon which, at 676-feet above sea level, is located at the highest part of Washington.

Situated on 57 acres, the Washington Cathedral features the National Cathedral School for girls and the St. Alban's School for boys.

- Deaf-and-blind educator Helen Keller and her devoted teacher, Annie Sullivan, are both buried in the cathedral.
- Like the Library of Congress, the Washington Cathedral has a 1455 edition of the Gutenberg Bible.
- Legend has it that the cremated ashes of a stone carver's wife are buried within the church's walls, because the bishop refused the worker permission to bury his wife in the cathedral. The exact location of those remains is unknown.
- The body of Woodrow Wilson is buried here. His grandson Francis Sayre served as dean of the cathedral.

Washington Hebrew Congregation
Massachusetts Avenue and McComb Street, N.W.

The building's cornerstone was laid by President Harry S Truman in 1952. The dedication was heard by President Dwight D. Eisenhower two years later.

PRESIDENTIAL FACTS

- The fathers of Presidents Chester A. Arthur, Grover Cleveland, and Woodrow Wilson were ministers.
- First Lady Abigail Fillmore was the daughter of a Baptist minister.
- More Presidents have been Episcopalian than any other religion— George Washington, James Madison, James Monroe, William Henry Harrison, John Tyler, Zachary Taylor, James Pierce, Chester A. Arthur, Franklin D. Roosevelt, and Gerald Ford.

- The only Catholic President to date has been John F. Kennedy.
- Herbert Hoover and Richard Nixon were the only Quaker Presidents.
- Presidents Thomas Jefferson, Abraham Lincoln, Andrew Johnson, and Rutherford Hayes had no religious affiliation.

SCHOOLS

Washington is home to several world-famous universities: American University, Catholic University, Georgetown University, Howard University, and George Washington University.

American University
Massachusetts Avenue and Nebraska Avenue, N.W.

The 75-acre-campus American University was incorporated in 1893 by act of Congress, under Methodist auspices, with Bishop John Fletcher Hurst serving as its first administrator. Hurst Hall, completed in 1898, was the campus's first building. American University features a museum of contemporary American art work, the Watkins Gallery, the Opera Theatre, the Gaston Hall, and the Welchester Theatre. The Civil War army post of Fort Gaines stood on the grounds of the what today is the university's campus.

- Actress Goldie Hawn attended American University for two years.
- In 1978 Ray Voelkel of American University set a modern-day major-college basketball record when he made 25 consecutive field goals (during nine games) for one season.

Capitol Page School
10 First Street, S.E.

There are 81 pages employed on Capitol Hill: 51 by the House, 26 by the Senate, and 4 by the Supreme Court. The pages, ranging in age from sixteen to eighteen in the House and fourteen to sixteen in the Senate, attend the Capitol Page School at the Library of Congress. School begins at 6:30 A.M., in order for the pages to be out of school in time to perform their duties at the Capitol. Some of their duties include delivering government documents, distributing current bills, running errands, and keeping the Senate snuffboxes filled. Until 1971, when the sex barrier was broken, all pages were male.

- Daniel Webster and Henry Clay, in 1829, appointed the first page, a lad just nine years old.
- Senator Robert Baker served as a page in his youth.
- A rule stating that pages could be no taller than the high-backed chairs of the justices of the Supreme Court has been abolished.
- Dickie Jones played a Senate page in the 1939 Frank Capra movie *Mr. Smith Goes to Washington,* in which James Stewart played Senator Jefferson Smith.

Catholic University of America
620 Michigan Avenue, N.E.

This 150-acre-campus college was founded in 1887 by Maryland Cardinal James Gibbons originally as a school of theology. On the grounds is located the National Shrine of the Immaculate Conception. The University also features the Hartke Theatre. There is a nuclear reactor in the institution's Mechanical-Aeronautical Engineering Building.

- The university is affiliated with a number of colleges, some of which are located on the university's grounds, such as the Catholic Sisters College. When this institution was established in 1911 it became the first institution to train nuns for parochial school teachers.
- Academy Award-winning actor Jon Voight graduated from Catholic University with a B.A. degree in art.

Franklin School
13th Street and K Street, N.W.

This award-winning building was designed in 1896 by Adolph Cluss, who was praised at several World's Fairs for its construction. The public school was attended by the children of U.S. Presidents Andrew Johnson and Chester A. Arthur.

- It was from this building that inventor Alexander Graham Bell made his first wireless telephone call on June 3, 1880. The signal was sent on a beam of light to a building on L Street.

Gallaudet College
Florida Avenue and 7th Street, N.E.

Built in 1864 on designs of Calvert Vaux and Frederick Law Olmsted, this was the world's only accredited liberal arts college for the hearing impaired. The school was founded by Edward Miner Gallaudet and named in honor of his father Thomas Hopkins Gallaudet. The school, which was founded by act of Congress in 1864, began as the National Deaf Mute College, a department of the Columbia Institution for the Instruction of the Deaf, Dumb and Blind, and was incorporated on February 16, 1857. The name was changed to the Columbia Institution for the Deaf, then in 1894 to Gallaudet College. In 1865 blind students were also admitted, and in 1867 women students began to attend.

- It was at Gallaudet College that the football huddle was invented, in the 1890s, so that the deaf players could exchange hand signals without the other team's seeing them.
- Gallaudet is the only accredited college for the deaf in the world that offers a degree in liberal arts.

Georgetown University
37th Street and O Street, N.W.

This school was founded in 1789 by America's first bishop, John Carroll, who would also become America's first archbishop. The 100-acre-campus university was organized with the help of John Quincy Adams, who helped to obtain personal loans for its construction. Georgetown University, originally named Columbian University, is the oldest Catholic college in the United States. The school has been run by the Jesuits since 1805 and is the oldest Jesuit school in the United States. Courses on service in foreign countries for diplomats and embassy workers are popular. In 1826 Georgetown University opened Washington's first law school.

The Georgetown University Law Center, which was opened in 1871, is located at 600 New Jersey Avenue, N.W., just a few blocks from the White House.

- In 1879 Healy Building was completed. It was named for Patrick Healy, the first black man to earn a Ph.D. in the United States. His grandson served as the school's president.

- The school's founder, John Carroll, originally considered building the university on Jenkins Hill, which is today the site of the Capitol.
- On July 24, 1849, Professor Henry Dielman of Georgetown University was awarded the first doctorate in musical arts.
- During World War II, Georgetown University's star tackle and shot-put champion Lieutenant Al Blozis was killed in action at the Vosges Mountains in France.
- Lorne Greene portrayed the school's founder, John Carroll (1735–1815), in the 1980 TV movie *A Time for Miracles*.

George Washington University
2121 I Street, N.W.

Founded in 1821 as Columbian College, in 1904 this school was renamed George Washington University in honor of the nation's first President, who had given fifty shares of his Potomac Canal Company stock in order to help finance the establishment of the institute. George Washington University is the largest private owner of real estate within Washington, D.C. In 1825 George Washington University opened the city's first medical school. In 1826 George Washington University's law school opened. On November 15, 1898, the university opened the world's first foreign service school, called the School of Comparative Jurisprudence and Diplomacy.

- Some of the dignitaries present at the university's first commencement services in 1824 were President James Monroe, John Quincy Adams, the Marquis de Lafayette, Henry Clay, and John C. Calhoun.
- Jacqueline Bouvier studied American history at George Washington University prior to her marriage to John F. Kennedy.
- George Washington University offered the world's first journalism course, beginning in 1869. It was taught by Professor Williard Fiske.

Howard University
2400 6th Street, N.W.

Howard University, the largest black college in the United States, was founded on March 2, 1867, as the Howard Normal and Theological Institute for the Education of Teachers and Preachers, by Oliver O. Howard, a white Union general and leader of the Freedmen's Bureau, to educate the newly freed slaves. Howard served as the university's first president from 1869 to 1874. The school's orginal building, at 607

Howard Place, was once Howard's home. General Howard had served as the head of the Freedmen's Bureau, a federal agency established for the rehabilitation of slaves who were liberated after the Civil War. The school's first students were the five daughters of faculty and trustee members, ironically all white. Mordecai W. Johnson was the school's first black president. Alpha Kappa Alpha was the school's first sorority. The school features the Howard University Gallery of Art.

- At one time, half the nation's black lawyers, dentists, engineers, architects, and physicians were graduates of Howard University.
- The school graduated America's first black lawyer, Charlotte E. Ray, who was admitted to the Washington bar in 1872, the year of her graduation.
- Singer Roberta Flack won a full scholarship to Howard University, majoring in music education. After graduation she taught school in Washington.

Other Washington Schools

Benjamin Franklin University, District of Columbia Teachers College, Federal City University, Holy Name College, Immaculate College, Johns Hopkins International University, Mount Vernon College, National War College, Trinity College, St. Paul's College, University of District of Columbia, and Wesley Theological Institute.

There are a number of law schools. In addition to the university law schools, Washington is home to Antioch School of Law, George Mason School of Law, and the Georgetown Law Center, among others.

WASHINGTON, D.C., SCHOOL FACTS

- In the early 1800s, only white children were given public education in Washington. The pupils were taught reading, writing, arithmetic, and grammar. Those children whose parents could afford an additional fee were also taught geography and Latin. A lottery was used as early as 1812 to raise money for public education, enabling the city to open several new schools.
- The first school for black children was started by three black dock workers—George Bell, Nicholas Franklin, and Moses Liverpool—in 1807. The three built a small schoolhouse, and hired their first instructor, a white teacher named Mrs. Mary Billings. The school was called the Bell School after George Bell, one of the founders. In 1864, at the conclusion of the Civil War, the first black public elementary school was opened in Washington.

- In 1873 the first black high school to open its doors in the United States was Dunbar High School, named for Paul Lawrence Dunbar. The school building was torn down during the 1970s. Some of the school's graduates have been Edward W. Brooke, the first black U.S. Senator since reconstruction; Charles Drew, the discoverer of blood plasma; William Haste, the first black federal judge; Richard T. Green, the first black Harvard graduate (1870), and Harvard's second black graduate, Robert H. Terrell; Mary Jane Patterson, who, in 1862, became the first black female college graduate (Oberlin College) in the United States, and later joined the Dunbar faculty; and Benjamin O. Davis, Sr., the first black American general. Christian A. Fleetwood, a black sergeant-major, who had won the Congressional Medal of Honor during the Civil War, taught drill for the cadet corps at Dunbar.
- In 1872 the red brick Sumner School was built at 17th and M Streets, N.W. Designed by Adolph Cluss, the building served as the school for black children in the District and later as the headquarters for the black school system of Washington. The school had been named for U.S. Senator Charles Sumner, who had been attacked by Representative Preston Brooks of South Carolina on May 22, 1856, as Sumner sat in the Senate. Sumner had just delivered a speech condemning slavery. Sumner died of his injuries on December 5. His body was laid in state in the Capitol Rotunda, a privilege accorded to only twenty-four other persons.
- The first national Parent-Teachers Association was founded by Alice McLellan Birney and Phoebe Hearst on February 17, 1897, in Washington, D.C., under the name of the National Congress of Mothers.
- On September 22, 1890, the world's first high school for business education, Business High School, was opened in Washington D.C., in an abandoned elementary-school building. The principal was Allan Davis.
- It was at the Hickman School of Expression in Washington that screen star Joseph Cotten first studied acting.
- At age sixteen, John Barrymore was expelled from the Georgetown Academy after he was seen entering a bordello where he and several other boys had gone to celebrate Washington's Birthday.
- Actress Tallulah Bankhead attended Fairmont Seminary in Washington, D.C.
- Baseball commissioner Bowie Kuhn played basketball for Theodore

His coach was Red Auerbach.

led Washington D.C. Drama School.

FACTS

United States never attended college:
George Washington
Andrew Jackson
Martin Van Buren
Zachary Taylor
Abraham Lincoln
Andrew Johnson
Grover Cleveland
Millard Fillmore
Harry S Truman

- Andrew Johnson never attended school a day in his life. It was his wife who taught him to read and write.
- The following Presidents were college dropouts:
  William Henry Harrison
  William McKinley
  James Monroe

- Four Presidents graduated from law school:
  Rutherford B. Hayes
  William Howard Taft
  Richard M. Nixon
  Gerald Ford

- Three Presidents were college presidents:
  Woodrow Wilson, of Princeton University.
  James A. Garfield, of Hiram College.
  Dwight D. Eisenhower, of Columbia University.

- Three Presidents were college chancellors:
  George Washington, of William and Mary College.
  John Tyler, of William and Mary College.
  Millard Fillmore, of Buffalo University.

- Herbert Hoover was a member of Stanford University's first graduating class.
- President Dwight Eisenhower's brother Milton Eisenhower served

as president of three universities: Kansas State, Penn State, and Johns Hopkins.

- Thomas Jefferson established, as well as designed, the buildings of the University of Virginia.
- Several U.S. Presidents were once school teachers:

> John Adams
> Millard Fillmore
> John Garfield
> Chester A. Arthur
> William McKinley
> Warren G. Harding
> Lyndon B. Johnson

- John Quincy Adams taught rhetoric at Harvard.
- First Lady Grace Coolidge was a teacher of the deaf.
- Woodrow Wilson is the only U.S. President to have earned a Ph.D.
- Chester A. Arthur was a Phi Beta Kappa president in college.
- Amy Carter became the first child of a President to attend a public school in Washington, when she was enrolled at Thaddeus Stevens Elementary School in 1976.

PARKS AND GARDENS

The Metropolitan area of Washington, D.C., is the location of 753 parks spread out over 7,725 acres. In 1901 a Senate Park Commission (also called McMillan Commission) was established to oversee the construction and maintenance of the District's more than 90 parks.

The United States Botanic Gardens
1st Street, Independence Avenue and Maryland Avenue, S.W.

This 9,000-square-foot glass and aluminum conservatory located at the foot of Capitol Hill was constructed in 1902 as a home for those plants and trees brought back by a number of botanical expeditions to foreign countries. The greenhouse, designed by the architectural firm of Bennett, Parsons, and Frost, was built in the Victorian style.

The Botanic Gardens, which feature a large collection with 500 varieties of orchids, have many types of flowers, such as dahlias, chrysanthemums, tulips, roses, poinsettias, and gladioli. Also growing in the Gardens are lemon, lime, and banana trees. There is even a waterfall. The gardens' most prized possession is the azalea collection.

The Botanic Gardens supply the Capitol with many of its plants.

- While serving as George Washington's Secretary of State, Thomas Jefferson, in 1792, was given the honor of having a plant named for him, the Jeffersonia diphylla.

107

Constitution Gardens

The Mall, Next to Constitution Avenue, N.W.

This 45-acre park, with 500 trees, is located next to the Reflecting Pool. The park's 7½-acre lake is home for numerous ducks. Before the site was turned into the present park, it was known as West Potomac Park. Constitution Gardens, designed by the architectural firm of Skidmore, Owings, and Merrill, was completed in 1976 as part of the Bicentennial project.

• Office buildings built during World War I, and used again in World War II, were situated on this site until 1966.

• An elevated passageway over the Reflecting Pool allowed office workers to go to buildings that stood on the other side of the pool. All traces of these ugly wooden buildings are gone today.

Ellipse

Completed in 1884, this oval park was named for its circular roadway on the south side of the White House, sometimes referred to as President's Park South. On the east side, tourists line up for White House tours. Tourists also enjoy events and concerts, including a Twilight Tattoo every Wednesday evening during the summer months. On the west side numerous softball games are held during the summer evenings.

The Zero Milestone, sculpted by Horace W. Peaslee, is the official point from which all distances within the United States to and from Washington, D.C., are determined. "Point for the measurement of distances from Washington on highways of the United States" reads the description of the Zero Milestone.

On the 15th Street side, there stands a granite memorial, designed by Andrew Jackson Downing, to the nineteen landowners who once owned the land that today encompasses the city of Washington.

The nineteen men are:

William Atcheson
Ninian Beall
Andrew Clarke
Richard Evans
Walter Evans
Walter Houp
William Hutchison
Henry Jowles
John Langworth
John Lewger

John Peere
Richard and William Pinner
Francis Pope
George Thompson
Walter Thompson
Robert Troope
Zachariah Wade
John Watson

Also located on the Ellipse is the 12-foot-high bronze Boy Scout Memorial, which was erected in 1964, designed by William Henry Deacy and sculpted by Donald DeLue. On the face of the pedestal is carved the Boy Scout oath.

The Ellipse is the location of the National Christmas Tree, a 32-foot-tall blue spruce. The tree is decorated and lit each Christmas, a tradition dating back to the 1920s. The tree was not lighted in 1979, and again in 1980, by orders of President Jimmy Carter as a reminder that fifty-two Americans were being held hostage in Iran.

• The Ellipse was the landing site of Klaatu's (Michael Rennie) spacecraft with his 8-foot-tall robot in the classic 1951 motion picture *The Day the Earth Stood Still.*

Lafayette Park

This 7-acre park is situated on the north side of the White House, which was constructed on the site of a cherry orchard. In the park can be found ninety-seven varieties of trees, including American elm, ash, bronze beech, fir, basswood, spruce, redwood, and magnolia, many park benches, and numerous pigeons. The park is where protestors with signs and banners can display their cause.

In 1853, a statue of Andrew Jackson tipping his hat astride his horse was erected. The sculpture was made by Clark Mills, who also sculpted the equestrian statue of George Washington. The statue of Jackson holds the distinction of being the first equestrian statue ever sculpted in the United States. Mills used the bronze from British cannons captured by Jackson during the War of 1812. The names of the four 870-pound cannons at the base of the statues are El Egica, El Aristo, El Apolo, and Witiza.

At the four corners of the park are located 8-foot-high statues, one of General Freidrich Von Steuben, one of the Marquis de Lafayette, one of Jean-Baptiste Rochambeau, and one of Thaddeus Kosciuzsko, four Europeans who aided the Colonies during the Revolutionary War.

In 1825 the park was officially named Lafayette Park. Formerly it had been called President's Square. In 1859, in the park, Congressman Daniel Sickle murdered Philip Barton Key, the son of Francis Scott Key, who had been having an affair with Sickle's wife.

Satirical columnist Art Buchwald posed sitting on a Lafayette Park bench, with the White House in the background, for the cover of his twentieth book, *Laid Back in Washington,* published in 1981.

- The uniform worn by Jackson on his statue is the one that the general wore at the Battle of New Orleans in 1814.
- For some reason, President Abraham Lincoln saw humor in the statue of Andrew Jackson atop his horse in Lafayette Park, nicknamed "the Hobby Horse Statue." President Lincoln would break into laughter every time he viewed the general on his steed.

Lincoln Park
East Capital Street, N.E.

Located in Lincoln Park is the Emancipation Monument, sculpted by Thomas Beall in 1876, as well as a sculpture of black educator Mary McLeod Bethune.

Malcolm X Park
16th Street, between Florida Avenue and Euclid Street

Formerly named Meridian Hill Park, this was named for militant black leader Malcolm X (born Malcolm Little), who was assassinated on February 21, 1965. The park, designed in 1920 by Horace Peaslee, is the location of the 9-foot-tall bronze statue of Joan of Arc—the only equestrian statue of a female in Washington—which was sculpted by Paul Dubois and erected in 1922.

- Malcolm X's autobiography was co-written in 1965 by Alex Haley, author of *Roots.*
- The original statue of Joan of Arc, of which the one in Malcolm X Park is a copy, stands in front of Rheims Cathedral in France.

The Mall

A 1½-mile-long grassy strip of land lined on each side with the museums of the Smithsonian Institution, the Mall was once a pasture called the Commons. The first building constructed along the Mall was the Smithsonian building called the Castle. The western end of the Mall features the Lincoln Memorial, while the Capitol is located at the eastern end. During the Civil War the Mall had cattle pens down its length.

In 1964 plans were made by the Department of the Interior to improve the Mall. The Reflecting Pool was built, trees were planted, and the World War I buildings were torn down.

• In 1968 the Mall was the site of Resurrection City, the name given to the hundreds of temporary dwellings erected to house the poor during the People's March.

• On October 7, 1979, Pope John Paul II held an outdoor mass on the mall across the street from the Castle for 175,000 people.

• In 1832 Congress seriously considered selling off the Mall land for private building lots. Back then, the Mall was an undeveloped wasteland.

• During the 1960s, it was planned to run the George Washington Memorial Parkway leading to the Lincoln Memorial down one side of the Mall.

National Arboretum
24th Street and R Street, N.E.

This 440-acre garden was established by Act of Congress, in 1927, to cultivate trees, plants, shrubs, and flowers. The garden is also the home to over 70,000 azaleas. Among the thousands of plants from around the world is a collection of unusual plants that is located in the Cryptomeria Valley of the Garden Clubs of America. Seen here is the Franklin Tree, which, upon its discovery in 1765, was named for inventor/statesman Benjamin Franklin. The citizens of Japan presented the United States with the beautiful National Bonsai Collection on display in the garden.

National Zoological Park (Washington Zoo)
3000 Connecticut Avenue, N.W.

This 176-acre home to over 3,000 mammals, reptiles, and birds is located in Rock Creek Park. It was founded in 1889 through the direction of Samuel Langley, then the Secretary of the Smithsonian Institution. The zoo's first curator was William T. Hornaday. Its first head keeper was William H. Blackburne (formerly of the Barnum and Bailey Circus).

There are several animal houses to visit:

Mammal House
Small Mammal House
Great Ape House
Monkey House
Reptile House
Elephant House

Lion House
Bear Pits

There are several trails for visitors to follow:

Elephant Trail
Raccoon Trail
Lion Trail
Crowned Crane Trail
Zebra Trail
Polar Bear Trail

Also featured are a Zoolab and a Birdlab.

The zoo is also the home to several celebrity animals, such as a pair of giant pandas named Hsing-Hsing ("Bright Star") and Ling-Ling ("Cute Little Girl"), which were a gift from the People's Republic of China to the United States in 1972, following President Richard M. Nixon's trip to China in February 1972. The United States had presented to China a gift of two musk oxen, named Matilda and Milton. When Hsing-Hsing and Ling-Ling were first put on display at the park on April 20, 1972, so many tourists came to see them that it was estimated that 1,000 people each hour filed past their display.

The "space chimp" Ham spent his remaining days at the zoo. Ham, whose name was an acronym for Holloman Aerospace Medical Center, became the first U.S. animal to orbit the earth, when he was launched by a Redstone 2 rocket into suborbital flight on January 31, 1961. Ham died at the zoo in January 1983, at the age of twenty-six.

The zoo's most celebrated resident is Smokey the Bear. The original Smokey was discovered in New Mexico's Lincoln National Forest after a forest fire in 1950. The six-month-old American black bear cub, originally named Hot Foot Teddy, was rescued by the National Park Service and sent to the National Zoo. When he died on November 9, 1976, he was buried at the Smokey Bear Historical Park in Capitan, New Mexico, near the spot where he had been found. In 1975 the 6-foot-tall Smokey had been "retired" from service, when his age equaled the human mandatory retirement age of seventy. A five-year-old male, Little Smokey, took over for the original Smokey. Since 1950, Smokey the Bear has been the symbol for the fire prevention program of the U.S. Forest Service.

- Smokey the Bear had his own private Zip Code, 20252.
- Congress owns the copyright to Smokey's image and name. To date they have made over $2 million in royalties.

- Smokey's mate at the zoo was named Goldie, but they produced no cubs.
- A cartoon "Smokey the Bear" once appeared on a TV commercial for BIC lighters, but it proved very unpopular with the public.
- In public service commercials, Jackson Weaver provided the voice of Smokey from 1950 to 1976. Actor Roger C. Carmel, who played the role of Harry Mudd on TV's "Star Trek," later provided Smokey's voice.
- In 1952 Gene Autry recorded the song "Smokey the Bear."
- In the 1973 film *The Ballad of Smokey the Bear,* produced by the Forest Service for school children, featured James Cagney as its narrator.

NATIONAL PARK ZOO FACTS

- It is believed by some historians that the first animals to be given to the National Zoo were two royal jackasses, which had previously been presented to George Washington by Charles III of Spain. As these were the first two jackasses in America, George Washington is credited with having been the first person to raise jackasses in the United States.
- The first inhabitant of the National Zoo was a turtle named Pigface, which was brought there in 1937 from an African expedition.

Rock Creek Park

The park consists of 1,800 acres of preserved land located along the course of Rock Creek. It was at the mouth of the creek that inventor Robert Fulton tested early models of his steamboats. A California-type log cabin can be viewed here. Much of the original forest in the park was destroyed during the Civil War. President Theodore Roosevelt often enjoyed riding his horse through Rock Creek.

Theodore Roosevelt Island

This 88-acre island located in the middle of the Potomac River, accessible only by footbridge, has 3½ miles of trails. On the island, originally called Analostan Island, is a 17-foot-tall bronze statue of President Theodore Roosevelt, sculpted by Paul Manship. For years the park has been the haven for thousands of birds, but many have left due to the noise of jet aircraft lifting off from Washington National Airport.

- During the Civil War black soldiers were quartered on Analostan Island, away from the white troops.
- Legend has it that the lush vegetation on the island was used as the model for the Pacific island on which the crew of the *Minnow* were stranded on the TV series "Gilligan's Island."

Tidal Basin

The Tidal Basin was built in 1897 in order to obtain water from the Potomac River for the Washington Channel.

- In 1921 the Tidal Basin became the site of the first bathing-beauty contest ever held in the United States. Atlantic City liked the idea so much that they put on their own contest that same year, won by Margaret Gorman, Miss Washington, D.C.

West Potomac Park

Salvaged from swampy land, this area includes the Jefferson Memorial, the Tidal Basin, the Lincoln Memorial, the Reflecting Pool, Sylvan Theater, Constitution Gardens, the Ellipse, and the Washington Monument.

OTHER PARKS

Some of the 90-plus parks within Washington are Folger Park, Garfield Park, Benjamin Bannecker Park, Suitland Parkway, Glover Archbold Parkway, Lady Bird Johnson Park, Shepherd Parkway, Fort Mahan Park, Fort Totten Park, Fort Stanton Park, Fort Davis Park, Oxen Run Parkway, Soapstone Valley Park, Melvin C. Hazen Park, Montrose Park, Kenilworth Aquatic Gardens, Anacostia Park, and Bishops Garden, just to name a few.

THEATERS

LEGITIMATE THEATERS

Washington is a cultural town that offers something for every entertainment taste. Listed below are some of the major theaters that feature live performances by both local and visiting talents.

Arena Stage
6th Street and M Street, S.W.

This theater was built in 1961 by producer-director Zelda Fichandler for the Arena Stage Repertory Company, of which she is the founder. The 800-seat theater-in-the-round was designed by Harry Weese. In 1970 the accompanying 500-seat Kreeger Theater was constructed. The Old Vat Room features a cabaret-style theater with entertainment presented as the audience enjoys drinks and snacks. The Old Vat Room took its name from its former location, the Heurich Brewery, in Washington, which today is the site of the John F. Kennedy Center for the Performing Arts.

- It was on the Arena's stage that actor Michael Tucker met his future wife, actress Jill Eikenberry, in 1970. The two play lawyers in love on the TV series "L.A. Law."

Carter Barron Amphitheater
16th Street near Colorado Avenue, N.W.

Located here is the 4,500-seat outdoor Rock Creek Park Theater, which is operated by the National Park Service. During the summer months, jazz, pop, and rock festivals are popular.

Constitution Hall
Daughters of the American Revolution
18th Street and D Street, N.W.

Washington's largest auditorium is the Daughters of the American Revolution's Memorial Constitution Hall, with a seating capacity of 4,001. The hall has been the site of musical presentations and lectures, and has served as the home of the National Symphony Orchestra.

The hall, which was first opened in 1921, became the site of the first Arms Limitation Talks.

- In 1946 twelve-year-old Shirley MacLaine performed with a ballet group presented by the National Symphony Orchestra.
- In 1939 black singer Marian Anderson was banned by the DAR from appearing in a concert at the hall. When First Lady Eleanor Roosevelt heard of this, she resigned from the organization and sponsored an appearance by Miss Anderson at the Lincoln Memorial. In the Interior Department building there is a mural depicting Marian Anderson's recital at the memorial.

Ford's Theatre
511 10th Street, N.W.

Ford's Theatre was built in 1863 by John T. Ford, replacing Ford's Antheneum, which had burned down. The theater was a popular entertainment spot for Washingtonians, but it wasn't until the evening of April 14, 1865, during a performance of Tom Taylor's celebrated comedy *Our American Cousin,* that Ford's Theatre became a part of history. During the performance, Washington actor John Wilkes Booth entered balcony box number 7, where he shot President Abraham Lincoln in the back of the head. Booth then jumped to the stage, yelling "Sic semper tyrannis" ("Thus always to tyrants"), and escaped from the theater. The President was taken across the street to William Petersen's house, where he died the following morning at 7:22 A.M.

In June 9, 1893, tragedy occurred again in Ford's Theatre. This time the third floor collapsed, killing twenty-two government workers and injuring sixty-five others. At the time the building was being used as the Army Medical Museum.

The theater remained unused for a number of years, until the federal government purchased it, converting the structure into offices, and later into a warehouse for the government's publications. In 1933 the National Park Service obtained the structure. The theater was finally restored by the Park Service to its appearance on the evening of Lincoln's assassination in 1865. It was opened to the public on February 13, 1968.

A museum displaying the derringer used by John Wilkes Booth, the rocking chair used by President Lincoln, and other Lincoln memorabilia is located in the theater's basement. The museum is based on the Oldroyd Collection of Lincolniana, which was organized in 1932. The clothes that Lincoln was wearing that evening are also on display. Also shown are the plaster casts of Lincoln's hands made by Leonard Volk in 1860.

Today performers at the theater are sponsored by the Ford's Theatre Society. The theater is open to the public free of charge, as is the Petersen house across the street.

- John Wilkes Booth appeared at Ford's Theatre eleven months earlier, as a performer in the Shakespearean play *Richard III*.
- Robert Todd Lincoln, the President's son, had just arrived in Washington, after which he went to Ford's Theatre to join his parents. He arrived just as his father was being taken to the Petersen house. This was only the first involvement in three historic assassinations that Robert Lincoln would experience. On July 2, 1888, as the Secretary of War, he arrived to join President James Garfield just as the body of the just-shot President was being carried away. The third occurred on September 6, 1901; he was present at the Pan American Exposition in Buffalo, New York, when Leon Czolgogz shot and killed President William McKinley.
- Assassin John Wilkes Booth's brother, Edwin Thomas Booth, was a popular actor at the time. He had been elected to the Hall of Fame of Great Americans.
- Just one of the many similarities between the deaths of Presidents Lincoln and Kennedy is that Lincoln was assassinated in Ford's Theatre and John F. Kennedy was assassinated in a Ford automobile—a Lincoln.

Gladsby's Tavern
128 N. Royal Street, Alexandria

This small tavern is home of the Little Theatre during August and September each year.

Hartke Theatre
Harewood Road, N.E.

This drama school theater is located on the grounds of Catholic University.

John F. Kennedy Center for the Performing Arts
2700 F Street, N.W.

Located on the banks of the Potomac River, where the old Heurich Brewery once stood, the $72 million National Cultural Center construction was financed entirely from subscriptions and donations. The complex, which was designed by Edward Durrell Stone, uses the color scheme of cream, gold, and crimson. The initial work on the center began in 1958, when Congress voted to establish a center for the performing arts in Washington. In 1964 it was named for the slain American President John F. Kennedy, whose bronze bust by sculptor Robert Berks stands on display in the lobby. Leonard Bernstein debuted his *Mass* at the center's gala opening.

The center is decorated with works of art from countries around the world, such as bronze panels on the main door from Germany, chandeliers from Ireland, furniture from Denmark, and marble from Italy.

The Opera House has a 2,200-seat auditorium, featuring huge crystal snowflake chandeliers, gifts from Austria.

The Concert Hall has a seating capacity of 2,750. Its stage was dedicated to the memory of John Philip Sousa. The red-and-gold stage curtains were donated by Japan. The chandeliers were a gift from Norway.

The Eisenhower Theater has a seating capacity of 1,100. The first performance there was Ibsen's *A Doll's House,* starring Claire Bloom. The red-and-black stage curtains were donated by Canada.

The Terrence Theater was a gift from Japan for the U.S. bicentennial year of 1976. Performances of chamber music or poetry reading are held in this 500-seat, third-floor theater.

The theater laboratory, also located on the third floor, seats approximately 100 people for readings of plays and poetry recitals.

Two great halls, the Grand Foyer and the Entrance Plaza, feature the flags of many of the nations of the world (Hall of Nations) in the order in which they established diplomatic relations with the United States, as well as the states of the Union (Hall of States), in the order in which they joined the Union.

- Within the center, there is no Row I, as it is too often confused with the number 1.
- The Kennedy Center began a tradition of awarding an honor to American performers. The first five recipients were singer Marian Anderson, dancer Fred Astaire, choreographer George Balanchine, composer Richard Rodgers, and pianist Arthur Rubinstein.

Lisner Auditorium
21st Street and H Street, N.W.

This theater, located on the campus of George Washington University, serves as the home of the American Light Opera Company. The auditorium features some of the best acoustics to be found in Washington.

National Theatre
1321 Pennsylvania, N.W.

Built in 1835, the 1,672-seat National Theatre is one of the oldest theaters in the United States. Four fires have gutted the building, and each time the theater has been rebuilt on the same site. The latest structure was completed in 1886. The theater has seen thousands of performances, from plays and musical presentations to vaudeville routines. Jenny Lind, "the Swedish Nightingale," sang there. In the summer of 1946, air conditioning was added for the comfort of the audience as well as the performers. During the 1950s, the National Theatre had to feature motion pictures after the Actors' Guild refused to perform there while the theater continued its segregation policies. For several years the theater was closed for renovation, and reopened in the fall of 1983 with David Merrick's *42nd Street*.

Segregation existed at the National Theatre for many years. Even in 1933, when the all-black play *Green Pastures* was performed, no blacks were allowed to attend.

In her youth, the "First Lady of the Theater," actress Helen Hayes, attended the National Theatre, where she watched her first play.

- The lighted front of the National Theatre can be seen at night in a scene of the 1986 Michael Mann film *Manhunter*.
- Some believe that a ghost haunts the National Theatre, supposedly the spirit of an actor, John McCollough, who was murdered by another actor and then buried in the theater's basement.
- On the night of President Abraham Lincoln's assassination, the President had originally planned to attend a performance at the National Theatre but instead decided to see the play *Our American*

Cousin at the Ford's Theatre. John Wilkes Booth, it is believed, followed him from the National Theatre to Ford's Theatre that fatal night.

• Academy Award-winning actress Shirley MacLaine was once employed as an usherette at the National Theatre while her brother, Warren Beatty, who also became an Academy Award winner, worked as a doorman.

New Playwright's Theatre
1742 Church Street, N.W. (Dupont Circle)

Readings of new plays as well as their performances are featured here.

National Sylvan Theatre
15th Street and Independence Avenue, N.W.

This outdoor theater, located on the grounds of the Washington Monument, was established in 1917 by Congress at the suggestion of Mrs. Alice Pike Barney, who had also founded the Neighborhood Settlement House. Along with the various performances here of concerts and plays during the summer months, the Sylvan Theatre is the site of the annual Shakespeare Festival. The audience area is located on the sloping grass.

• The first plays presented at the Sylvan Theatre were those written and produced by Alice Barney, the woman instrumental in the founding of the National Sylvan Theatre.

Trapier Theatre
3543 Garfield Street, N.W.

Located at St. Albans School on the grounds of the Washington Cathedral, the Trapier features classic plays.

Warner Theater
513 13th Street, N.W.

This 2,000-seat theater originally opened as a vaudeville palace in 1926. In 1948 it was purchased by Warner Bros., which made it into a popular playhouse.

Other theaters in Washington are the Smithsonian, The Studio, the Trinity, and the Washington Projects Arts.

OTHER THEATER FACTS

- For many years the Watergate Amphitheater, located on the Potomac River along Ohio Drive, was the site of concerts presented by the Army, Navy, and Marine Corps bands.
- It was at the Lafayette Square Opera House that singer Lillian Russell appeared in a play, *The Brigands,* in the 1890s.
- Tragedy struck the Knickerbocker Theater in 1922, when a snowstorm caused the roof to cave in, killing ninety people inside.
- The Washington Theatre, which opened in 1822, introduced opera to the citizens of Washington. Both John Wilkes Booth and Edwin Booth performed here on stage, as they had on other Washington stages, such as Ford's Theatre. The Washington Theatre was closed in 1836.
- Washington's first playhouse was the United States Theatre, first located at Blodgett's Hotel, which later became the site of the Patent Office.
- The late actor Forrest Tucker began his career in entertainment during the 1930s, acting as emcee for the Gayety Burlesque Theatre in Washington, D.C.
- According to some sources, it was Washington Bullets coach Dick Motta who coined the now-famous saying, "The opera isn't over until the fat lady sings."
- Prior to appearing in his first motion picture in 1935, Henry Fonda appeared with the National Junior Theater in Washington, performing in plays for the city's children during the winters of 1928 and 1929.
- It was at the defunct Capitol Theatre, in the summer of 1938, that comedian Red Skelton emceed the program in which President Franklin D. Roosevelt launched his historic March of Dimes Infantile Paralysis Program, to help the crippled children of the United States.
- In 1953 Washington theaters and movie houses were integrated.

MOVIE THEATERS

In addition to the usual movie theaters, Washington features some smaller theaters showing rather specialized films.

American Film Institute Theatre
2700 F. Street, N.W.

This 227-seat theater of the Hollywood-based American Film Institute is located at the John F. Kennedy Center for the Performing Arts.

Ecology Theater
National Museum of Natural History
10th Street and Constitution Avenue, N.W.

A fifteen-minute film titled *Blue Planet* is shown in the Ecology Theater.

Langley Theater
National Air and Space Museum

The museum, which opened on July 4, 1976, features two theaters: the Langley Theater, with films shown on its Imax Motion Picture Projection System, such as *To Fly, Living Planet, On the Wing,* and *The Dream Is Alive;* and the highly advanced five-story-high and seven-stories-wide Albert Einstein Spacearium. This 220-seat planetarium is a Zeiss Model VI, which was presented to the United States as a bicentennial gift from the Federal Republic of Germany.

Mary Pickford Theatre
Library of Congress

Located in the James Madison Building, the Mary Pickford Theatre, which seats only sixty-four people, charges no admission.

MILITARY FACILITIES

Bolling Air Force Base

Bolling Air Force Base, without a single runway or aircraft, is located on the eastern side of the Potomac River. It was named for Col. Reynal C. Bolling, who was killed in World War I. Adjoining the base to the north is the U.S. Naval Station Washington, established in 1918, which does have a heliport.

Fort Myer
Arlington, Virginia

This military post, adjacent to Arlington National Cemetery, was the site of the first aircraft accident when Orville Wright crashed his airplane, killing his passenger, Lieutenant Thomas Selfridge, history's first airplane fatality. Lieutenant Selfridge was buried in Arlington National Cemetery. Selfridge Field was named for him and he is honored here by a monument.

Funeral processions to Arlington National Cemetery originate at Fort Myer, which oversees the military affairs of the cemetery.

On the grounds of Fort Myer is buried Blackjack, the horse that took part in the funerals of Presidents Herbert Hoover, John F. Kennedy, and Lyndon Johnson.

Naval Observatory

Observatory Circle, Massachusetts Avenue, 34th Street, N.W.

This 72-acre science facility sits on top of a soapstone quarry once used by the early Indians. The fifty-building complex is the determination of standard time within the United States. In 1877, Dr. Asaph Hall discovered the two moons of Mars, Deimos and Phobos, using the observatory's 26-inch telescope.

The grounds were originally constructed in 1893 to serve in part as the home of the Superintendent of the Naval Observatory, and the superintendents did live there from 1928 until 1968. In 1974 the Admiral's House was redesigned to serve as the home of the Vice President of the United States.

- The first woman astronomer to work at the U.S. Naval Observatory was George Washington University graduate Eleanor Annie Lamson, who worked there from 1900 until her death in 1932.
- The original Naval Observatory was built where the Lincoln Memorial now stands, but the ground proved too unstable due to the swampy land near the Potomac banks.
- The observatory was established with the help of Lieutenant Matthew Fontaine Maury, whose wife's brother was married to the sister of President Chester A. Arthur.
- The Superintendent of the Naval Observatory traditionally holds the rank of captain.

Marine Barracks

8th Street and I Street, S.E.

This, the oldest Marine Corps Post in the United States, is located on a small rectangular plot of land that President Thomas Jefferson selected in 1801.

The two-and-a-half-story commander's house, located at 810 G Street, was constructed in 1805, the only original building still present on the site. Every commandant of the U.S. Marines has lived here since 1805.

The barracks are also the home for the Marine Corps Drum and Bugle Corps. It was here that Bandmaster John Phillip Sousa led the Marine Corps Band.

- Aaron Burr was imprisoned in the marine barracks while he awaited his trial on charges of treason.
- It was on March 4, 1821, at President James Monroe's second inaugural, that the Marine Band made its first public appearance at an official ceremony.

Navy Yard
11th Street and O Street, S.E.

This 155-acre facility was built in 1799 on the Anacostia River as the first Navy Yard in the United States. At the appointment of Thomas Jefferson, Benjamin H. Latrobe designed twenty of the buildings.

Located in Building 76 is the U.S. Navy Memorial Museum, where over 4,000 Navy-related historical items are on display. Visitors can see hundreds of model ships, some of which were borrowed from President John F. Kennedy's personal collection. Midget submarines used during World War II can also be seen, as well as tanks.

The World War II submarine U.S.S. *Drum* is moored permanently in the Navy Yard as a training vessel for Navy reservists. Also on display is the deep-sea-diving sub *Trieste,* as well as replicas of the two atomic bombs, Little Boy and Fat Man, that were dropped on Hiroshima and Nagasaki to end the war with Japan.

In Building 67 is a recorded history of the U.S. Navy and Marine Corps, on canvas.

- When the British invaded Washington on March 24, 1814, the commander of the Navy Yard had all the ships under construction destroyed so they would not fall into the hands of the British.
- It was at the Navy Yard's gun factory that the 14- and 16-inch guns used on the modern-day battleships were manufactured.
- One of the halls at the U.S. Naval Academy at Annapolis is named for Admiral John Dahlgren, who invented the Dahlgren naval gun and who commanded the Navy Yard during the Civil War. During the war, Dahlgren lost one of his legs, which was placed in the wall of a foundry under construction. A plaque on the foundry wall commemorates Colonel John Dahlgren.
- On November 12, 1912, the Navy Yard became the site of the first airplane to be catapulted. The plane, a Curtiss, was piloted by Lt. Theodore Gordon Ellyson.

Other military facilities in and around Washington are the Army Medical Center (see Walter Reed Hospital); the Naval Medical Center in Bethesda, Maryland; Fort Andrew McNair, the site of the National War College (one of the nation's oldest forts); Anacostia Naval Air Station; Bolling Field Air Force Base; and Andrews Air Force Base. At Andrews are kept both Air Force One Boeing 707s, plus additional military aircraft, government planes, V.I.P. aircraft, and the CIA's own fleet of various airplanes.

CIVIL WAR FORTS

During the Civil War, the District was surrounded by dozens of military forts to repulse any invasion by the Confederate Army. Toward the conclusion of the war, sixty-eight forts and twenty-two batteries surrounded Washington.

The forts included:

Fort Greble	Fort Williams	Fort Ellsworth
Fort Carroll	Fort Cross	Fort Lyon
Fort Snyder	Fort Kirby	Fort Farnsworth
Fort Stanton	Fort Davis	Fort Weed
Fort Ricketts	Fort Gaines	Fort O'Roarke
Fort Baker	Fort Kemble	Fort Willard
Fort Wagner	Fort C. F. Smith	Fort Stevens
Fort Davis	Fort Bennett	Fort Jackson
Fort Dupont	Fort Strong	Fort Kingsbury
Fort Meigs	Fort Corcoran	Fort Albany
Fort Chaplin	Fort Morton	Fort de Russy
Fort Lincoln	Fort Woodbury	Fort Runyon
Fort Mahan	Fort Cass	Fort Smead
Fort Thayer	Fort Whipple	Fort Richardson
Fort Saratoga	Fort Tillinghast	Fort Kearny
Fort Bunker Hill	Fort Buffalo	Fort Berry
Fort Totten	Fort Ramsay	Fort Reno
Fort Mt. Pherson	Fort Barnard	Fort Slocum
Fort Bayard	Fort Ward	Fort Craig
Fort Simmons	Fort Worth	Fort Mansfield

The vast majority of the forts no longer exist today; however, there are a few remains found within Washington. The remnants of the Battery Kemble can be seen at the Chain Bridge. Fort Reno, now a reservoir, is the highest land point in Washington, at 39th and Ellicott Streets, N.W. Fort de Russy is located in Rock Creek Park. Fort Slocum is located at 3rd and Kansas Streets, N.W., and Fort Totten is preserved north of the Soldier's Home.

At 4301 W. Braddock Road in Alexandria can be found the Fort Ward Museum and Park, where the Civil War facility was partially rebuilt and today serves as a museum and park with displays of the history of the war, military uniforms, and firearms. Only the ramparts remain of Fort Stevens on 13th Street.

- A popular bit of American folklore is the story of President Abraham Lincoln visiting Fort Stevens during an attack by Lieutenant General Jubal Early's raiders. As Lincoln was watching the battle from the fort, a physician standing nearby was shot and killed. An officer yelled to Lincoln, "Get down, you fool," after which Lincoln ducked down. The officer was Lieutenant Colonel Oliver Wendell Holmes.

GOVERNMENT DEPARTMENTS

Washington, D.C., is home to the Department of the Army, Department of the Navy, and the Department of the Air Force, all of which fall under the authority of the Department of Defense.

- Henry Knox served as the first Secretary of War in 1789.
- The Navy Department was first organized in 1789.
- Benjamin Stoddert served as the first Secretary of the Navy in 1798.
- The Department of the Army was part of the Department of Defense when both were created in 1947.
- Secretary of the Navy Frank Knox (1940–1944) was the father of screen actress Elyse Knox, who married football great Tom Harmon. Their son is actor Mark Harmon, and their daughter Kristin was married to singer Ricky Nelson. They are the grandparents of TV actress Tracy Nelson.
- The only man in U.S. Navy history ever hanged for mutiny on the high seas was Philip Spencer, who caused a mutiny onboard ship in December 1842. He was the son of Secretary of War John C. Spencer.
- Secretary of the Navy James Webb has authored a number of best-selling novels, including *Fields of Fire*.
- Actress Elizabeth Taylor was married to former Secretary of the Navy John Warner, from 1976 to 1981. He later became a U.S. Senator.

MILITARY FACTS ABOUT THE PRESIDENTS

- Twelve Presidents have held the rank of general: George Washington, Andrew Jackson, William H. Harrison, Zachary Taylor, Franklin Pierce, Andrew Johnson, Ulysses S. Grant, Rutherford B. Hayes, James A. Garfield, Chester A. Arthur, Benjamin J. Harrison, and Dwight D. Eisenhower.

- About two-thirds of all U.S. Presidents have served in the various military branches.
- Five U.S. Presidents have served in the Navy: John F. Kennedy, Lyndon B. Johnson, Richard M. Nixon, Gerald Ford, and Jimmy Carter, all having served consecutively as Presidents.

ORGANIZATIONS

Washington, D.C., is home to hundreds of lobby groups, clubs, nonprofit charities, religious organizations, labor organizations, research institutes, historic groups, and many others.

Listed below are just a few of the organizations found within Washington.

AFL–CIO Headquarters

815 16th Street, N.W.

The lobby mural here has been regarded as one of the best examples of WPA art in Washington.

Amalgamated Transit Union

5025 Wisconsin Avenue, N.W.

This building was designed in 1981 by Hellmuth, Obata, and Kassabaum.

American Legion Building

1608 K Street, N.W.

World War II Medal of Honor winner Lieutenant Hulon Whittington served as the model for the statue of the soldier on the building's facade.

Brookings Institute
1775 Massachusetts Avenue, N.W.

This "think tank" was founded by Robert S. Brookings, who had made his fortune manufacturing clothespins.

Catholic War Veterans
2 Massachusetts Avenue, N.W.

This religious group was founded in 1935 in an old Childs Restaurant.

Chamber of Commerce of the United States
Connecticut Avenue and H Street, N.W.

This national organization has been located here since 1925.

- When President Calvin Coolidge dedicated this building on October 23, 1924, his speech was the first national radio broadcast to be heard on the West Coast.

Cosmos Club
212 Massachusetts Avenue, N.W.

Since 1964, this organization has presented the Cosmos Club Award to further the club's cultural objectives and honor significant contributions in science, literature, and the learned professions of public service. Biologist Elwin C. Stakman was selected as the first winner of their citation of $1,000.

- This private men's club was instrumental in the founding of the International Club in 1964, when the Cosmos denied membership to black journalist Carl Rowan.

Daughters of the American Revolution (D.A.R.)
Constitution Hall
1776 D Street, N.W.

Constructed at a cost of $1.57 million, this building, located opposite the Ellipse, serves as the home of the D.A.R. The organization, founded on October 11, 1890, is made up of descendants of soldiers who fought in the Revolutionary War. The society's seal is Rembrandt Peales's portrait of George Washington.

- President Benjamin Harrison's First Lady, Caroline Scott Harrison, served as the first President-General of the D.A.R.

Eastern Star Temple

1618 New Hampshire Avenue, N.W.

Built in 1909 by Perry Belmont at a cost of $1.5 million, this was originally built as a private estate called the Belmont House. During the Depression, in 1937, the 54-room house was sold to the Order of the Eastern Star for only $100,000.

- Builder Perry Belmont was the grandson of Commodore Matthew C. Perry, who, in November 1852, opened Japan to trade with the West.
- The Order of the Eastern Star is an organization of 2,500,000 women who are related to Master Masons. It is associated with freemasonry.

International Brotherhood of Teamsters, Chauffeurs, Warehousemen, and Helpers

25 Louisiana Avenue, N.W.

This union headquarters was nicknamed the James Bond Building because of the numerous push-button devices built into the structure.

Masonic Temple (House of the Temple)

16th and S Streets

Designed by John Russell Pope and Elliott Woods, this $1.8 million building, completed in 1915, is the headquarters of the Supreme Council of the Southern Jurisdiction of the Thirty-third Degree of the Ancient and Accepted Scottish Rite of Free Masonry.

- The building has 33 columns, each 33 feet high.
- The temple was constructed on Suter's Hill, which at one time was the site of the Dulany County Estates. Prior to the selection of Jenkins Hill for the site of the Capitol, Suter's Hill was seriously considered.
- The building's cornerstone was laid in 1911 using the same silver trowel, gavel, candlesticks, and Bible that George Washington had used when he laid the cornerstone of the Capitol on September 18, 1793.

National House Center

15th and M Streets, N.W.

This is the headquarters of the National Association of Home Builders. Open to the public, it features exhibits of housing developments on its first floor.

National Press Club
National Press Building
529 16th Street, N.W.

Founded in 1908, the Press Club was where Ronald Reagan announced his candidacy for President on November 20, 1975.

National Rifle Association of America (NRA)
1600 Rhode Island Avenue, N.W., at Scott Circle

Incorporated in 1871, the NRA was founded by Civil War General, and later Governor of Rhode Island, Ambrose Burnside, who served as the first president of the NRA. The motto of the organization is the constitution's dictum that "The right of the people to keep and bear arms should not be infringed."

The building, which also houses a museum of over a thousand antique and modern firearms, was designed by Antonio C. Ramos.

- President John F. Kennedy was a member of the NRA.
- The NRA's first president, Ambrose Burnside, lent his name to the style of facial hair now referred to as sideburns. During the Civil War, President Abraham Lincoln said of Burnside—after his defeat at Fredericksburg—"Only Burnside could have managed such a coup, wringing one last spectacular defeat from the jaws of victory."

National Women's Party (NWP)
Sewall-Belmont House
2nd Street and Constitutional Avenue, N.E.

Built in the late 1600s, the Sewall-Belmont House was partially burned by the British on the night of August 24, 1814.

Since 1929, the restored house has served as the headquarters of the NWP. It is open to the public as a museum of American women's political accomplishments, such as that of Alice Paul, who authored the Equal Rights Amendment.

- In this building Thomas Jefferson's Secretary of Treasury Albert Gallatin worked out the plans for the Louisiana Purchase from France in 1803 for $15 million.

Organization of American States (OAS)
(Previously the Pan American Union)
17th Street and Constitution Avenue, N.W.

This Georgia marble building was completed in 1910 for $1,100,000, based on the designs of Paul Cret and Albert Kelsey, with funds contributed by Andrew Carnegie. The building, which has been the site of numerous social events, is located in the exact geographical center of the District of Columbia.

The OAS building, also called the House of Americas, is constructed on the site of Davey Burnes's farm and later site of the John Van Ness house, which was designed by Benjamin Latrobe.

On the second floor is the Hall of the Americas and the Hall of Heroes and Flags. The three chandeliers in the Hall of Heroes were designed by Louis Comfort Tiffany.

For the bicentennial of the United States, the Museum of Modern Art of Latin America was created for the OAS building.

The courtyard fountain was designed by Gertrude Vanderbilt Whitney. The nearby Peace Tree was planted by President William Howard Taft in 1910.

- The organization of American states was founded in 1890 and now consists of twenty-seven member countries. The OAS employs 1,400 people with an annual budget of $80,000.
- The first Pan American Conference in the United States was held in Washington, D.C., on October 2, 1889. It was headed by Secretary of State James G. Blaine.

Society of the Cincinnati
2118 Massachusetts Avenue, N.W.

The Society of the Cincinnati, founded in 1783, originally was comprised of officers who had served in the Continental Army during the American Revolutionary War. The Society itself was named after Roman leader Lucius Quinctius Cincinnatus, whom George Washington greatly admired. Membership in the organization is limited to eldest sons of eldest sons down through the generations. George Washington served as the society's first President-General. The society's insignia was designed by Pierre L'Enfant.

The Society of the Cincinnati is located in the Anderson House. The house, which has been made available to the State Department for diplomatic receptions, has an 80-foot-long ballroom.

The society also features a museum that displays the uniforms of the French regiments who were allies of the Americans during the Revolutionary War. Also of note are the beautiful marble floors and the seventeenth-century tapestries. The house has a 10,000-volume library with books pertaining to the early history of the United States.

- Larz Anderson, the original owner of the house, served as the U.S. Minister to Belgium.
- The Ohio city of Cincinnati was named after the society by a member.

Sulgrave Club
1801 Massachusetts Avenue, N.W.

This private women's club, founded in 1932, is named for George Washington's birthplace, Sulgrave Manor in Great Britain.

OTHER WASHINGTON ORGANIZATIONS

- The Boy Scouts of America was chartered by Congress in 1916.
- The YMCA is located at 1711 Rhode Island Avenue, N.W.
- The YWCA is located at 624 9th Street, N.W.
- The first black YMCA was founded on May 31, 1853.
- The National Congress of Mothers was founded by Alice M. Barney and Phoebe Hearst, the mother of William Randolph Hearst.
- On December 4, 1867, the Order of Patrons of Husbandry, a secret society for agriculturalists, was founded.
- On December 17, 1895, the Anti-saloon League was organized.
- Washington, D.C., is also home to a number of consumer advocate organizations, including the one headed by Ralph Nader.
- President Jimmy Carter boycotted the exclusive Alfalfa Club because of their policy of allowing males only.

MUSEUMS AND ART GALLERIES

It was George Washington who, in 1789, urged the Congress to use its "best endeavors to improve the education and manners of a people to accelerate the progress of art and science; to patronize works of genius, to confer rewards for inventions of utility and to cherish institutions favorable to humanity." It was Washington's philosophy that was the inspiration behind the U.S. government's support of the arts.

Anacostia Neighborhood Museum
(Smithsonian Institution)
2405 Martin Luther King, Jr., Avenue, S.E.

This small museum was founded in 1968 and is located in the former Carver Theatre. It is the smallest branch of the Smithsonian Institution. The museum is dedicated to black history, black art, and the history of the Anacostia area of Washington.

Anderson House
2118 Massachusetts Avenue, N.W.

Built in 1900, the building, which is today the headquarters of the Society of the Cincinnati, was the home of the Anderson family from 1902 to 1905. On his deathbed, in 1937, Minister to Belgium Larz Anderson bequeathed the house to the society.

The house, which has been made available to the State Department for diplomatic receptions because of its 80-foot-long ballroom, now serves as a museum of uniforms of the French regiments who were allies of the Americans during the Revolutionary War. Also to be seen are marble floors and seventeenth-century tapestries, as well as a 10,000-volume library.

Arts and Industries Building
(Smithsonian Institution)
900 Jefferson Drive, S.W.

Originally named the National Museum, this red-brick and Ohio sandstone building, which is the second oldest on the Mall, was designed by Adolph Cluss and constructed at a cost of $250,000. It first opened its doors in 1881 with "1876: A Centennial Exhibition," featuring the best from that exhibit, previously seen in Philadelphia. In March of that year, it was the site of President James Garfield's inaugural ball.

The building was restored in 1976 and features the 1876 Centennial exhibits on both its first- and second-floor galleries. The museum has seven areas of display: Government, Women's Exhibition, Foreign, Nature, Transportation, Medicine, and Machinery and Industries. Some of the exhibits are Samuel Morse's telegraph, the Santa Cruz Railroad's 35-ton locomotive and tender, the locomotive *Jupiter,* and the 45-foot-long model of the U.S.S. *Antietam,* a Navy cruiser.

B'nai B'rith Klutznick Museum
("Sons of the Covenant")
1640 Rhode Island Avenue, N.W.

This eight-story Hebrew facility is the headquarters for the nation's largest and oldest service organization. Featured is the Klutznick Exhibit Hall with its collection of books, clocks, coins, and items pertaining to the history of the Jewish people. The museum has a 1790 letter written by George Washington to a Hebrew congregation in Newport, Rhode Island, about democracy.

The Franklin D. Roosevelt's Four Freedoms Library has thousands of volumes about the history of the Jewish people, as well as books written by them.

Capital Children's Museum
800 3rd Street, N.E.

This is a must-see for children. The museum was created by Ann White Lewin with a $1.7 million grant from the Department of Housing and

Urban Development. Each year new exhibits have been added from different commercial organizations and sponsors throughout the country since the museum first opened in 1979. The museum is an international learning place with exhibits from various parts of the world, including a Mexican marketplace and a miniature Indian village.

There are many displays for children to touch and climb. They can taste the foods of other nations as well as type on a Braille typewriter. A small Penny Exchange shop allows the children to purchase souvenir toys.

The Castle
(Smithsonian Institution)
1000 Jefferson Drive, S.W.

This unusual red building is also called "the Red Castle on the Mall" and "the Castle on the Mall." The building, constructed of red sandstone, was the original Smithsonian Institution building in Washington. James Renwick designed the building in 1874 to resemble a Norman castle. It was completed in 1852, but fire gutted the structure in January 1865, after which it was rebuilt.

The tomb of institution founder James Smithson rests in a chapel-like room just inside the building's Jefferson Drive entrance.

Outside the Castle stands a statue of Joseph Henry, who had served as the first Secretary of the Smithsonian Institution.

• In the cornerstone of the Castle are copies of the New Testament, the Declaration of Independence, the Congressional Directory of 1847, and a medal with James Smithson's likeness on it.

Corcoran Gallery of Art
17th Street and New York Avenue, N.W.

This gallery is the home of the art collections of banker William Wilson Corcoran and of Senator William Andrews Clark, the latter's collection having been added in 1928. Guarded on each side by two bronze lions, the building was constructed in 1897 on designs by Ernest Flagg. The Corcoran School of Art is located in the building's north section.

Among the hundreds of paintings on display are two portraits of George Washington by Gilbert Stuart.

Daughters of the American Revolution Museum
1776 D Street, N.W.

This museum was founded by the Daughters of the American Revolution in 1890, in order "to perpetuate the memory and spirit of the men and women who achieved American independence."

The building, which is also headquarters of the D.A.R., features twenty-eight period rooms in an eighteenth-century interior. A number of the museum's exhibit rooms are named for states of the Union, such as the California Room, the Rhode Island Music Room, the Indiana Room, the Oklahoma Room, the New Jersey Room, the Maryland Room, the Massachusetts Room, and the New Hampshire Children's Attic, with collections of period pieces, from furniture to toys, musical instruments, cooking utensils, and even a chest of tea from the Boston Tea Party. There is also a collection of dolls that date back over a hundred years, from corncob dolls to those made of wood.

Diaries, letters, wills, and other written history can be found in the Americana Room, which also displays the signatures of a number of U.S. Presidents. A painting by Grandma Moses can be seen hanging in the room.

One of the best genealogical libraries in the United States is found in the museum, with over 72,000 volumes. Many family histories, dating back to the *Mayflower,* are located in this room.

- It was in the D.A.R.'s library that author Alex Haley spent a number of years researching his family tree, which he put together into a best-selling book called *Roots.*

Doll's House and Toy Museum
5236 44th Street, N.W.

Flora Gill Jacobs founded this museum for children in 1975. It features toys, games, dolls, and doll houses that date back to the Victorian age. Dolls are not the only toys featured—stuffed animals, cars, games, and miniature houses are also displayed. A game of the Presidents, manufactured in 1884, can be seen.

On festive occasions throughout the year the museum features special displays, such as on Easter, Halloween, and Christmas.

Folger Shakespeare Library
East Capitol Street, S.E.

This library and museum is a showcase of Shakespearean memorabilia (see Libraries).

Ford's Theatre Museum
511 10th Street, N.W.

Located in the basement of Ford's Theatre is Osborn H. Oldroyd's Collection of Abraham Lincoln memorabilia (see Theaters).

Francis Scott Key Mansion
3518 M Street, Georgetown

This house was built in 1805 by Francis Scott Key. It was while living here that the young attorney wrote "The Star-Spangled Banner" aboard the British flagship H.M.S. *Minden* on September 12, 1814.

Freer Gallery of Art
(Smithsonian Institution)
12th Street and Jefferson Drive, S.W.

This art gallery was donated to the Smithsonian by Charles Lang Freer (1856–1919). The museum features Far- and Near-Eastern Art. Its library features 35,000 books and pamphlets. The beautiful Peacock Room was designed by James Abbott Whistler. The gallery has the world's largest collection of Whistler paintings.

- Decorator Henry Jeckyll had gone on a trip, leaving James Whistler in charge of the Freer Gallery. After receiving official permission, Whistler spent six months during 1876 and 1877 repainting one of Jeckyll's rooms with peacocks; this has become known as the Peacock Room. Upon Jeckyll's return, he was so shocked by Whistler's work that he fell into a state of depression and was admitted to an asylum for the insane, where he died soon after entering.

Hillwood Museum
Rock Creek Park

This 25-acre estate features a Georgian mansion, rose garden, greenhouses, a pet cemetery, a Japanese garden, a French garden, and a Friendship Walk through a beautiful landscape. The forty-room house, which is today a museum, was once owned by Marjorie Merriwether Post, the heiress to the Post cereal fortune.

This museum has the largest collection of Russian decorative art outside of the Soviet Union.

Hirshhorn Museum and Sculpture Garden
(Smithsonian Institution)
Independence Avenue and 8th Street, S.W.

This modern building is the home of 4,000 paintings and 2,000 sculptures in addition to other works of art, with works of Pablo Picasso, Edgar Degas, Alexander Calder, Henri Matisse, Winslow Homer, Auguste Rodin, and hundreds of other artists on display. It has the largest public collection of sculptures by Henry Moore in the United States.

The building is 82 feet high and 231 feet in diameter, and opened in October 1974. Called "the Doughnut," the gallery is supported by four 14-foot-tall piers. Inside is featured a 70-foot-long balcony. The third floor's Abram Lerner Room was named for the museum's founding director.

A 6-foot, 10½-inch statue of *The Burghers of Calais,* sculpted by Francois Auguste Rodin in 1886, stands outside the front of the Hirshhorn.

On the Mall, across the street from the Hirshhorn Museum, is the Sculpture Garden situated from 6 to 14 feet below the surface of the Mall.

- Among the hundreds of artists represented in the Hirshhorn is Robert De Niro, Sr., the father of Academy Award–winning actor Robert De Niro.

Museum of African Art
(Smithsonian Institution)
The Mall

This museum was founded in 1964 by Warren Robbins, and since 1979 has been under the authority of the Smithsonian Institution. It was originally located at 318 A Street, N.E., but was moved to the National Mall in 1986.

Featured are textiles, musical instruments, and traditional sculptures of African heritage.

- Among the nine Victorian row houses that make up the original complex on A Street was one in which abolitionist Frederick Douglass lived.

National Air and Space Museum
(Smithsonian Institution)
Independence Avenue and 6th Street, S.W.

This is the world's most visited museum. It is a modern, up-to-date branch of the Smithsonian, offering some of the most impressive exhibits found anywhere in any museum. The museum has a cafeteria on the fourth floor and a gift shop. There are twenty-six galleries covering two floors, each with hundreds of displays:

FIRST FLOOR		SECOND FLOOR	
Gallery	*Exhibit*	*Gallery*	*Exhibit*
100	Milestones of Flight	201	Einstein Spacearium
102	Air Transportation	203	Sea-Air Operations
103	Vertical Flight	205	World War II Aviation
104	West Gallery	206	Balloons and Airships
105	Golden Age of Flight	207	Exploring the Planets
106	Jet Aviation	208	Pioneers of Flight
107	Early Flight	209	World War I Aviation
108	South Lobby	210	Apollo to the Moon
109	Flight Testing	211	Flight and the Arts
110	Satellites	213	Flight Technology
111	Stars	215	Theater
112	Lunar Exploration Vehicle		
113	Rocketry and Space Flight		
114	Space Hall		
115	Theater		

Some of the most interesting displays are:

- Flyer: The Wright brothers' actual aircraft, which became the first sustained power aircraft to fly, at Kitty Hawk on December 17, 1903.
- *Spirit of St. Louis:* In this small aircraft Charles Lindbergh won the hearts of the peoples of the world when he flew the Atlantic Ocean solo on May 20 and 21, 1927, flying 33 hours and 20 minutes from New York to Paris.
- Lockheed Vega: The red single-engine aircraft in which Amelia Earhart made the first solo flight by a woman across the Atlantic Ocean in 1932.
- *Winnie Mae:* Wiley Post's Lockheed Vega in which he flew around the world in July 1933, covering 15,596 miles in 7 days, 18 hours and 49½ minutes.
- *Glamorous Glennis:* The orange bullet-shaped Bell X-1 in which

Chuck Yeager officially broke the sound barrier on October 14, 1947.

- *Friendship 7:* The first manned U.S. space capsule, in which astronaut John Glenn orbited the earth on February 20, 1962.
- *Gemini 4:* The space capsule from which astronaut Ed White became the first American to walk in space on June 3, 1965.
- *Apollo 11* Command Module Columbia: It was from this lunar capsule that Neil Armstrong became the first person to set foot on the moon, July 20, 1969.
- *Gossamer Condor:* The first human-powered aircraft, which was piloted by Bryan Allen on August 23, 1977, for 6 minutes, 22.05 seconds. The aircraft was powered by pedaling.
- *Double Eagle II:* The first manned hot-air balloon, piloted by Americans Ben Abruszzo, Maxie Anderson, and Larry Newman, crossed the Atlantic Ocean in August 1978.

Some other the other aircraft hanging from the ceiling are a 17,500-pound DC-3, a Learjet, and a Ford Tri-Motor.

- Senator William Proxmire, who, beginning in 1975, gave out the monthly Golden Fleece Award for excessive government spending and waste, gave the Smithsonian Institution an Award of Merit because the Air and Space Museum not only was built under budget, with added features, but was opened on July 1, 1976, four days ahead of schedule.
- An interesting comparison: There has never been a President of the United States who was an only child, while twenty-one of the first twenty-three American astronauts in space were either the only child or the firstborn son in their families.

National Gallery of Art
(Smithsonian Institution)
Constitution Avenue and 6th Street, N.W.

This large art gallery consists of two buildings, the original West Building and the newer East Building. The museum was given to the American people in 1936 by Andrew W. Mellon, who had served as the Secretary of Treasury from 1921 to 1932. It was opened to the public in 1941. The nucleus of Mellon's generous gift was 126 paintings and 26 sculptures. Since 1936, over 30,000 additional works of art have been added to the gallery's collection.

On the main floor are featured European paintings and sculptures from the thirteenth through the nineteenth centuries, as well as American art.

The West Building is connected to the East Building by an underground people-mover under 4th Street. The Cascade Cafe and a gift shop with thousands of art books are located in the underground mall. In the Great Rotunda is a fountain with a figure of the god Mercury.

- The West Building is situated on the site of the old B & O Railroad Station, where, on July 2, 1881, President James A. Garfield was shot by Charles Julius Guiteau. Garfield survived for eighty days before his death.
- The museum features Leonardo da Vinci's *Ginevra de Benci,* the only painting by the Italian master within the United States. It was purchased from Liechtenstein on February 20, 1967, for an undisclosed sum, estimated by some at $5 million.

National Museum of American Art

(Smithsonian Institution)

8th and G Streets, N.W.

This art gallery, formerly the National Collection of Fine Arts, is located in a building that is shared by the National Portrait Gallery and the Archives of American Art. Featured are over 30,000 works by such artists as Albert Ryder, Thomas Cole, Albert Bierstadt, Georgia O'Keeffe, Morris Louis, and Winslow Homer. The Lincoln Gallery was the site of President Abraham Lincoln's second inauguration reception.

The library also features a 40,000-volume library of history, art, and artists' biographies.

National Museum of American History

(Smithsonian Institution)

Constitution Avenue and 14th Street, N.W.

It was this museum that writer Mark Twain nicknamed "The Nation's Attic." On display here is memorabilia of the United States, including models of cotton gins, automobiles, trains, and hundreds of other exhibits, from the gowns worn by the First Ladies to memorabilia of American movies and television. The fifteen-stripe American flag about which Francis Scott Key wrote in "The Star-Spangled Banner" is on display.

- Archie and Edith Bunker's two living-room chairs from Norman Lear's popular TV series "All in the Family" are on display.
- Dorothy Gale's ruby slippers from the 1939 movie *The Wizard*

of Oz, and the marionette Howdy Doody and the dummy Charlie McCarthy, are on display here.

• It was in this museum that President Richard Nixon held his inaugural ball.

• Singer Michael Jackson was once given a private tour of the museum during the evening hours.

National Museum of Natural History
(Smithsonian Institution)
Constitution Avenue and 10th Street, N.W.

This museum, built at a cost of $3.5 million, designed by the firm of Hornblower and Marshall, has become the home of over 81 million objects, ranging from the Ice Age to the present, since it opened in 1910. President Ulysses S. Grant laid the cornerstone on June 2, 1874. Prior to 1980 the museum was called the National Museum of History and Technology. At the Mall entrance, a 25-foot-long life-size model of a Triceratops dinosaur, sculpted by Louis Paul Jones, is featured. He has been given the nickname of Uncle Beazley.

THE GROUND FLOOR

Ecology Theater
Special Exhibits
Spencer F. Baird Auditorium
Birds of Washington, D.C.

THE FIRST FLOOR

Rotunda
Fossils: The History of Life
Splendors of Nature
Dynamics of Evolution
Native Peoples of Americas
Discovery Room
Mammals
Birds of the World
Life in the Sea
Cultures of Asia and Africa
Ice Age Mammals and the Emergence of Man

THE SECOND FLOOR

Rotunda Balcony Gallery
Minerals and Gems
Earch, Moon, and Meteorites
South America: Continent and Culture
Human Origin and Variation
Western Civilization: Origins and Traditions
Bones
Reptiles
Insect Zoo
Prehistoric People of North America
North American Archeology
Jade
Gems
Minerals

- The 12-ton stuffed African elephant that stands in the Rotunda is the largest elephant ever shot.
- The world-famous 45.5-carat Hope Diamond can be seen in the Hall of Gems.

National Portrait Gallery
(Smithsonian Institution)
G Street and 7th Street, N.W.

Situated in the Old Patent Office Building, which was constructed in 1837 and designed by William Elliott and Robert Mills, the museum features portraits of over 4,500 Americans ranging from Pocahontas to President Ronald Reagan. The gallery shares the building with the National Museum of American Art and the Archives of American Art.

The Hall of Presidents features paintings by Gilbert Stuart and John Trumbull. Stuart's paintings are the only surviving complete set of portraits of the first five Presidents. Civil War photographer Mathew Brady's photographs are on display in the Meserve Gallery.

- Time magazine covers are given their own display.
- In 1857 G. P. A. Healy was the first artist commissioned to paint a series of presidential portraits. This series of paintings led to the establishment of the National Portrait Gallery.

Naval Memorial Museum
Building 76 in the Washington Navy Yard
(See Military Facilities)

Phillips Collection
1600 21st Street, N.W.

When this art gallery opened in 1921, it became the first permanent museum of modern art in the United States. In 1907 a wing was added to this four-story brownstone building and a second-floor skylight gallery was completed in 1917.

Some of the artists featured are El Greco, Francisco Goya, Honoré Daumier, Vincent Van Gogh, and Giorgione.

Renwick Gallery
(Smithsonian Institution)
Pennsylvania Avenue at 17th Street, N.W.

This museum, located across the street from the White House, is a curatorial department of the Smithsonian's National Museum of American Art. The building was designed in 1859 by James Renwick as a home for banker William Wilson Corcoran's art collection, and served as the city's first art museum. It was the original location of Corcoran's Gallery of Art until the Corcoran collection proved too large for the structure and was moved to the Corcoran Gallery on 17th Street. The building then became the home of the U.S. Court of Claims. President John F. Kennedy saved the structure from being demolished in 1965. In January 1972 the building reopened as the Renwick Gallery.

At the time of its construction it was the largest building ever erected in the United States to serve solely as an art museum. The structure was a copy of the Tuilleries addition of the Louvre in Paris.

- When the building was completed, William Wilson Corcoran couldn't move his art treasures into the building because it had been taken over by the Union Army's Quartermaster Corps, who were using it in their battle against the Confederacy. Corcoran finally got access to the building in 1871.

Smithsonian Institution

This is the world's largest museum complex, consisting of thirteen museums and the Washington National Zoo. The Smithsonian was established in 1846 on funds bequeathed by James Smithson, who never visited the United States. The money that English chemist Smithson gave to the United States arrived in Philadelphia in 1838 in nine boxes containing a total of 1,000 gold sovereigns, and 105 bags and one box containing 960 sovereigns, eight shillings, and sixpence.

The Smithsonian's board of trustees was established in 1846. The Chief Justice of the Supreme Court serves as Chancellor of the Smithsonian Institution's board of regents. The Vice President, three Senators, three Representatives, and nine private citizens make up the regents board.

The Smithsonian Institution is made up of the following museums:

Freer Gallery of Art
National Museum of American History
National Museum of Natural History
The Arthur M. Sackler Gallery
National Museum of American Art
National Portrait Gallery
National Air and Space Museum
Hirshhorn Museum and Sculpture Garden
Arts and Industries Building
Renwick Gallery
National Museum of African Art
National Zoological Park
Anacostia Neighborhood Museum
Cooper–Hewitt Museum (New York City)

The Smithsonian Institution acquired 942,000 new items in 1986, including an oil painting of Jimmy Carter and Warren G. Harding's top hat.

Textile Museum
2320 S Street, N.W.

This unusual museum was founded in 1925 by George Hewitt Myers in order to display his collection of textiles. It is the only museum of its kind in the United States. The museum features a vast collection of fabrics, mainly from the Orient, as well as ancient Persian, Egyptian, Indian, and Spanish remnants, for a collection of 8,500 textiles with over 800 rugs. The museum also features a technical reference library.

Additional museums and art galleries within Washington, D.C., include:

American Friends of the Middle East
1607 New Hampshire Avenue, N.W.

American University's Watkins Gallery
American University

The Association for the Study of Negro Life and History
1538 9th Street, N.W.

Columbia Historical Society
1307 New Hampshire Avenue, N.W.

Decatur House
748 Jackson Place, N.W.

Dumbarton Oaks
1703 32nd Street, N.W.

Franciscan Monestery
14th and Quincy Street, N.E.

Howard University Gallery of Art
Howard University

Kenilworth Aquatic Gardens
42nd Street and Douglas Street, N.E.

The Octagon House
1799 Massachusetts Avenue, N.E.

Truxton-Decatur Naval Museum
1610 H Street, N.W.

Washington Gallery of Modern Art
1503 21st Street, N.W.

Woodrow Wilson House
2340 S Street, N.W.

Unusual Museums

At 4th and E Streets, S.W., is the Wax Museum with displays of Presidents, historical figures, actors, villains, and various figures in wax reproductions.

The tongue-in-cheek Potato Museum can be found at the brownstone home of Tom and Meredith Hughes. The couple's entire home is dedicated to the spud, with such displays as Mr. Potato Head, pictures of potatoes, potato peelers, cookbooks, and even a clock that runs on the electrical power generated from two potatoes.

The reason that every museum and art gallery found in Washington, D.C., can't possibly be listed in this section is that the entire city is in essence a museum and an art gallery. There is history everywhere you look and in every building you visit. Art is everywhere in this city and not confined solely to galleries and collections. Washington, D.C., is the museum of the United States.

(*See also:* Theaters, Military Facilities, Government Buildings, Cemeteries, Churches, Parks, Organizations, Schools, and Medical Facilities chapters for additional museums.)

MEMORIALS AND MONUMENTS

There is no lack of memorials and monuments in Washington, D.C. Many of the statues in Washington came from the efforts of widows and veteran groups after the Civil War. Ironically, only eleven Presidents are memorialized in Washington, compared to thirteen Civil War heroes. Motilal Nehru, Prime Minister of India, once said of Washington's memorials: "Here are real temples, to which each general must pay tribute and, in doing so, must catch something of the fire that burnt within the hearts of those who were the torch bearers of freedom not only for his country, but for the world."

Boy Scout Memorial
The Ellipse at 15th Street, N.W.

Erected in 1964, this monument marks the site where the first National Boy Scout Jamboree was held in Washington, in 1937. Unveiled on November 7, 1964, the 12-foot-high bronze figures represent American Manhood and Womanhood, standing next to a Boy Scout.

Columbus Memorial Fountain

This fountain can be found in front of Union Station. Scupted by Lorado Z. Taft between 1912 and 1914 from designs by Daniel H. Burnham, who also designed Union Station. (See Union Station.)

The Confederate Memorial
(Memorial to Confederate Dead)
Arlington National Cemetery
This memorial to the Confederate soldiers who died during the American Civil War is but one of a number of memorials located at Arlington National Cemetery.

First Division A.E.F. Monument
The Ellipse
This 80-foot-high memorial with its 15-foot-version of Winged Victory was designed by Cass Gilbert and his son Cass Gilbert, Jr., with Daniel Chester French as the sculptor. The statue, situated on a 65-foot monolithic column, was dedicated to the First Division of the American Expeditionary Force and includes the names of the 5,599 men of the division who were killed in World War I. The monument was dedicated by President Calvin Coolidge on October 4, 1924.

- In a ceremony on August 24, 1957, the names of the division's 4,365 men killed in World War II were added.

Grant Memorial
East end of the Mall
This 252-foot-long bronze statue to President Ulysses S. Grant was authorized by Congress in 1901 and finally dedicated on April 27, 1922. The 17-foot-high bronze statue, which is situated downhill from the Capitol, looking west over the Mall, was sculpted by Henry Merwin Shrady, the son of Dr. George Shrady, who was Grant's physician.

- Architect Henry Shrady spent twenty-one years on the design and the construction of the Grant Memorial and spent more money on the project than the government reimbursed him. He also joined the New York National Guard in order to learn as much as he could about the Civil War. Shrady died of exhaustion just two weeks prior to the statue's dedication.

Jefferson Memorial
This beautiful monument to President Thomas Jefferson is situated at the south banks of Washington's Tidal Basin, the last monument to be erected on the Mall. It was dedicated by President Franklin D. Roosevelt in 1943, on the two-hundreth anniversary of Jefferson's birth.

Designed by John Russell Pope, this monument is loosely based on the Roman Pantheon, in the similar style that Jefferson used when he designed the Rotunda at the University of Virginia as well as his home Monticello, in Charlottesville, Virginia. It has fifty-four Ionic columns, each weighing 45 tons, that surround the structure.

The 19-foot-tall statue of Thomas Jefferson, by Rudulph Evans, is at the center of the Memorial Room on a Minnesota black granite pedestal. The structure's dome is constructed of Indiana limestone, and white Georgia marble encases the interior. The floors are made of gray and pink Tennessee marble.

There are four panels on the walls with inscriptions from Thomas Jefferson's writing.

DECLARATION OF INDEPENDENCE

> . . . We hold these truths to be self-evident: that all men are created equal, that they are endowed by their Creator with certain inalienable rights, among these are Life, Liberty and the pursuit of Happiness. That to secure these rights Governments are instituted among men. We . . . solemnly publish and declare, that these colonies are and of right ought to be free and independent states . . . And for the support of this declaration, with a firm reliance on the protection of Divine Providence, we mutually pledge our lives, our fortunes and our sacred honour.

VIRGINIA STATUTE FOR RELIGIOUS FREEDOM

> Almighty God hath created the mind free. All attempts to influence it by temporal punishments or burthens . . . are a departure from the plan of the Holy Author of our religion . . . No man shall be compelled to frequent or support any religious worship or ministry or shall otherwise suffer on account of his religious opinions or belief, but all men shall be free to profess and by argument to maintain, their opinions in matters of religion. I know but one code of morality for men whether acting singly or collectively.

ON SLAVERY

God who gave us life gave us liberty. Can the liberties of a nation be secure when we have removed a conviction that these liberties are the gift of God? Indeed I tremble for my country when I reflect that God is just, that his justice cannot sleep forever. Commerce between master and slave is despotism. Nothing is more certainly written in the book of fate than that these people are to be free. Establish the law for educating the common people. This it is the business of the state to effect and on a general plan.

ON GOVERNMENT

I am not an advocate for frequent changes in laws and constitutions, but laws and institutions must go hand in hand with the progress of the human mind. As that becomes more developed, more enlightened, as new discoveries are made, new truths discovered and manners and opinions change, with the change of circumstances, institutions must advance also to keep pace with the times. We might as well require a man to wear still the coat which fitted him when a boy as civilized society to remain ever under the regimen of their barbarous ancestors.

FACTS:

- It was during World War II that the Jefferson Memorial was dedicated. Since bronze was in short supply, a plaster model of Jefferson was used until it could be replaced with the real bronze statue after the war was over.
- On the monument's quotations from the Declaration of Independence, some words are omitted.

Lincoln Memorial

The plans for a monument to honor President Abraham Lincoln began as far back as 1867, when Congress authorized the Lincoln Memorial Association. But it wasn't until 1911 that Congress again authorized a commission, headed by President William Howard Taft, to build the monument. A site was chosen, designs were agreed upon, and construction began.

This beautiful Greek-style structure was designed by architect Henry Bacon, who was inspired by the Parthenon in Athens, Greece. The thirty-six Ionic columns, each standing 44 feet tall, represent the thirty-six states of the Union at the time of Abraham Lincoln's death in 1865. On the wall of the right side of the chamber is engraved Lincoln's Second Inaugural Address, which he delivered just forty-one days before his death, and on the left side of the chamber is engraved the Gettysburg Address. The mural of the Angel of Truth was painted by Jules Guerin. The names of all forty-eight states of the Union (in 1922) are shown in festoons on the outside parapet of the monument. When completed in 1922, and dedicated on Memorial Day of that year, the structure cost $3 million. Fifty-six steps lead from the sidewalk to the statue, one for each year of Lincoln's life.

- The 19-foot-high statue of the seated Abraham Lincoln was designed by Daniel Chester French, who originally wanted to make the statue only eight feet tall. He carved the work in four years from twenty-eight blocks of white marble.
- The Lincoln Memorial has appeared on the reverse side of the U.S. penny since 1959, and on the back of the U.S. five-dollar bill since 1928.
- When the memorial was dedicated, in 1922, the city was segregated with Jim Crow laws. President Woodrow Wilson had a separate stand constructed to seat the city's black dignitaries away from the white officials.
- In 1939 black singer Marian Anderson gave a concert on the steps of the memorial to a crowd of approximately 74,000 people. She had been invited to sing at the memorial by Secretary of the Interior Harold L. Ickes, after she had been refused permission to perform at the D.A.R.'s Constitution Hall.
- The Lincoln Memorial was the site of the famous peaceful black demonstration led by the Reverend Martin Luther King, Jr., on August 28, 1963, where he addressed an estimated crowd of 200,000 people. His speech was his brilliant "I Have a Dream" speech. Gospel songs were performed by Mahalia Jackson, Marian Anderson, and Odetta.
- Speaker of the House Joseph "Uncle Joe" Cannon once proclaimed that he would "never let a memorial to Abraham Lincoln be erected in the goddamned swamp." Cannon did live long enough to see the Lincoln Memorial dedicated in 1922, on land that had indeed previously been swamp.

- The Lincoln Memorial was the only structure in Washington to be hit by gunfire during World War II, when an antiaircraft missile, which had been misfired, hit the monument in the location of the Maryland engraving on the parapet, knocking out a chunk of marble.
- It is estimated that if the seated Abraham Lincoln were to stand up, he would be 28 feet tall.
- A bill was introduced in Congress to add the latest two states, Alaska and Hawaii, to the names of the other forty-eight on the monument, but the proposal was defeated.
- The famous "I Have a Dream" speech delivered by Nobel Prize winner Reverend Martin Luther King on the steps of the Lincoln Memorial reached the number 88 position on the Billboard record charts in May 1968, the only charted recording that ever originated from a memorial.
- Daniel Chester French, who sculpted the Lincoln Memorial statue, was the son of Judge Henry Flagg French, who had served as the assistant Secretary of the Treasury. Daniel French later married May Alcott, the sister of *Little Women* author Louisa May Alcott.

National Guard Memorial
National Guard Hermitage Gallery
1 Massachusetts Avenue, N.W.

This building was dedicated in 1959 with designs by Louis Justement. In front is a 20-foot-tall statue of a Minute Man, sculpted by Felix de Weldon.

Navy and Marine Memorial
George Washington Memorial Parkway on Columbia Island

The 35-foot-tall aluminum-and-bronze memorial shows seven seagulls hovering over an ocean wave as a tribute to the American sailors and marines who had died at sea during World War I.

The monument was designed in 1922 by Harvey W. Corbett and sculpted by Ernesto Begni del Piatta.

Nuns of the Battlefield
Rhode Island Avenue and M Street, N.W.

This bronze monument, designed by Ward Brown and sculpted by Jerome Connor, was erected by the Ladies' Auxiliary of the Ancient Order of the Hibernians in 1924.

Measuring 6 feet high by 9 feet wide, the bronze relief is dedicated "to the memory and in honor of the various orders of sisters who gave their services as nurses on battlefields and in hospitals during the Civil War."

The Peace Monument
1st Street and Pennsylvania Avenue, N.W.

This marble memorial is dedicated to the sailors who died during the American Civil War. It was sculpted in 1877 by Franklin Simmons with the inscription "They died that their country might live."

Second Division A.E.F. Memorial
Constitution Avenue and 17th Street,

This memorial is for the U.S. Army Second Division's 17,669 who lost their lives during the three wars. The sculpture of bronze hands holding a flaming bronze sword was designed by James Earle Fraser. The monument, which was designed by John Russell Pope, was dedicated by President Franklin D. Roosevelt on July 18, 1936.

Robert A. Taft Memorial
U.S. Capitol Grounds

This 100-foot-high bell tower was constructed as a memorial to Senator Robert A. Taft, who was affectionately called "Mr. Republican." The tower, seen breaking through the tops of the surrounding trees, is located on a 5-acre lot on the Mall side of the Fountain Plaza and is the only memorial on Capitol Hill. Designed by Douglas W. Orr, the tower, which was constructed of Tennessee marble, consists of twenty-seven bells, which chime twice each day. The 10-foot-tall statue of Senator Taft was designed by Wheeler Williams.

- Senator Robert A. Taft was the son of William Howard Taft, the twenty-sixth President of the United States and a former Chief Justice of the Supreme Court.

Titanic Memorial
Washington Channel Park
4th Street and P Street, S.W.

This 18-foot-high figure, standing on a 6-foot pedestal, was designed by Henry Bacon, the architect of the Lincoln Memorial. The memorial was erected in 1931 in tribute to those men and women who perished on board the British ocean liner *Titanic*, on the evening of April 15, 1912, including such distinguished people as Isadore Strauss, Benjamin Guggenheim, John Jacob Astor, author Jacques Futrelle, and the ship's builder, Thomas Andrews. Clarence Moore, another passenger, built the house at 1746 Massachusetts Avenue, which today serves as the Canadian Chancery.

- In 1986 President Ronald Reagan declared the newly located *Titanic* a national monument. The sunken battleship U.S.S. *Arizona*, at the bottom of Pearl Harbor, is also a national monument.

Vietnam Veteran's Memorial
Constitution Gardens

This 494-foot-long polished black granite stone wall features the names of almost 58,000 Americans who died during the war in Southeast Asia, from 1959 to 1975. It rises 10 feet high and bends at an angle of 125 degrees so that one end is pointing toward the Washington Monument and the other toward the Lincoln Memorial. The beautiful monument, which was dedicated on November 11, 1982, is located on a 2-acre site in the western half of the Constitution Gardens. The monument is sometimes affectionately referred to as simply "The Wall."

Vietnam veteran Jan C. Scraggs, who served in Vietnam in 1969 and 1970, was inspired to build a memorial to the men and women who had died in Vietnam after he saw the 1978 movie *The Deer Hunter*. As a student at American University in Washington, he met attorney Robert W. Doubek, with whom he founded the Vietnam Veteran's Memorial Fund. After long efforts to begin his drive for support and money, the ground for the monument was finally broken on March 26, 1982. Renderings in a competition for the monument's final design were submitted by 1,421 artists. Twenty-one-year-old Maya Ying Lin—a senior at Yale University and entry number 1,026—was selected as the winner. Frederick E. Hart's 7-foot-tall bronze sculpture of three American soldiers (one Caucasian, one black, and one Hispanic) was unveiled at the site in November 1984.

The names on the monument are listed chronologically from 1959 through 1975, with Dale R. Buis as the first name listed and Richard Vande Geer as the last. Diamonds next to some names denote confirmation of their death. Crosses next to some names denote that they are MIA (Missing in Action).

New names were added in November 1987.

Two names on the monument are those of men who are still alive; they were listed by mistake.

- Many consider the Vietnam Memorial the most beautiful and inspiring memorial in Washington, yet its designer, Maya Ying Lin, received only a B minus in her art studies at Yale for the project.
- On the monument can be seen the name of Arthur John Rambo, one of the soldiers killed in Vietnam.
- Of the names presently listed on the Vietnam Memorial, eight are women.
- The Vietnam Memorial was pictured on a 20-cent U.S. postage stamp on November 10, 1984.
- The granite used in the memorial came from Bangalore, India.

Washington Monument
The Mall

This is the tallest masonry structure in the world, set west to east, on the Mall, between the Lincoln Memorial and the Capitol and north to south between the White House and the Jefferson Memorial.

It was designed by Robert Mills, who submitted his design after a public invitation to American architects. In his original design there was a 100-foot-high Greek temple at the base of the obelisk, but it was later abandoned due to a lack of funds.

The monument rises 555 feet, 5⅛ inches high, on a 36-foot-deep foundation. When this 81,120-ton structure was completed in 1878, it surpassed the world's tallest structure, Cologne Cathedral, by 43 feet. Inside the tower are 898 steps to the observation deck, with 202 carved tribute blocks along the way. These massive stones are from all fifty states, twenty-two municipalities, a number of countries, such as Brazil, Japan, China, Turkey, Switzerland, Siam, and Wales. Even a block from the ruins of the Parthenon was sent by Greece. The National Park Service, which is in charge of the monument, have closed the stairs to the public, making the elevator the only means to ascend and descend from the observation deck. Windows were installed at the summit after five people had jumped to their deaths from the deck. Twenty-five tourists are allowed at one time to ride the elevator on its 70-second journey to the top, and crowds encircle the monument during tourist season, in all weather. In 1958 flashing red lights to warn aircraft were installed. Fifty flags, representing each of the states, have encircled the base of the Washington monument since 1959.

The cornerstone was laid for the monument on July 4, 1848, by Masonic Grand Master Benjamin B. French, who wore the same apron as had George Washington when he laid the cornerstone of the Capitol, fifty-five years earlier. Some of those present in the crowd of 20,000 were President James Polk, George Washington Parke Custis, former First Lady Dolley Madison, and Mrs. Alexander Hamilton.

The first congressional bill for the monument was introduced by Representative John Marshall, future Supreme Court Chief Justice. He also served as the first president of the Washington National Monument Society. James Madison served as the second, after which each President of the United States, by law, served as the society's president. Construction was begun in 1848 but stopped in 1859, due to a lack of funds caused by the War between the States. Abandoned at the 150-foot level, the monument remained uncompleted until 1876 after which construction was resumed under the control of Lieutenant Colonel Thomas Casey, builder of Civil War forts. The monument was completed in 1878. Because of a lack of Maryland marble, Massachusetts marble had to be used above the 150-foot level for the next 26 feet, at which time the original Maryland marble became available. This accounts for the slightly different color of those 26 feet. On September 10, 1888, after reaching a total cost of $1,187,710, the Washington Monument was opened to the public.

- The 3,300-pound aluminum tip at the monument's peak was the largest piece of its kind ever cast. Prior to its installation, it had been on display in the window of Tiffany's jewelry store in New York City.
- When the steam elevator was first installed in the Washington Monument, it was considered so dangerous that women and children were not allowed to ride in it. The men could ride up, a five-minute trip, while women and children had to walk the 898 steps to the top. The present elevator, installed in 1959, takes only 70 seconds to reach the top and only 60 seconds to descend.
- On August 31, 1886, an earthquake occurred that actually raised the monument 1/2000th of an inch.
- In 1854 a stone sent as a gift by Pope Pius IX was stolen from the grounds and dumped into the Potomac River. It has never been found.
- Gabby Street of the Washington Senators baseball team once caught a baseball dropped by Washington newspaperman Pres Gibson from

the top of the Washington Monument. He caught the thirteenth and last ball dropped. Earlier, on August 29, 1892, Billy "Pop" Shriner, the Senators' first baseman, became the first player to catch a ball dropped from the monument.

- On December 8, 1982, a nuclear arms protestor threatened to blow up the Washington Monument by crashing a dynamite-filled truck into the structure. He was shot and killed by the police.
- President Zachary Taylor celebrated July 4, 1850, on the grounds of the Washington Monument, sitting in the hot sun. He became ill and died five days later as a result of consuming too many cherries and iced milk.
- Between May 3 and June 24, 1967, the Poor People's March, led by Reverend Ralph Abernathy, camped at Resurrection City, near the Washington Monument.
- Prior to the closing over of the open windows on the observation level, four men and one woman had committed suicide. Others have jumped down the elevator shaft.

LIBRARIES

The Library of Congress
Thomas Jefferson Building (Main Building)
John Adams Building (2nd Street and Independence Avenue, S.W.)
James Madison Memorial Building (101 Independence Avenue, S.W.)

The Library of Congress was founded by an act of Congress on April 24, 1800, with an appropriation of $5,000. The facility, which was created "for the purchase of such books as may be necessary for the use of both Houses of Congress," was originally situated in the basement of the Capitol. Thomas Jefferson contributed a list of works that he thought imperative for the library to have available. After the British set fire to the original library on August 24, 1814, destroying most of its treasures, Thomas Jefferson agreed to sell his personal library to get the institution back on its feet. In 1815, 6,487 volumes of Jefferson's own books were added to the library's inventory. The books were purchased from Jefferson for $23,950.

Today the Library of Congress is the world's largest library, with 80 million books on over 550 miles of bookshelves housed in three large buildings. Each day, in addition to 400 new volumes, 550 U.S. and 1,120 foreign newspapers are catalogued and added to the ever-increasing inventory. There are 3.6 million musical scores, 500,000 books on music, and over 800,000 recordings. Its law library, which was started in 1832 with 2,011 books (639 from the library of Thomas Jefferson), presently consists of over 1.7 million volumes. The library is home to the world's largest collection of comic books, five Stradivarius violins, and three Gutenberg Bibles.

In the Rare Book and Special Collections Division can be found thousands of interesting items, such as the items that President Abraham Lincoln had in his pockets the evening that he was shot at Ford's Theatre. Also displayed is a dollar bill that Charles Lindbergh carried with him in his famous flight across the Atlantic Ocean in the *Spirit of St. Louis*, in 1927.

The Library of Congress is divided into seven major departments: Management, National Programs, Research Services, Processing Services, Copyright Office, Law Library, and Congressional Research Service.

The Library of Congress is situated in three large buildings. The Thomas Jefferson Building, which is the original building, was designed after the Paris Opera House. It has 2,000 windows and 275 miles of shelving, and was constructed between 1886 and 1897 after designs by John L. Smithmeyer and Paul J. Pelz. Its dome rises to a height of 160 feet above the reading room floor. The next addition to be constructed was the John Adams Building, which was completed in 1939. On its heavy bronze doors are depicted twelve figures who have aided in the education of the people of the United States. In 1980 the largest of the three buildings was completed, covering the area of more than thirty-five football fields. Named the James Madison Memorial Building, the nine-story facility features 46 acres of display, work, and office space.

In addition to the severe fire of 1814, the Library of Congress has experienced two conflagrations. A fire occurred on the evening of December 22, 1825, causing some minor damage, and another fire on the evening of December 24, 1851, destroyed approximately 35,000 volumes.

To date, twelve men have held the office of Librarian, beginning with John James Beckley, who also served as the Clerk of the House of Representatives. After Beckley's appointment as Librarian on January 29, 1802, he served until his death on April 8, 1807. Until 1815, when George Watterston was appointed Librarian, all the Librarians were also required to serve as the Clerk of the House of Representatives.

In front of the main library building is the 50-foot *Fountain of the Court of Neptune* with a 12-foot-tall bronze figure of Neptune, the god of the sea, and two Nereids riding a pair of sea horses. This impressive work was sculpted by Roland Hinton Perry in 1898 from the designs of architects J. L. Smithmeyer, Paul J. Pelz, and Edward Pearce Casey. It has been suggested that the fountain was inspired by the famous Trevi Fountain in Rome, Italy.

RELATED FACTS:

- When the Main Reading Room was opened to the public on November 1, 1897, the very first book that was borrowed was *The History of the City of New York* by Martha Lamb. It was lent to an employee of the Department of Agriculture.
- The copy of the Declaration of Independence on display was not the original drawn up by Thomas Jefferson. The original had a clause denouncing slavery, but in order to get the southern colonies to sign, the clause was removed. The Declaration of Independence is considered to be the Library of Congress's most valued possession.
- President Franklin D. Roosevelt unsuccessfully attempted to get the dome of the Library of Congress building torn down, as he thought it was "out of line" with the surrounding architecture.
- One of the Library's Gutenberg Bibles was purchased in 1930 for the sum of $300,000. The Gutenberg Bible, which was produced in Gutenberg, Germany (circa 1450–1455), was the first book in the western world to be printed with movable type.
- Abraham Lincoln's famous Gettysburg Address is also safely kept at the Library of Congress.

Washington, D.C., has more general and specialized libraries than any other city in the United States. The following facilities contain libraries.

American Pharmaceutical Associates
Army Medical Library
Army War College
Commerce Department
Department of Health, Education, and Welfare
Department of Justice
Dumbarton Oaks
Federal Reserve System
Folger Shakespeare Library
Freer Gallery
Geological Survey Library
Interstate Commerce Commission
John F. Kennedy Center

Labor Department
Library of Congress
Marine Corps Museum
Martin Luther King Memorial Library
National Archives
National Gallery of Art
Old District of Columbia Library
Organization of American States
Red Cross Library
Smithsonian Institution
St. Elizabeth's Hospital
Treasury Department
U.S. Naval Observatory
U.S. Supreme Court
White House
World Bank

Additional libraries can be found in museums, churches, and private organizations as well as in the District's schools and colleges, such as the Howard University Founders' Library, and the George Washington University Law Library, Georgetown University, and Catholic University.

B'nai B'rith Women's Four Freedoms Library
1640 Rhode Island Avenue, N.W.

The Franklin D. Roosevelt Four Freedoms Library consists of books on such subjects as liberation movements and labor movements, and many volumes relating to the history of the Jewish people as well as the history of the United States.

- The library proudly displays a 1790 letter written by George Washington to a Hebrew congregation in Newport, Rhode Island, about democracy.

Columbia Historical Society Library
1307 New Hampshire Avenue, N.W.

Library facilities here feature a history of Washington, D.C.

Department of Justice
Constitution Avenue and 10th Street, N.W.

This two-story law library features, in addition to thousands of books, twenty panels painted by Maurice Sterne. The library is mainly used by the attorneys employed by the Department of Justice.

Folger Shakespeare Library
201 E. Capitol Street, S.E.

This museum, founded by Standard Oil executive Henry Clay Folger, Jr., is owned and administered by Amherst College, featuring over a quarter of a million volumes relating to the works of William Shakespeare, including many rare editions of the Bard's plays. The museum, which has the largest collection of Shakespeariana in the world, was dedicated on April 23, 1932, on the 368th anniversary of Shakespeare's birth.

The library is also the home of the Folger Theater Group, which performs in a small-scale reproduction of London's famous Globe Theatre.

In the garden stands a fountain statue of the *Midsummer Night's Dream* character Puck, sculpted in 1932 by Brenda Putnam.

- Founder Henry Clay Folger first became interested in the works of Shakespeare after hearing a WPA lecture by Ralph Waldo Emerson while Folger was a student at Amherst College.
- Shakespeare's *The Comedy of Errors* is the only one of his plays that mentions America (Act III, Scene 2).
- Although the library has the world's most extensive collection of Shakespeariana and possesses seventy-nine of the Folios, the library does not possess a single play in Shakespeare's own handwriting.
- The library's founder didn't live long enough to see his dream emerge, as he died just two weeks after the building's dedication.

Frederick Douglass Museum of African Art Library
318 A Street, N.E.

In this one-time home of Frederick Douglass is a 100,000 photograph collection of Eliot Elisofon. This small museum and library became a part of the Smithsonian Institution in 1979 and was relocated to a new site of the Mall in 1986.

Georgetown University Libraries
37th and O Streets, N.W.

The school's Healy building contains several libraries, including the Riggs Memorial Library and the Hurst Library. Mark Twain's handwritten manuscript of *The Adventures of Tom Sawyer* is considered to be the most valuable item of the school's library collection.

Hubbard Memorial Library
1146 16th Street, N.W.

This library was constructed in 1902 in the Romanesque style by architects Hornblower and Marshall.

Kennedy Center of the Performing Arts Library
Kennedy Center

On the center's top floor is located a library, operated in association with the Library of Congress, which specializes in theater and film arts.

Martin Luther King, Jr., Memorial Library
901 G Street, N.W.

Designed by Ludwig Mies van der Rohe and opened in 1972, this library serves as the main branch of the District of Columbia public libraries. Featured are a black studies department and a Washingtonian room. The Anteroom Gallery displays a collection of paintings, sculptures, and photographs.

The library has twenty-four branch libraries throughout the city.

Masonic Eastern Star Temple
1618 New Hampshire Avenue, N.W.

Featured here is the world's largest collection of Masonic literature.

Mooreland-Spingarn Research Center
6th and College Streets

This facility features a black heritage library.

National Anthropological Archives
Smithsonian Museum of Natural History
10th Street and Constitutional Avenue, N.W.

The library specializes in the study of anthropology and related subjects of the earth's environment, past and present.

National Genealogical Society Library
1921 Sunderland Place, N.W.

This library is dedicated to genealogical research, useful in tracing a person's family tree.

National Society of the Daughters of the American Revolution Library

1776 D Street, N.W.

This library includes a genealogical reference collection for the tracing of American ancestry.

Old District of Columbia Central Library

Mt. Vernon Place
Massachusetts Avenue at 8th and K Streets, N.W.

Although now vacant, when it opened in 1903 this building served as Washington's first public library. It was donated to the city by Andrew Carnegie, who, with President Theodore Roosevelt, attended its dedication.

Society of the Cincinnati

2118 Massachusetts Avenue, N.W.

This private society, located in the Anderson House, features a geneology reference collection, as well as volumes relating to early American history, especially the Revolutionary War era.

U.S. Navy Observatory

In addition to many volumes relating to the history of the U.S. Navy, 800 pre-nineteenth century books are housed in this facility.

OTHER LIBRARY FACTS

- The first public library in the United States was established in Peterborough, New Hampshire, in 1833.
- It was statesman and inventor Benjamin Franklin who established the world's first take-out library, which he opened in Philadelphia in 1731.
- Harvard University has nine million volumes, making it the largest school library in the United States.
- Our thirteenth president, Millard Fillmore, is not known to have accomplished a great deal as head of state, but it was he who added a library to the White House when he and his family resided there.

EMBASSIES

A quarter of the embassies in Washington, D.C., are located on Massachusetts Avenue in a section called "Embassy Row." Washington law states that embassy office buildings can be constructed in high-density commercial zones.

There are 132 countries represented in Washington, with over 2,200 diplomats:

Afghan Embassy
2001 24th Street, N.W.

Algerian Embassy
2118 Kalorama Road, N.W.

Argentinian Embassy
1600 New Hampshire Avenue, N.W.

Australian Embassy
1601 Massachusetts Avenue, N.W.

Austrian Embassy
2343 Massachusetts Ave., N.W.

Bahamian Embassy
600 New Hampshire Avenue, N.W.

Bahraini Embassy
3502 International Drive, N.W.

Bangladeshi Embassy
2201 Wisconsin Avenue, N.W.

Barbadian Embassy
2144 Wyoming Avenue, N.W.

Belgian Embassy
3330 Garfield Street, N.W.

Beninese Embassy
2737 Cathedral Avenue, N.W.

Bolivian Embassy
3014 Massachusetts Avenue, N.W.

Botswanan Embassy
4301 Connecticut Avenue, N.W.

Brazilian Embassy
3006 Massachusetts Avenue, N.W.

British Embassy
3100 Massachusetts Avenue, N.W.

Bulgarian Embassy
1521 22nd Street, N.W.

Burmese Embassy
2300 S Street, N.W.

Cameroonian Embassy
2349 Massachusetts Avenue, N.W.

Canadian Embassy
1746 Massachusetts Avenue, N.W.

Cape Verde Embassy
3415 Massachusetts Avenue, N.W.

Central African Republic
1618 22nd Street, N.W.

Chadian Embassy
2002 R Street, N.W.

Chilean Embassy
1732 Massachusetts Avenue, N.W.

Chinese (People's Republic) Embassy
2300 Connecticut Avenue, N.W.

Colombian Embassy
2118 Leroy Place, N.W.

Congolese Embassy
4891 Colorado Avenue, N.W.

Costa Rican Embassy
2112 S Street, N.W.

Cypriot Embassy
2211 R Street, N.W.

Czechoslovakian Embassy
3900 Linnean Avenue, N.W.

Danish Embassy
3200 Whitehaven Street, N.W.

Dominican Embassy
1715 22nd Street, N.W.

Ecuadorian Embassy
2535 15th Street, N.W.

Egyptian Embassy
2310 Decatur Place, N.W.

El Salvadoran Embassy
2308 California Avenue, N.W.

Ethiopian Embassy
2134 Kalorama Road, N.W.

Fijian Embassy
1140 19th Street, N.W.

Finnish Embassy
3216 New Mexico Avenue, N.W.

French Embassy
4101 Reservoir Road, N.W.

Gabonese Embassy
2034 20th Street, N.W.

Gambian Embassy
1785 Massachusetts Avenue, N.W.

German Embassy
4645 Reservoir Road, N.W.

Ghanaian Embassy
2450 16th Street, N.W.

Greek Embassy
2221 Massachusetts Avenue, N.W.

Grenadan Embassy
1701 New Hampshire Avenue, N.W.

Guatemalan Embassy
2220 R Street, N.W.

Guinean Embassy
2112 Leroy Place, N.W.

Guyanese Embassy
2490 Tracy Place

Haitian Embassy
2311 Massachusetts Avenue, N.W.

Honduran Embassy
4301 Connecticut Avenue, N.W.

Hungarian Embassy
3910 Shoemaker Street, N.W.

Icelandic Embassy
2022 Connecticut Avenue, N.W.

Indian Embassy
2107 Massachusetts Avenue, N.W.

Indonesian Embassy
2020 Massachusetts Avenue, N.W.

Iranian Embassy
16th Street, N.W.

Iraqi Embassy
1801 P Street, N.W.

Irish Embassy
2234 Massachusetts Avenue, N.W.

Israeli Embassy
3514 International Drive., N.W.

Italian Embassy
1601 Fuller Street, N.W.

Ivory Coast Embassy
2424 Massachusetts Avenue, N.W.

Jamaican Embassy
1850 K Street, N.W.

Japanese Embassy
2520 Massachusetts Avenue, N.W.

Jordanian Embassy
2319 Wyoming Avenue, N.W.

Kenyan Embassy
2249 R Street, N.W.

Korean Embassy
2320 Massachusetts Avenue, N.W.

Kuwaiti Embassy
2940 Tilden Street, N.W.

Laotian Embassy
2222 S Street, N.W.

Latvian Embassy
4325 Tilden Street, N.W.

Lebanese Embassy
2560 28th Street, N.W.

Lesotho Embassy
1601 Connecticut Avenue, N.W.

Liberian Embassy
5201 16th Street, N.W.

Lithuanian Embassy
2622 16th Street, N.W.

Luxembourgian Embassy
2200 Massachusetts Avenue, N.W.

Madagascan Embassy
2374 Massachusetts Avenue, N.W.

Malawian Embassy
1400 20th Street, N.W.

Malaysian Embassy
2401 Massachusetts Avenue, N.W.

Malian Embassy
2130 R Street, N.W.

Maltese Embassy
2017 Connecticut Avenue, N.W.

Mauritanian Embassy
2129 Leroy Place, N.W.

Mauritian Embassy
4301 Connecticut Avenue, N.W.

Mexican Embassy
2829 16th Street, N.W.

Moroccan Embassy
1601 21st Street, N.W.

Nepalese Embassy
2131 Leroy Place, N.W.

Netherlands Embassy
4200 Linnean Ave., N.W.

New Zealand Embassy
37 Observatory Circle, N.W.

Nicaraguan Embassy
1627 New Hampshire Avenue, N.W.

Nigerois Embassy
2204 R Street, N.W.

Nigerian Embassy
2201 M Street, N.W.

Norwegian Embassy
2720 34th Street, N.W.

Omani Embassy
2342 Massachusetts Avenue, N.W.

Pakistanian Embassy
2315 Massachusetts Avenue, N.W.

Panamanian Embassy
2862 McGill Terrace, N.W.

Paraguayan Embassy
2400 Massachusetts Avenue, N.W.

Peruvian Embassy
3001 Garrison Street, N.W.

Philippine Embassy
1617 Massachusetts Avenue, N.W.

Polish Embassy
2300 Foxhall Road, N.W.

Portuguese Embassy
2310 Tracy Place, N.W.

Qatar Embassy
600 New Hampshire Avenue, N.W.

Romanian Embassy
1607 23rd Street, N.W.

Rwandan Embassy
1714 New Hampshire Avenue, N.W.

Saudi Arabian Embassy
601 New Hampshire Avenue, N.W.

Senegalese Embassy
2112 Wyoming Avenue, N.W.

Sierra Leonean Embassy
1701 19th Street, N.W.

Singaporean Embassy
1824 R. Street, N.W.

Somalian Embassy
600 New Hampshire Avenue, N.W.

South African Embassy
3051 Massachusetts Avenue, N.W.

Soviet Embassy
1825 Phelps Plaza, N.W.

Spanish Embassy
2700 15th Street, N.W.

Sri Lankan Embassy
2148 Wyoming Avenue, N.W.

Sudanese Embassy
2210 Massachusetts Avenue, N.W.

Surinamese Embassy
2600 Virginia Avenue, N.W.

Swaziland Embassy
4301 Connecticut Avenue, N.W.

Swedish Embassy
600 New Hampshire Avenue, N.W.

Swiss Embassy
2900 Cathedral Avenue, N.W.

Syrian Embassy
2215 Wyoming Avenue, N.W.

Tanzanian Embassy
2139 R Street, N.W.

Thai Embassy
2300 Kalorama Road, N.W.

Togolese Embassy
2208 Massachusetts Avenue, N.W.

Trinidad/Tobago Embassy
1708 Massachusetts Avenue, N.W.

Tunisian Embassy
2408 Massachusetts Avenue, N.W.

Turkish Embassy
1606 23rd Street, N.W.

Ugandan Embassy
5909 16th Street, N.W.

United Arab Emirates Embassy
600 New Hampshire Avenue, N.W.

Upper Voltan Embassy
2340 Massachusetts Avenue, N.W.

Vatican Embassy
3339 Massachusetts Avenue, N.W.

Venezuelan Embassy
2445 Massachusetts Avenue, N.W.

Yemeni Embassy
600 New Hampshire Avenue, N.W.

Yugoslavian Embassy
2410 California Avenue, N.W.

Zairian Embassy
1800 New Hampshire Avenue, N.W.

Zambian Embassy
2419 Massachusetts Avenue, N.W.

Zimbabwean Embassy
2852 McGill Terrace, N.W.

EMBASSY FACTS:

- The Belgian Embassy building was previously owned by Mrs. Raymond T. Baker, whose husband was Director of the Mint under President Woodrow Wilson. King Albert of Belgium was the first reigning European monarch to visit the United States.
- The British Embassy is the second-largest embassy in Washington, surpassed only by the Soviet embassy. A statue of Prime Minister Winston Churchill stands in the front yard, erected over a time capsule that is to be opened in the year 2063. The statue stands with one foot on British-owned soil and one foot on American soil, just outside embassy territory, since Churchill was born to a British father and an American mother.
- Foreign ambassadors to Britain are officially titled Ambassadors to the Court of St. James. President John F. Kennedy's father, Joseph Kennedy, Sr., held this position.
- The Canadian Embassy, built in 1906 by Clarence Moore, was known as the Clarence Moore House until his widow sold the house to the Canadian government in 1927. The Canadian government has the oldest diplomatic mission in Washington, D.C.
- Vincent Massey, the brother of actor Raymond Massey, once served as the Governor General of Canada. In 1927 he became the first accredited envoy to Washington, D.C., from Canada.
- The Chilean Embassy was once a private home owned by the Daughters of the American Revolution. It has previously been the Bangladesh Embassy.
- The first female foreign minister from the United States was Ruth Bryan Owens, the daughter of William Jennings Bryan, when President Franklin D. Roosevelt appointed her minister to Denmark on April 13, 1933. In 1949 President Harry S Truman appointed

Eugenie Moore Anderson as the first woman U.S. ambassador. She served as Ambassador to Denmark.

- The Indonesian Embassy is located in the 60-room McLean Mansion built by Thomas Walsh in 1902. Vice President and Mrs. Thomas Marshall had entertained King Albert and Queen Elizabeth of Belgium in this house.

- The Japanese Embassy, built in 1931, features the Japanese Ceremonial Tea House and Garden called the "Ippakutei."

- It was the U.S. Minister to Mexico, Joel Poinsett, after whom the poinsettia flower is named. He brought the flower to the United States from Mexico.

- The *New York Times* called the Peruvian Embassy at 3001 Garrison Street, N.W., "the Jewel Among Embassies." It is situated on the site of the old Civil War fortress Battery Terrill.

- The largest embassy in Washington is the Soviets'. It is located on a hill that provides the possibility to spy via telephone lines, radio signals, satellite signals, and other listening devices. Numerous antennas, satellite dishes, and other listening devices are located on the building's roof, but the embassy denies any illegal activity.

- The Iranian Embassy has been closed since shortly after Iran took American Embassy personnel in Tehran hostage on November 4, 1979.

- The Greek Embassy is located in a 35-room mansion built in 1906 by Hennen Jennings, the leading mining engineer of the time.

- The German Embassy, constructed in 1964, was the first building erected in the United States by the German government.

- The Egyptian Embassy was built in 1907 by Mrs. Margaret K. C. Beale and was sold to the Egyptian government in 1928 for $150,000.

- The Philippine Embassy mansion was purchased by the Philippine government in 1941 from Mrs. Stella Stapleton, who had helped build Father Flanagan's Boys Town in Nebraska. The embassy had previously been located in two buildings, one of which was owned by the mother of actor Douglas Fairbanks, Jr. Two streets near the chancery are appropriately named Bataan and Corregidor.

- The Italian Embassy is a reflection of the artwork of Italy. The embassy describes its decor as representing three typical Italian cities: Venice, for its ornamental decorations; Florence, for its artistic value; and Rome, for its historical significance.

- In the Polish Embassy the work of Polish artists can be seen, as well as bronze busts of George Washington and Benjamin Franklin. The embassy is an art gallery of works by Polish painters and sculptors.

- The Turkish Embassy has been called one of the city's most beautiful homes. The house, built in the architectural elements of eighteenth-century Europe with Romanesque and fifteenth-century Italianate details, was designed by George Oakley Totten, Jr., in 1908 and was completed in 1915. It is furnished in Louis XVI and Regency pieces.

- The Embassy of the People's Republic of China is located in the old Windsor Park Hotel, which was converted into offices and a chancery.

- The Taiwan Embassy occupies the house that inventor Alexander Graham Bell once called home.

- Until the end of 1935, 16th Street was referred to as "Embassy Row," after which many embassies moved to Massachusetts Avenue.

HOSPITALS AND MEDICAL FACILITIES

American Pharmaceutical Association Building
Constitution Avenue between 22nd and 23rd Streets, N.W.

This is the home of the American Institute of Pharmacy, the only nongovernment building on Constitution Avenue. It was designed by John Russell Pope and was completed in 1934. The entrance features a statue of William Proctor, Jr., "The Father of American Pharmacy," sculpted by Richard Burge. The Association features a museum for tourists.

- Vice President Hubert H. Humphrey was employed as a pharmacist after graduation from the Denver College of Pharmacy.

American Red Cross Building
17th and D Streets, N.W.

This building, with stained-glass windows designed by Louis Tiffany, features a museum of World War I memorabilia including an ambulance similar to those driven by American soldiers in Europe.

- Some of the men who served as ambulance drivers in Europe during World War I were Walt Disney, Ernest Hemingway, Louis Bromfield, e. e. cummings, John Dos Passos, Dashiell Hammett, W. Somerset Maugham, Archibald MacLeish, and Sidney Howard.
- General George Marshall, whose Marshall Plan rebuilt Europe after World War II, served as the president of the American Red Cross.

Georgetown University Hospital
Georgetown University

Congress granted Georgetown University the right to award degrees in medicine beginning in 1851.

George Washington University Hospital
901 23rd Street, N.W.

Founded in 1825, the George Washington School of Medicine is located in a 5-story structure adjacent to the University Hospital.

Walter Reed was once the head of the school's bacteriology division. Two other distinguished men of medicine, Fredrick Russell and Theobald Smith, also held that position.

- The George Washington University Hospital is where President Ronald Reagan was taken after he had been shot by John Hinckley on the afternoon of March 30, 1981. Press Secretary James Brady, who was also wounded in the assassination attempt, was also taken there.

St. Elizabeth's Hospital
Nichols Avenue, S.E.

The 168 buildings on this 800-acre site comprise the grounds of St. Elizabeth's Hospital, established by Congress in 1855.

Two well-known men have been incarcerated at St. Elizabeth's:

- Poet Ezra Pound was held here for a period of twelve years, including the duration of World War II, after it was determined that he was not mentally fit to stand trial for treason.
- John W. Hinckley, Jr., was incarcerated here in 1982, after he was found not guilty by reason of insanity in the shooting of President Ronald Reagan in May of 1981.

Walter Reed General Hospital
(Army Medical Center)
6825 16th Street, N.W.

This medical facility was established as an Army hospital in 1898, with the Army Medical Center facility opening three years later. In 1908 a section was added that featured the first hospital with a 120-bed capacity. The current 7-story facility was finally completed in 1979.

On the grounds, at Building 54, is the Armed Forces Medical Museum, which features among its many unusual displays bottled Siamese twins, mummified heads, a bone fragment from the head of Abraham Lincoln, and James Garfield's spinal column fragment, as well as General Daniel Sickle's right leg bone, which he himself contributed. John Wilkes Booth's cervical vertebrae and spinal cord are on display at the Armed Forces Institute of Pathology.

The 215,000-square-foot, windowless building, dedicated by President Dwight Eisenhower on May 23, 1955, was the first atom-bomb-resistant federal building in the United States. It was to have been the prototype of structures that could withstand an atomic bomb attack.

- On June 16, 1921, Walter Reed Hospital graduated the first class of U.S. Army nurses. 402 graduates were in this premier class.
- Every Easter Sunday, sunrise services are held on the grounds.
- In the 1951 movie *The Day the Earth Stood Still*, Klaatu (played by Michael Rennie) was taken to Walter Reed Hospital after being shot. He stayed in room 306.
- In 1949 James Forrestal, the first U.S. Secretary of Defense, jumped to his death from a window of the hospital. A U.S. Navy aircraft carrier, the U.S.S. *Forrestal*, was named in his honor.
- Former President Dwight D. Eisenhower died at Walter Reed Hospital on March 28, 1969.

The American College of Surgeons

This organization was founded in Springfield, Illinois, in 1912 but was first organized in Washington, D.C. on May 5, 1913. The ACS was "organized to elevate the standard of surgery to establish a standard of competency and of character for practitioners of surgery, and to educate the public and the profession to understand that the practice of surgery calls for special training."

WASHINGTON-BORN CELEBRITIES

Edward Albee	Playwright	March 12, 1928
Elgin Baylor	Basketball player	September 16, 1934
Carl Bernstein	Journalist	February 14, 1944
Edward Brooke	U.S. Senator	October 26, 1919
Billie Burke	Actress	August 7, 1885
Anita Colby	Actress	August 5, 1914
Robert Considine	Columnist	November 4, 1906
Benjamin Oliver Davis	Soldier	July 1, 1877
John Foster Dulles	Secretary of State	February 25, 1888
Duke Ellington	Composer	April 29, 1899
Marvin Gaye	Singer	April 2, 1939
Jane Greer	Actress	September 9, 1924
Goldie Hawn	Actress	November 21, 1945
Alan Hale, Sr.	Actor	February 10, 1892
Helen Hayes	Actress	October 10, 1900
J. Edgar Hoover	FBI Chief	January 1, 1895
Michael Learned	Actress	April 9, 1939
John Lodge	Actor and politician	October 20, 1903
Anthony McCauliffe	U.S. Army general	July 2, 1898
Roger Mudd	Journalist	February 9, 1928
Frederick Patterson	Educator	October 10, 1901
John Howard Payne	Actor and writer	April 9, 1852
Chita Rivera	Dancer	January 23, 1933
Peter Tork	Monkees member	February 13, 1944
John Warner	Secretary of the Navy	February 18, 1927
Robert Weaver	Government official	December 29, 1907

- John Lodge was a Hollywood actor who later went into politics, serving as a Representative, Governor of Connecticut, Ambassador to Spain, and Ambassador to Argentina.

WASHINGTON MEDICAL FACTS

- During the Civil War, American Red Cross founder Clara Barton, author Louisa May Alcott, and poet Walt Whitman served as nurses in Washington D.C. hospitals. Besides the soldiers' wounds, the doctors and nurses had to treat typhoid, dysentery, and scarlet fever during the war. At the start of the War, Washington had one hospital, shortly afterward the city had thirty-six hospitals, one of which was located within the Capitol itself.

- President William Henry Harrison studied medicine for a time under the tutelage of famous Philadelphia physician Dr. Benjamin Rush. Harrison dropped out his first year in order to become an Indian fighter.
- Jimmy Carter was the first U.S. President to be born in a hospital.
- Ironically, it was Surgeon General Joseph K. Barnes who attended to both Presidents Abraham Lincoln and John Garfield after they were shot.
- When George Washington planned to build the Capitol he hired physician William Thornton, instead of a trained architect.
- The first group hospital–medical cooperative in the United States was created in 1937 by the Group Health Association, Inc., of Washington, D.C.
- In 1865 Dr. Mary Walker of Washington became the only woman ever awarded the Medal of Honor for her heroic work as a surgeon during the Civil War. In order to perform her job, Dr. Walker had to dress as a man. Her medal was taken away from her in 1917, but in 1977 it was restored by the U.S. Army.
- The first Capitol physician, Dr. George Wehnes, served in the 70th Congress. A retired rear admiral, he was officially called "the attending physician."
- On January 26, 1961, Dr. Janet Graeme Travell became the first woman to be appointed as a personal physician to a President. She served President John F. Kennedy.
- On the TV series "Temperatures Rising," James Whitmore headed the fictitious Capitol General Hospital in Washington, D.C.

OTHER MEDICAL FACILITIES

Washington has many other medical facilities and schools, including District of Columbia General, Sick Children's Hospital, Veteran's Administration, Washington Center, Freedman's Hospital, Children's Hospital, Howard University Hospital, and Columbia Hospital for Women.

HOTELS

There is no shortage of hotels in Washington, D.C. However, at one time Washington had so few hotels and boarding houses that when the first Congress convened in November 1800 only the Speaker of the House, Theodore Sedgwick, could find a bedroom for himself, while other members of Congress were forced to double up. It was from Conrad's boarding house on New Jersey Avenue that Thomas Jefferson walked to his own inauguration in March 1801.

Following are some of Washington's historic hotels, many of which have gone with the wind.

Beveridge's Hotel
Geronimo once slept at this hotel on 3rd Street.

Blodgett's Hotel
This establishment was built in the late 1790s on E Street at 8th Street, as a prize in a Washington lottery. When the winner saw the unfinished hotel he attempted to sue Blodgett, who had just left town. The structure burned down in 1836.

Capital Hilton
16th and K Streets, N.W.
It was outside this hotel, located just two blocks from the White House,

that President Ronald Reagan was shot by John Hinckley on March 30, 1981.

Hotel Washington
15th Street and Pennsylvania Avenue

The first successful hotel on Pennsylvania Avenue was opened in 1801 on what is today the site of the Hotel Washington. It was in this hotel that Al Pacino and Diane Keaton's characters stayed in the 1974 movie *The Godfather*.

Indian Queen Hotel

Built by Jesse Brown, and no longer standing, it was at this hotel on Pennsylvania Avenue that Indians who came to Washington on business often stayed. Pocahontas was depicted on the hotel's signpost. It was at the Indian Queen Hotel that Vice President John Tyler was sworn into office as President on April 6, 1841, upon the death of President William Henry Harrison.

Kirkwood Hotel

Andrew Johnson was sworn in as President of the United States here on April 15, 1865, after the assassination of Abraham Lincoln.

Marriott Hotel
(J. W. Marriott)
1331 Pennsylvania Avenue, N.W.

The super-deluxe hotel is the flagship of the Marriott Hotel chain. It was also the first hotel built by John Willard ("Bill") Marriott on the site of his A&W Root Beer stand, which he had opened in 1927. There are two other Marriott Hotels in Washington, the Marriott Washington and the Marriott-Key Bridge.

The Marriott Corporation is the largest private employer in Washington.

Mayflower Hotel
1127 Connecticut Avenue, N.W.

This 800-room hotel was completed in 1924 and served as the site of President Calvin Coolidge's gala inauguration ball as its grand opening. The Mayflower was designed by the architectural firm of Warren and Westmore, which had previously designed New York City's Grand Central Station.

- Franklin D. Roosevelt and his family stayed in rooms 776 and 781 while waiting for Herbert Hoover and his family to vacate the White House in 1933.
- Each day, FBI Chief J. Edgar Hoover left his headquarters to have lunch at the Mayflower. He performed this ritual every working day for twenty years, until his death in 1972.
- The Mayflower has even published its own magazine.
- While the hotel's foundation was being dug, the remains of a cypress swamp were discovered.
- During World War II, in 1942, a member of a Nazi sabotage team that had landed in the U.S. on a German submarine surrendered to FBI agents in room 351.

Washington Hotel
Pennsylvania Avenue and 15th Street
This 350-room hotel was built in 1918.

Watergate
2650 Virginia Avenue, N.W.
This hotel is located next to the more famous Watergate apartment complex, which had been the site of the Democratic Headquarters. The infamous break-in occurred on the evening of September 15, 1972.

- At one time the Vatican owned stock in an Italian company that built the Watergate in 1965. In 1970 the Vatican sold their interest.
- When Attorney General John Mitchell was sentenced to prison after the Watergate break-in and cover-up, he became the highest-ranking government official ever sent to prison.
- Room 733 in the Howard Johnson Motor Inn across the street from the Watergate is where G. Gordon Liddy and E. Howard Hunt set up electronic listening devices to bug the Watergate offices of the Democrats.

Willard Hotel
14th Street and Pennsylvania Avenue
This is the most famous hotel in Washington, D.C. Located just a few blocks from the White House, it has more history associated with it than any other hotel in the city, and possibly any hotel in the nation. Author Nathaniel Hawthorne once wrote that "it may much more justly be called

the center of Washington and the Union than either the Capitol, the White House, or the State Department."

The original Willard Hotel, which consisted of a row of houses called Fuller's City Hotel, was opened in 1816. In 1850 Henry Willard purchased the houses and converted the site into a 100-room hotel, naming it after himself. A newer Willard Hotel was built on the site in 1901, standing fourteen stories high. Since 1816 there have been twelve major renovations or new buildings constructed on the site.

Opera star Jenny Lind, "the Swedish Nightingale," sang there in 1851. In 1861 Abraham Lincoln stayed there the night before his inauguration, having to wear women's clothing to sneak in. Julia Ward Howe penned "The Battle Hymn of the Republic" there one day in 1861, after Dr. James Clarke had suggested that she write a poem to be sung to the tune of "John Brown's Body." The hotel was so popular that it produced its own guidebook, titled *Willard's Guidebook to Washington*.

Mr. and Mrs. Tom Moore were the last guests to check out of the hotel before it closed in 1968. They were later the first couple to sign in at 11 A.M. on August 19, 1986, when the hotel was reopened after a $74 million renovation.

- Legend has it that Henry Clay introduced the mint julep drink to Washington at the hotel's Round Robin Bar.
- Legend says that Ulysses S. Grant coined the term "lobbyist" because the lobby of the hotel was used for many meetings. Grar had his own private dining room in the hotel.
- Calvin Coolidge stayed at the hotel while waiting to move into the White House after President Harding's death. One evening he captured a cat burglar in his room, but decided to let him go.
- First Lady Abigail Fillmore died in 1853 in the same room in which her husband, Millard Fillmore, had succeeded Zachary Taylor as President in 1850.
- Emanuel Leutze, the artist who, in 1851, painted the masterpiece *Washington Crossing the Delaware*, collapsed in front of the Willard on July 18, 1868, dying that evening.

In the 1880s some of Washington's most popular hotels were the Ebbitt House, the Metropolitan Hotel, the National Hotel, Rigg's Hotel, the Willard Hotel, and the Wormley Hotel.

Today there is no lack of hotels in Washington, from the Embassy Row, which caters to foreign visitors, to the elegant 203-room Four Seasons. Two deluxe hotels, the Jefferson and the Madison, are even named for Presidents. Hotels in Washington run from the very expensive to inexpensive. Five Holiday Inns and several Ramada Inns are convenient for families on a budget.

Cary Grant and Sophia Loren stayed at the Continental Hotel in the 1958 movie *Houseboat,* but don't look for it, because it exists only on film.

HISTORIC HOUSES

There are hundreds of beautiful historic houses in and around Washington, D.C. Unfortunately, hundreds of others have been destroyed throughout the years in order to make room for the sprawling office buildings and stores of the modern-day city. Every type of house in America is represented, including Colonial, Georgian, Victorian, Gothic revival, Romanesque revival, neo-classic, and modern. Many historic houses constructed of brick have fallen into disrepair. The most elegant row of houses in Georgetown, called Cox's Row, was built in 1805 by Colonel John Cox on the corner of N Street and 34th Streets. Houses in Washington were first given street address numbers in 1854.

Remember that some of the historic houses are private residences, and are not open to the public.

Anderson House
2118 Massachusetts Avenue, N.W.

Today's home of the Society of Cincinnati was built in 1905 by Larz Anderson. At the time of his death the house was bequeathed to the society. (See Organizations; Museums.)

Art Club of Washington
2017 I Street, N.W.

President James Monroe and his wife, First Lady Elizabeth, lived here, from his March 1817 inauguration until the refurbished White House was available in December.

Belmont House
1618 New Hampshire Avenue, N.W.

Master mason Perry Belmont built the house in 1909. In 1937 the building became the home of the Order of the Eastern Star (*see* Organizations).

Blaine Mansion
2000 Massachusetts Avenue, N.W.

Built in 1881 by newspaper editor James G. Blaine, who had served as Speaker of the House (1869–1875), U.S. Secretary of State (1881, 1889–1892) and three-time presidential candidate. The house was later owned by George Westinghouse, the millionaire inventor of the railroad airbrake.

Blair-Lee Houses
1651 Pennsylvania Avenue, N.W.
1653 Pennsylvania Avenue, N.W.

Blair House was constructed from 1824 to 1827 by Dr. Joseph Lowell, the first Surgeon General of the United States Army. It is today the President's official guest house. The building's second owner, who purchased it in 1836 for $6,500, was Francis Preston Blair. The Blair family and its descendants resided in Blair House from 1836 until 1942, at which time it was purchased by the U.S. government. President Harry S Truman and his family lived in Blair House during the renovation of the White House from 1948 to 1952. It was outside the front door of the house that on November 1, 1950, two Puerto Rican Nationalists were shot and killed after they had shot and killed a policeman. During President Jimmy Carter's term, he commuted the life sentence of one of the Puerto Ricans.

The Lee House, adjoining Blair House, was constructed in the early 1860s for the Blairs' daughter.

- It was at Blair House in April 1861 that Francis Preston Blair requested Robert E. Lee to take command of the Union Army as the inevitable war between the North and the South grew closer. Lee turned the offer down, choosing instead to accept the command of the Confederate Army.

- In 1862 David Farragut attacked New Orleans, which was being defended by Confederate forces commanded by General Mansfield Lowell, the son of Joseph Lowell, the builder of Blair House. Ironically, it was at Blair House that Farragut was given his orders to attack New Orleans, only a few months earlier.
- The Reagans stayed at Blair House while waiting for the Carters to vacate the White House, before Ronald Reagan's inauguration.

Bodisco House
3322 O Street

This house—in which Baron Alexander der Bodisco, the Russian envoy to the U.S., married teenaged Harriet Williams—later served as the Russian Embassy for many years. The facilities also feature an impressive garden.

Cedar Hill
14th and W Streets, S.W., in Anacostia

Once the home of black leader Frederick Douglass, this historical house is operated by the National Park Service and was maintained for many years by the Frederick Douglass Memorial and Historical Association.

Codman House
2145 Decatur Place, N.W.

This house was once the home of Dwight F. Davis, who served as the governor of the Philippines and who lent his name to tennis's Davis Cup, which he donated. Codman House was constructed in 1907 by Martha Codman of Boston.

Custis-Lee Mansion
(Arlington House)
Arlington National Cemetery

Built in 1802 by George Washington Parke Custis, the grandson of Martha Washington, this was the home of Robert E. Lee and his wife, Mary Ann Randolph Custis from 1831, when they inherited it, until April 20, 1861, when they chose to leave Washington for the South. In order to show contempt for Lee's decision to head the Confederate army, the federal government decided to turn the estate's grounds into a cemetery for the victims of the Civil War.

Decatur House

748 Jackson Place, N.W., in Lafayette Square

The house was built in 1818 by Commodore Stephen Decatur using the money accrued from his victories over the Barbary pirates. Before the house was finished, Commodore Decatur was killed in Bladensburg during a duel with Commodore James Barron. The house was designed by Benjamin Latrobe, who had also designed the nearby St. John's Episcopal Church. Decatur House, the first private dwelling constructed in Lafayette Square, has served throughout the years as an embassy for the British, French, and Russians.

- It was Commodore Stephen Decatur who gave the famous toast, "In her intercourse with foreign nations, may she always be in the right; but our country, right or wrong."
- The house had once served as the home of Secretary of State Martin Van Buren, who, it was rumored, would sometimes signal President Andrew Jackson at the nearby White House from the Decatur House attic window.

Dolley Madison House

Lafayette Park

Built in 1820, the Dolley Madison House served as the home of First Lady Dolley Madison until her death in 1849. The building once served as the headquarters for the famous Cosmos Club and still later as the headquarters for the National Aeronautics and Space Administration.

- A plan was actually drawn up in 1958 to have both the Dolley Madison House and the Decatur House torn down in order to replace them with government office buildings. Thanks in part to President John F. Kennedy, the two buildings were not only saved, but restored.

Dumbarton House

2715 Q Street, N.W., Georgetown

The Dumbarton House was built by Samuel Jackson, circa 1799, and remodeled by Benjamin Latrobe in 1805. Prior to 1915 the house was located 100 yards south of its present location. It was jacked up, put on rollers, and moved in order to make room for Q Street. Known as Bellevue until 1932, the Dumbarton House has served as the permanent headquarters of the National Society of Colonial Dames of America, whose efforts went into the house's restoration.

- While fleeing the White House on the evening of August 24, 1814, with as many artifacts as she could carry, including Gilbert Stuart's famous unfinished portrait of George Washington, First Lady Dolley Madison stopped at the Dumbarton House for a short time.

Dumbarton Oaks

3101 R Street, Georgetown

Dumbarton Oaks, built in 1891 by William Hammond Dorsey, was called "America's most civilized square mile." It was named for Scotland's Rock of Dumbarton, which is located in the River Clyde. The estate was designed by Beatrix Farrand on sixteen acres of land, ten of which consist of formal gardens. The house was owned and remodeled by drug manufacturer Robert Woods Bliss from 1920 to 1940. His ashes as well as those of his wife, Mildred, are buried in the rose garden. It was Mildred Bliss who, with the aid of Beatrix Ferrand, laid out and designed the estate's beautiful gardens.

In 1944 the mansion was the headquarters for the conference in which the proposals for the United Nations Charter were drawn up.

Dumbarton Oaks, which today is owned by Harvard University, has served as a museum of Byzantine jewelry and pre-Columbian art since 1963. It also has its own research library.

- Vice President John C. Calhoun once made Dumbarton Oaks his home.
- Violinist Igor Stravinsky's Concerto in E-flat was named the "Dumbarton Oaks Concerto" after it was first performed in the music room of Dumbarton Oaks.
- It was in the Dumbarton Oaks' reading room that the plans were drawn up for the Manhattan Project, which developed the atomic bomb, as well as for the Los Alamos laboratories.

Everett House

1606 23rd Street, N.W.

This estate was built in 1908 by George Oakley Totter for "The bottle top king" Edward H. Everett, who had created the bottle cap used for Coca-Cola bottles. In 1936 the Everett House was sold to the Turkish government to be used as their embassy.

Green House

1625 K Street

The Green House became a legend during the years of Prohibition, serving as a popular speakeasy.

Guston Hall
Near Mr. Vernon

Built in 1758, Guston Hall served as the home of "the father of the Constitution's Bill of Rights," George Mason, a signer of the Declaration of Independence.

Kennedy House
3217 P Street, N.W.

This house is where Senator John F. Kennedy and his bride, Jacqueline Lee Bouvier, lived.

Laird-Dunlop House
3014 N Street, N.W.

This house, also called the John Laird Mansion, was once owned by Robert Todd Lincoln, the son of President Abraham Lincoln. The house was built in 1799 by John Laird, a tobacco merchant.

Law House
6th and N Streets, S.W.

The Law House was built to serve as the honeymoon house of Thomas Law and his bride, Elizabeth Parke Custis, the granddaughter of Martha Washington, after their marriage in 1796.

Meridian House
1630 Crescent Place, N.W.

Designed by John Russell Pope, the house was constructed in 1920 by Irwin Laughlin, who later served as the U.S. Minister to Greece and Ambassador to Spain. Today the Meridian House Foundation maintains the historic structure.

Miller House
2201 Massachusetts Avenue, N.W.

Today called the Argyle Guest House, this four-story structure was designed by Paul J. Pelz and constructed in 1901. The house featured the very first garage in Washington, called an automobile house. The house features the "Farragut Window," which honors Admiral David Farragut, whom the house's owner, Commander Miller, had admired.

National Paint and Coating Association
1500 Rhode Island Avenue, N.W.

This 40-room brick building was constructed in 1876 by John Brodhead with John Fraser as the architect. In 1912 the structure was remodeled by John Russell Pope. In 1882 the National Geographic Society founder, Gardiner Greene Hubbard, bought the house as a wedding present for his daughter and her groom, inventor Alexander Graham Bell. Until 1887, the couple resided in this house, which featured the first elevator in Washington to be installed in a private dwelling.

The building served as the Russian Embassy from 1903. The embassy's hostess, Marguerite Cassini, was the mother of fashion designer Oleg Cassini and columnist Igor Cassini.

Octagon House
1799 New York Avenue, N.W.

This three-story house facing Rawlings Square, located one block west of the White House, is the oldest private mansion in Washington. Designed by architect Dr. William Thornton in 1789, and constructed between 1798 and 1800 for horsebreeder and planter Colonel John Tayloe as his "Virginia Winter" house, the house served as the living quarters of President Madison and First Lady Dolley Madison for several months in the fall and winter of 1814 and 1815 after the British had burned the White House. President James Madison signed the Treaty of Ghent in this house on February 17, 1815, concluding the War of 1812. During that war, the house had been spared the torch of the British because it was the headquarters for the French foreign ministry and flew the French flag from its roof. During the Civil War, the Octagon House served as a hospital for wounded soldiers. Since 1902 the Octagon House has been the headquarters of the American Institute of Architects.

- The Octagon House has been featured in Robert L. Ripley's "Believe It or Not!" column, stating that the house in reality has only six sides.
- Legend has it that the daughter of Colonel Tayloe's daughter who committed suicide by leaping from a staircase, haunts the house.
- At one time there was an underground tunnel that connected the Octagon House with the White House. For security reasons the tunnel has now been sealed over.

Old Soldier's Home
Webster and 3rd Streets, N.W.

Located across the street from St. Paul's, the Old Soldier's Home holds the distinction of being the oldest military retirement facility in the United

States. The cottage was built in 1842 by banker George Washington Riggs as a country house.

- Legend has it that General Winfield Scott built the facility with money that he had taken out of Mexico City during the United States' war with Mexico.

Old Stone House
3051 M Street, N.W., in Georgetown

This small two-story, four-room house built in 1765 consists of a parlor, kitchen, dining room, and bedroom, furnished with period pieces. Constructed by Christopher Layhman, it is the oldest surviving structure in Washington. Cassandra Chew purchased the house after Layhman's death in 1765, adding several rooms and a kitchen. In 1950 the house was restored by the National Park Service and has been open to the public as a museum since 1960. Prior to the purchase of the house by the National Park Service, the land nearby had been a used-car lot.

- Washington, D.C., designer Pierre L'Enfant used the Old Stone House as his headquarters during the planning of the construction of the Federal City.

Petersen House
516 10th Street, N.W.

Known today as "the house where Lincoln died," the red brick Petersen House is located across the street from Ford's Theatre. The house was owned by William and Pauline Petersen when, on the evening of April 14, 1865, President Abraham Lincoln was taken from Ford's Theatre and placed in a bed in a back room on the ground floor. Lincoln's wife, Mary Todd Lincoln, stayed in the parlor that last night of Lincoln's life.

From 1893 until 1896, Osborn H. Oldroyd featured his Collection of Lincolniana in a museum in the home. In 1896 the government purchased the house, making it a national monument. In 1928 the room in which President Lincoln died was restored.

- The bed seen today is not the real bed in which Lincoln died, but a model. The actual bed is now on display at the Chicago Historical Society Museum, in Chicago.
- The basement of the Petersen House is where Louis Schade published the *Washington Sentinel* newspaper in the late 1870s.

Surratt House
604 H Street, N.W.

The Surratt House, which is located in Washington's Chinatown, is the house in which John Wilkes Booth and three co-conspirators met to plan the assassination of several government officials, including President Abraham Lincoln. Mary Eugenia Surratt, the owner of the house, was accused of being among the conspirators and, on July 7, 1865, became the first woman hanged in the United States. Although her guilt is still questioned by some, it is known that her son John was a spy for the Confederacy.

Tayloe-Cameron House
21 Madison Place, Lafayette Square

This house was built in 1828 by Benjamin Ogle Tayloe, who had constructed the Octagon House. It was built as an annex to the Cosmos Club. The house had been nicknamed "the Little White House" while President William McKinley's advisor Mark Hanna lived there. The house was sold to the U.S. government in July 1941.

Townsend House
2121 Massachusetts Avenue

This house was built in 1899 by Richard Townsend, one-time president of the Erie and Pittsburgh Railroad. President William Howard Taft and the Marine Corps Band attended a marriage in the home in 1910. The Cosmos Club purchased the Townsend House in 1949.

Tudor Place
1644 31st Street, Georgetown

This house, which was built in 1795, was designed for the married couple of Thomas Peter and Martha Parke Custis, the granddaughter of Martha Washington.

Walsh-McLean House
2020 Massachusetts Avenue, N.W.

Built in 1903, this mansion was designed by Henry Anderson. Vinson Walsh McLean, daughter of Evalyn Walsh and Edward McLean, whose family owned the *Washington Post,* was born in the house. While living here, she purchased the famous Hope Diamond, starting a strange chain of tragic events that became known as the Hope Diamond curse.

- The Walsh-McLean House has served as the Indonesian Embassy.

Wheat Row

1313–1321 4th Street, S.W.

This row of red-brick houses—built by James Greenleaf, Robert Morris, and John Nicholson—was constructed from 1794 to 1795. It was one of Washington's first groups of row houses.

Woodrow Wilson House

2340 Q Street, N.W.

Built in 1915, this house served as President Woodrow Wilson's retirement home from 1921 until his death there in 1924. The house was a gift from Wilson to his wife, Edith, on their fifth wedding anniversary. The historic site is owned by the National Trust for Historic Preservation. On display at the house are memorabilia of World War I as well as the furnishings present when the Wilsons lived there. In the house, Woodrow Wilson slept in a bed that was a replica of Abraham Lincoln's bed in the White House. Wilson died in the replica. President Wilson's typewriter, on which he typed his famous Fourteen Points, is on display. Upon her death in the house, on December 28, 1961, his widow bequeathed the house to the United States government.

- Woodrow Wilson was the only U.S. President who lived in Washington, D.C., after his term of office had expired.

Woodley Manor

3000 Cathedral Avenue, N.W.

Constructed in 1836 by Francis Scott Key's nephew, this house was the summer home of Presidents Martin Van Buren, John Tyler, James Buchanan, and Grover Cleveland. Today the estate is used as a private school. Maret School purchased the manor in 1941.

PUBLICATIONS

Next to government, publishing is the largest industry in Washington, D.C.

BOOKS

There has never been a shortage of books emanating from Washington. Listed below are only a handful of the thousands that have been written.

- Samuel Blodgett's book *Thoughts on the Increasing Wealth and National Economy of the United States* was the first book to be published in Washington (1801).
- Washingtonian Frances Hodgson Burnett wrote the 1886 best-selling novel *Little Lord Fauntleroy*.
- William "Fishbait" Miller, the doorkeeper to the House of Representatives for twenty-eight years, had his memoirs, *Fishbait*, published in 1977.
- In 1986 Abigail McCarthy, the former wife of Senator Eugene McCarthy, and Jane Muskie, the former wife of Senator Edmund Muskie, collaborated on a Washington novel, *One Woman Lost,* which ironically told about the Vice President of the United States selling arms to Iran.
- Margaret Truman, the daughter of President Harry S Truman, has

authored a series of best-selling murder mysteries set in Washington—*Murder in the White House, Murder on Capitol Hill, Murder in the Smithsonian, Murder in the Supreme Court,* etc.

- Elliott Roosevelt, the son of Franklin D. Roosevelt, published a novel in 1984 featuring his mother, First Lady Eleanor Roosevelt, as the heroine; its title was *Murder and the First Lady.*
- Art Buchwald's series of books, taken from his popular *Washington Post* column, gives his satirical comments on aspects of life in Washington.

MAGAZINES

National Geographic
17th and M Streets

The National Geographic Society was founded in Washington by Gardiner Greene Hubbard at the Cosmos Club in 1888. The magazine's first photos appeared in 1896 and their first color photo in 1906. The magazine's traditional yellow-bordered cover was introduced in February 1910.

The magazine's founder was the father-in-law of inventor Alexander Graham Bell. In 1899 Gilbert Grosvenor, the twenty-three-year-old son-in-law of Alexander Graham Bell, was chosen as the magazine's first editor, remaining in that job until 1954.

The National Geographic Building has been the home of the society since they moved from their 16th Street headquarters in 1964. The new facilities feature the Explorers Hall of Fame on the first floor, as well as a rotating 1,100-pound globe of the Earth eleven feet in diameter, a model of the solar system, and a number of other displays open to the public.

The society issues its own award, the Hubbard Medal, and produces its own syndicated television series, "National Geographic."

Smithsonian

The Smithsonian Institution also publishes a beautiful monthly magazine, *Smithsonian,* published only for members of the Smithsonian Associates, which anyone can join by becoming a member in either the National or Resident category.

NEWSPAPERS

Washington Post

1150 15th Street, N.W.

The morning newspaper was founded on December 6, 1877, by Stilson Hutchins. In 1933 Eugene Meyer bought the newspaper for $825,000, and his son-in-law, Philip Graham, took over for him. With a daily circulation of 584,500 it is the largest publicly held U.S. firm headed by a woman, Katharine Graham, the daughter of Eugene Meyer. The *Washington Post* has its own zip code, 20071.

In 1889, to honor the newspaper's fiftieth anniversary, John Philip Sousa composed the "Washington Post March."

In 1971 the *Washington Post* published the controversial Pentagon Papers, which told the public yet another side of the Vietnam War.

The *Post*'s political cartoonist "Herblock" (Herbert Block) has won three Pulitzer Prizes.

In 1981, *Post* reporter Janet Cooke was awarded the Pulitzer Prize in journalism, only to have it taken back when it was revealed that her story on "Little Johnny" had been fabricated.

The *Post* has had a great number of columnists throughout the years, including Art Buchwald and Judith Martin (Miss Manners).

The *Washington Post* publishes a guide to Washington, D.C.

The best-known *Post* reporters are Bob Woodward and Carl Bernstein, who together broke the Watergate break-in coverup. They were portrayed by Robert Redford and Dustin Hoffman in the 1976 movie based on the pair's bestselling book, *All the President's Men.* Jason Robards, Jr., portrayed editor Benjamin Bradlee in the film.

- Mrs. Evalyn McLean, one-time owner of the *Washington Post,* was also the owner of the famed Hope Diamond, which is now on display in the Smithsonian Institution. She auctioned off the famous gem in 1933.
- *Washington Post* reviewer Paul Hume once gave Margaret Truman, the daughter of President Harry S Truman, a bad review after a musical performance. The President was so upset with Hume's review that he sent him a nasty note that later was made public.
- Kitty Kelley, the author of such biographies as *Jackie O* and *His Way,* was a researcher for the *Post* in the 1960s.
- It was the *Washington Post* that strung a banner across the front of its building reading, "Mr. President, we are ready to eat crow when you are ready to serve it," after Harry Truman had won the presidential election.

Washington Times

This newspaper, owned by Reverend Sun Myung Moon's Unification Church, began publishing in 1982.

National Era

From 1851 through 1852, this Washington paper first serialized Harriet Beecher Stowe's *Uncle Tom's Cabin,* before it was released in book form.

National Intelligencer

This, the city's first newspaper, began publication in 1801 as America's first national newspaper. It was founded by Samuel Harrison Smith, son of a member of the Continental Congress. William W. Seaton, one of the newspapers co-owners, would serve as mayor of Washington from 1840 to 1850. When the British invaded Washington in 1814, they burned the newspaper's building.

Times and Potowmack Packet

This weekly, when first published in Georgetown in 1789, became Georgetown's first newspaper.

Washington Bee

This was the first black-owned newspaper in Washington, D.C.

Washington Star

225 Virginia Avenue, S.W.

This newspaper folded after 128 years of publication. The paper was founded in 1853 and later incorporated by a special act of Congress on July 27, 1868. On April 24, 1897, *Star* reporter William W. Price became the first White House reporter. On November 18, 1902, the *Star* ran a photograph of President Theodore Roosevelt with a female bear cub. The photo inspired Morris Michton to name his new toy, the Teddy Bear.

In 1974 the newspaper was purchased by Joe Allbritton for $35 million, only to sell it to Time Inc. in 1978 for $20 million.

When the *Washington Star* folded, the files were given to the Martin Luther King Library, which now features the *Star* Library.

Washington Times-Herald

Jacqueline Bouvier was employed by this newspaper as its Inquiry Camera Girl before she married John Kennedy.

After sixty years of publishing, this newspaper ceased publication on March 17, 1954.

PRESIDENTS IN PUBLISHING

- On a July morning in 1829, newspaper reporter Anne Royall forced President John Quincy Adams to give her an interview when she sat on his clothes as he bathed in the Potomac River.*
- Franklin D. Roosevelt was once the editor of the Harvard *Crimson*.
- President Warren G. Harding was the editor of the *Star* in Marion, Ohio.
- It was the *Chicago Tribune* that ran the famous headline "Dewey Defeats Truman." Harry Truman is seen holding up the paper with the incorrect headline in a popular photograph of the time.

*This legendary story makes for good reading, but some historians have pointed out that Miss Royall couldn't have seen Adams during the summer of 1829 as his term of office had ended in March of that year.

STREETS

Washington, D.C., is divided into quadrants—N.W., N.E., S.E., and S.W.—centered at the U.S. Capitol, with some streets existing in one or more quadrants. The diagonal streets were named for the thirteen original states. Streets running east and west are lettered alphabetically beginning with A Street. W Street is followed by streets with two-syllable names, again beginning alphabetically—Adams Street, etc., through the letter W, then followed by three-syllable names—Allison Street, etc.— followed by streets named alphabetically for flowers or trees—Aspen Street, and so on. Thomas Jefferson and his commission established that the numbered streets would run north and south, while the lettered streets would run east and west.

When Pierre L'Enfant planned Washington, he had 270 miles of streets running throughout the center of the city.

In the 1870s, Mayor Alexander Shepherd's aggressive administration graded and surfaced 118 miles of city roads and 39 miles of county roads. He had water lines, gas mains, sewage lines, and sidewalks installed and 50,000 trees planted throughout the city. Shepherd's improvements caused millions of dollars of debt, which he never seemed to worry about. He has been criticized for his wild spending and praised for the city's many improvements. The numbering of Washington's buildings began in 1870.

A congressional law, passed in 1910, prevented buildings from being constructed over 20 feet higher than the width of a street, with a maximum height of 130 feet. In 1931 B Street was renamed Constitution Avenue.

STREET FACTS

- There is no J Street in Washington. It is believed that the name was omitted as an insult to the first Chief Justice, John Jay. There are also no B, X, Y, or Z Streets.
- The only state that does not have a street named for it in Washington is the state of Washington.
- Tunlaw Street is actually walnut spelled backward, a name suggested by President Ulysses S. Grant.
- Xenia Street is the only street name in Washington that begins with the letter *X*.
- 16th Street, N.W. was named Avenue of the Presidents for only one year, in 1912.

TRAFFIC CIRCLES

French architect Pierre Charles L'Enfant planned the city's traffic circles after he had observed that in the streets of Paris mobs were allowed to tear through the city unhindered. He believed that circles would slow or stop any rampaging crowds.

Constitution Avenue, previously named B Street, was once a part of the C & O Canal. The canal was filled in and paved over when it became too polluted.

Logan Circle was previously named Iowa Circle.

Dupont Circle

In the center of this circle is a fountain designed by Daniel Chester French.

Sheridan Circle

At Sheridan Circle stands the equestrian statue of General Philip H. Sheridan mounted on his favorite horse, Rienzi, erected there in 1909. It was designed by Gutzon Borglum—the man who would one day sculpt four Presidents on Mount Rushmore.

The first house built on Sheridan Circle, at 2306 Massachusetts Avenue, is the Barney Studio House, which is today a part of the National Museum of American Art.

The city has other circles, including Scott Circle, Ward Circle, De-Witte Circle, and Washington Circle. An equestrian statue of Lieutenant General Winfield Scott stands at Scott Circle and a statue of Major General Artemus Ward overlooks Ward Circle.

STREET FACTS

- At the intersection of Idaho Avenue and Massachusetts Avenue there once stood Hamilton Circle, which was eliminated when Christ Church was built there in 1967.
- The most popular street name in the United States is Park. Washington is second, Lincoln is fifth, Jefferson is eighth, Madison is tenth, Jackson is fourteenth, and Adams is twenty-fourth.
- An unwritten rule for the planning of statues placed in the circles throughout Washington is that each statue should face the White House, no matter where in Washington it was erected.

Pennsylvania Avenue

The grand avenue connecting the "President's Palace" and the "Federal House" is Pennsylvania Avenue, the most popular street in Washington, which runs between the Capitol and the White House, a little over one mile. Washington, D.C.'s, building codes allow the city's tallest buildings to be built on Pennsylvania Avenue.

The street was first widened from 35 feet to 160 feet in 1800 and 1801. President Andrew Jackson had Pennsylvania Avenue paved for the first time. Once referred to as the Great Serbonian Bog, the street was paved with wooden blocks in 1871. It was a Washington publisher, Mayor Alexander Shepherd, who had asphalt laid. At one time, cable cars ran down Pennsylvania Avenue, as did streetcars until the 1960s.

During President John F. Kennedy's administration, plans were drawn up to have the avenue rebuilt. The first presidential funeral procession down Pennsylvania Avenue occurred in 1841, upon the death of President William Henry Harrison, who had died in office just thirty-two days after inauguration. Electric lights were first installed on Pennsylvania Avenue in 1887. In 1896 a Duryea became the very first automobile to drive along the avenue.

Pennsylvania Avenue has been the site of many gala inaugural processions, with many distinguished foreign visitors such as the Marquis de Lafayette and Queen Elizabeth of Great Britain.

PENNSYLVANIA AVENUE FACTS

- The first First Lady to ride with her husband down Pennsylvania Avenue in a carriage was Helen Taft.
- After the assassination of President John F. Kennedy in 1963, a change of name from Pennsylvania Avenue to John F. Kennedy Avenue was seriously considered.

Parades

Washington is a city of parades. Inauguration Day, Army Day, Memorial Day, Independence Day, St. Patrick's Day, Navy Day, and Halloween are only a few good reasons for a parade.

- The city's first official parade occurred on September 18, 1793, when George Washington and a large band of dignitaries, including drummers, marched from the President's Square up to Jenkins Hill, where he laid the Capitol's cornerstone.
- A huge parade took place on Pennsylvania Avenue on October 12, 1824, to honor the national guest—the Marquis de Lafayette— during his visit to the city. Lafayette became the first of only three foreigners ever granted honorary U.S. citizenship by the Congress. The other two were Winston Churchill and Raoul Wallenberg.
- On May 23, 1865, the largest parade in the city's history occurred when Union troops, led by General George C. Meade, returning home from the Civil War, marched sixty abreast down Pennsylvania Avenue for two days and two nights. During part of the event, they paraded in front of President Andrew Johnson and General Ulysses S. Grant, who were in the reviewing stands.
- Thirteen-year-old Al Jolson, in 1898, watched a parade of American soldiers marching down Pennsylvania Avenue to the music of a fife and drum. The troops were on their way to Cuba to avenge the deaths of American sailors and marines who had died when the battleship *Maine* was sunk in the Havana harbor.
- In 1919 a temporary Arch of Triumph was constructed to span Pennsylvania Avenue at 15th Street, so that the returning U.S. doughboys, led by General John J. Pershing could march under it as they had marched beneath the real Arch of Triumph (Arc de Triomphe) in Paris. In this World War I victory parade, Union and Confederate veterans marched together for the first time.
- In 1925, 50,000 members of the Ku Klux Klan marched down Pennsylvania Avenue.
- It was during President John F. Kennedy's inauguration parade on

January 20, 1961, when the newly elected President rode up Pennsylvania Avenue, that the seeds were first planted for the President's Council on Pennsylvania Avenue, appointed on June 1, 1982. Pennsylvania Avenue at the time was comprised of drab, worndown buildings.

• The avenue has seen parades for Spanish-American War hero Admiral Dewey in 1899, for aviator Charles Lindbergh in 1927, and for astronaut John Glenn in 1962.

Constitution Avenue is the site of the annual St. Patrick's Day parade and the annual Cherry Blossom Parade. The city's silliest parade is the Annual Gross National Parade sponsored by WMAL radio for the benefit of the District of Columbia Police Boys and Girls Club. Featured are the Synchronized Precision Briefcase Drill Team, as well as many other zany groups and acts—all for fun. (See the Calendar of Events for presidential inauguration parades.)

BRIDGES

Arlington Memorial Bridge

Constructed between 1926 and 1932, this bridge, which crosses the Potomac River, was designed by the architectural firm of McKim, Mead, and White. The bridge connects Arlington National Cemetery to Washington, D.C., just west of the Lincoln Memorial. Four equestrian statues designed by American sculptors were later added to the bridge. Cast in bronze and covered in gold, they were presented to the United States as a gift from Italy.

- Although plans to construct a bridge across the Potomac to Arlington had been studied for a number of years, a huge traffic jam on Armistice Day in 1921 was the catalyst that finally caused the bridge to be built.

Cabin John Bridge

The Cabin John Bridge is a single arch of 220 feet spanning Cabin John Creek. It was designed in 1857 by Captain Thomas Meigs in order to bring water from Great Falls into Washington. On the bridge, there is a plaque with the name of the President of the United States, Abraham Lincoln, and of the President of the Confederate States of America, Jefferson Davis. This is the only location of a plaque or memorial in Washington, D.C., to Davis.

Chain Bridge

In 1797, Chain Bridge was the first bridge built across the Potomac River. Originally called Falls Bridge, it was constructed at Little Falls above Georgetown. The bridge was rebuilt in 1937 and 1938 after the previous bridge, constructed in 1874, had flooded out.

Connecticut Avenue Bridge

Built in 1931 from a design by Paul Cret, this structure replaced an earlier trolley-car bridge. Eight large urns decorate the sides of this bridge, which spans Klingle Valley.

Dumbarton Bridge (Buffalo Bridge)

This bridge, which spans Rock Creek Park, was designed by father and son team Glenn and Bedford Brown, and was completed in 1914. The architecture features twenty-eight Indian heads on each side of the structure, which were modeled after the life mask of Chief Kicking Bear. The bridge is also called the Buffalo Bridge because of the four buffaloes, designed by A. Phimister Procter, which are situated at the ends of the span.

14th Street Bridge

This bridge, which connects Washington's 14th Street with Alexandria, has undergone several name changes. Through the years it has been known as Rochambeau Bridge, George Mason Memorial Bridge, and the Central Highway Bridge.

- It was into this structure that Air Florida 90, a Boeing 737, crashed after takeoff from Washington National Airport on January 13, 1982, killing seventy-four passengers and four people on the bridge. Only five passengers were pulled alive from the icy Potomac River.

Francis Scott Key Bridge

Better known simply as Key Bridge, this span was completed in 1923 on the site of the old aqueduct bridge.

- During the Civil War the aqueduct bridge was located on this site. In order to prevent a sneak attack by the Confederates at night, the planks of the aqueduct bridge were removed each evening and replaced each morning.

Taft Bridge

This bridge, located on Connecticut Avenue, was once referred to as the "Million Dollar Bridge." It stands next to the Calvert Street Bridge.

Theodore Roosevelt Memorial Bridge

This bridge, which crosses the Potomac River as well as Theodore Roosevelt Island, was built by the District of Columbia Highway Department. It is considered by many to be a rather unattractive structure. Near the bridge is a marker at the spot where General Edward Braddock crossed the Potomac River, landing at Braddock's Rock in 1755 during the French and Indian Wars.

Woodrow Wilson Bridge

On December 28, 1961, the day on which the Woodrow Wilson Bridge was dedicated, First Lady Edith Bolling Wilson died.

WASHINGTON BRIDGE FACTS

- None of the Washington bridges have overhead structures.
- One of the world's largest displays of model bridges of every conceivable design can be seen at the Smithsonian Institution's National Museum of American History.
- It was via the Long Bridge on May 24, 1861, that the Twelfth New York Regiment became the first Union soldiers to enter Virginia during the Civil War.

MUSIC

Washington, D.C., is a town that enjoys music, from jazz, rock, and country played in the many pubs and taverns to the more sophisticated symphonies at Constitution Hall or the Kennedy Center. To the beat of military music or the opera, this city caters to everyone's tastes.

Free concerts by the Smithsonian Performing Arts take place at the National Museum of Natural History.

The National Symphony Orchestra

Founded in Washington in 1931, the orchestra performs at Constitution Hall.

National Gallery Symphony Orchestra

Usually on Thursday and Friday evenings from October to April, the Juilliard String Quartet gives concerts at the Library of Congress playing the library's Stradivarius instruments.

Other concerts in Washington are performed at: Constitution Hall; John F. Kennedy Center; Library of Congress; Lisner Auditorium; National Gallery of Art; Pavillion (Old Post Office); Phillips Art Collection; and Renwick Gallery, among other locations. Concerts are given between April and September on Saturdays at 2 P.M. at the Netherlands Carillon at the Marine Memorial in Arlington National Cemetery.

Military Bands

The Marine Corps Band was established by an act of Congress in 1798, originally consisting of one drum major, one fife major, and thirty-two drums and fifes. The United States Marine Band, which is also called "The President's Own," has played at every presidential inauguration since Thomas Jefferson's in 1801.

John Philip Sousa joined the band when he was thirteen years old, in 1868. He served with them for the next seven years, becoming their bandmaster from 1880 to 1892. His father was also a member of the Marine Band.

At formal events, both the Air Force Strolling Strings and the Army's Strings perform.

"THE STAR-SPANGLED BANNER"

Surprisingly, it wasn't until March 3, 1931, when President Herbert Hoover signed the act into law, that "The Star-Spangled Banner" became the national anthem of the United States.

- President Woodrow Wilson's daughter, Margaret Woodward Wilson, recorded a version on Columbia Records, which appeared on the *Billboard* charts on May 8, 1915.
- In 1969 Jimi Hendrix performed a controversial instrumental version of the national anthem at Woodstock.
- In some states it is against the law to dance to "The Star-Spangled Banner."

ROCK 'N' ROLL

No matter how sophisticated many Washingtonians wish to keep their music, rock 'n' roll is here to stay. President Harry S Truman called it "that damn noise they play today."

- When the rock band The Guess Who played at the White House in 1970, they were requested not to play their hit song "American Woman."
- Secretary of the Interior James Watt caused quite a controversy in 1983 when he decided that the well-known rock band, the Beach Boys, could not play at the Fourth of July celebration in Washington, because they might draw the wrong element.
- In Martha Reeves and the Vandellas' 1964 hit song "Dancing In the Street," Washington is one of the cities mentioned in the lyrics.

- Kenny Inouye, the son of Senator Daniel K. Inouye of Hawaii, was a member of the punk rock group Marginal Man.
- Bill Minkin of the Hardly-Worthit Players charted a number-20 hit novelty record in 1967 with "Wild Thing," credited to "Senator Bobby," in which Minkin does a voice parody of Senator Robert Kennedy. Two months later, he barely charted another song by "Senator Bobby," "Mellow Yellow," which peaked at number 99.

WASHINGTON MUSIC FACTS

- The Starlight Vocal Band, which in 1976 charted the hit song "Afternoon Delight," hails from Washington, D.C., where they played the clubs before becoming nationally famous. They named their first hit after the appetizers at Clyde's restaurant in Washington.
- Multi-talented Benjamin Latrobe not only designed St. John's Episcopal Church, built in 1816, but he served as its first organist.
- Mousketeer Jimmy Dodd, host of TV's "Mickey Mouse Club," wrote Washington's official song.
- In 1956 comedian Carol Burnett recorded the novelty song "I Made a Fool of Myself Over John Foster Dulles."
- Duke Ellington's first jazz band was named The Washingtonians.
- Jazz guitarist Charlie Byrd played at the city's Showboat Lounge for many years.
- Edward Rutledge Hawn, the father of actress Goldie Hawn, played violin for presidential inaugurations and for embassy parties.
- President Richard M. Nixon had a music box on his Oval Office desk, which played "Hail to the Chief" when opened.
- The only song to go to number one on *Billboard*'s record charts that was about a former U.S. Congressman was the 1955 hit, "Ballad of Davy Crockett," by Bill Hayes, who later became a TV soap star.
- The only song to go to number one on *Billboard*'s record charts that was about a future American President was the 1959 hit song "The Battle of New Orleans" by Johnny Horton.
- Senator Everett Dirksen's recording of "Gallant Men" reached number 29 on the *Billboard* "Hot 100" record chart in January 1967.

PRESIDENTIAL MUSIC:

- The official song of the President of the United States is "Hail to the Chief," with words by Sir Walter Scott from "The Lady of the Lake,

Canto II." The Vice President's official song is "Hail Columbia," which was, ironically, written to the melody of "The President's March," composed in 1789 by Philip Phile.

- Thomas Jefferson enjoyed playing his violin, as much as four hours a day.
- President Abraham Lincoln was a lover of music. Upon receiving news of Robert E. Lee's surrender, he ordered his own military band to play the song "Dixie." He thought it was a great song.
- One of the more popular photographs of the 1940s was of actress Lauren Bacall sitting atop of a piano being played by President Harry S Truman. His favorite song was "Home on the Range."
- President Richard M. Nixon sometimes liked to dabble at the piano; he, too, enjoyed playing "Home on the Range."

NUMBERS

1	White House telephone number, installed for President Herbert Hoover.
2 years	Length of a single term of a Representative to Congress.
4 years	Length of a single term of the President of the United States.
6th Congress	Their second session was the first congressional session to meet in Washington, D.C., November 17, 1800.
6 years	Length of a Senator's single term.
8 years old	Age limit for children to take part in the annual White House lawn Easter Egg Roll. Prior to 1970 the age limit had been twelve years old.
9	Number of judges who sit on the Supreme Court.
11	Number of gun salutes that consul generals are given.
16½ acres	Floor space of the Capitol.
19 feet	Height of the Abraham Lincoln statue in the Lincoln Memorial.
19 feet	Height of the Thomas Jefferson statue in the Jefferson Memorial.
19½ feet	Height of the *Freedom* statue on the Capitol dome.

21	Number of gun salutes that heads of state and royalty are given.
32	Number of U.S. Senators in the Sixth Congress, the first to serve in Washington, D.C.
35	Number of words in the Presidential Oath.
35	Minimum age to be elected President of the United States.
36	Number of Presidents who served the United States before the people of Washington, D.C., were allowed to vote for the President.
40	Number of original boundary stones marking the District of Columbia. Today thirty-seven of the stones remain.
53 bells	Carillon in the Gloria in Excelsis Tower in the Washington National Cathedral.
$66.66	Price per acre paid by the government to the landowners for their land in Federal City. The land for streets was donated free of charge.
80 feet	Width of Washington streets as envisioned by Pierre L'Enfant.
90 degrees	Temperature of the White House swimming pool in which President John Kennedy swam.
100	Present number of Senators, two from each of the fifty states.
100th Congress	Session of Congress that convened in early 1987.
120	Number of beds in Walter Reed Hospital when it first opened in 1908.
142	Number of fountains in the Rainbow Pool on the Mall.
160 feet	Width of Washington avenues as envisioned by Pierre L'Enfant.
196	Number of U.S. Representatives in the Sixth Congress, the first to serve in Washington.
231 feet	Diameter of the Hirshhorn Museum on the Mall.
287 feet, 5½ inches	Height of the Capitol from the East Front base to the top of the *Freedom* statue.
291	Number of government workers in Washington in 1802 (138 of which were Congressmen).
435	Number of U.S. Representatives now serving in the House.

$500	Prize money offered in 1792 for the winning design of the Federal City.
540	Number of rooms in the Capitol.
625	Number of government workers in Washington in 1829 (273 of whom were Congressmen).
650	Number of cherry trees that are located on the Potomac Park Basin in Washington Park.
4,372	Pieces in First Lady Nancy Reagan's controversial White House china collection.
5793	Masonic year engraved on the silver plate laid with the Capitol cornerstone by George Washington in 1793.

SPORTS

FACILITIES

National Guard Armory
2001 East Capitol Street, N.E.

Built in 1947, this 133,000-square-foot structure has been the home arena for basketball games, hockey games, and ice skating.

Robert F. Kennedy Stadium
East Capitol and 22nd Street, N.E.

Constructed in 1961, with a seating capacity of 55,363 people, RFK Stadium is one of only two stadiums in the United States named for the two Kennedy brothers; the other, JFK Stadium, is in Philadelphia.

Washington Center
M Street and 3rd Street, N.E.

The Washington Bullets basketball team play their home games here.

Griffith Stadium (torn down)
7th Street and Florida Avenue, N.W.

The 32,000-capacity stadium was formerly the home of the Washington Senators and the Washington Redskins. Boxing matches were held there during the summer months.

It was at Griffith Stadium, on April 14, 1910, in a game between the

Senators and the Philadelphia Phillies, that President William Howard Taft began the tradition of throwing out the first baseball of the Senators' season. He had been asked by umpire Billy Evans if he would like to throw out the first ball and the President accepted Evans's suggestion. President Taft is also credited with introducing the "seventh-inning stretch," when, during a game against the Pittsburgh Pirates, President Taft stood up to stretch himself after the seventh inning. Everyone else in the stadium stood up to see what the President was doing, and a tradition was born.

BASEBALL

Washington Senators

The Washington Senators were owned by Clark Griffith from 1911 to 1955. Senators manager and shortstop Joe Cronin, who married Griffith's daughter, was later sold by his father-in-law to the Boston Red Sox for $250,000.

From 1912 to 1933, the Senators finished in the first division sixteen times, winning three pennants—1924, 1925, and 1933—and winning their only World Series in 1924. A popular little ditty at the time was "Washington, first in war, first in peace, and last in the American League."

The team's most outstanding player was Hall of Famer Walter Johnson, who was one of two major league players to win over 300 games with over 3,000 career strikeouts. Johnson had won 416 career games and struck out 3,508 batters. He pitched for the Senators in seven of the opening-day games. He once pitched 56 scoreless innings, a record that lasted for fifty-five years.

The Senators' Goose Goslin holds the unusual record of having played in all of the Senators' World Series games (19) from 1924 to 1933, winning the World Series in 1924, against the New York Giants, but losing in 1925, against the Pirates and in 1933, against the Giants.

In 1960, after seventy-one years in Washington, the original Washington Senators moved to Minnesota and became the Twins. The Senators again became a team with the expansion of the American League, but in 1972 the team moved again, this time to become the Texas Rangers.

The last game played by the Senators, September 30, 1971, had to be forfeited to the New York Yankees, because the Washington fans ran onto the field and wouldn't allow the game to continue. The forfeited score was 9 to 0.

- Washington Senators player Pete Cassidy, on April 7, 1896, was the first baseball player to be X-rayed (his wrist), when he was a member of the Louisville Colonels.
- Senators manager Joe Cantillon umpired the first American League game played in Washington.
- On October 9, 1915, President Woodrow Wilson became the first president to throw out a baseball to open the World Series.
- In September 1928, Ty Cobb made the last hit of his career a double against the Senators.
- Songwriter Harry Ruby once played second base for the Senators in a 1931 exhibition game against the Orioles.
- Cuban Premier Fidel Castro was given a tryout with the Washington Senators, who decided to pass on him as a player.
- On September 29, 1934, Senators pitcher Syd Cohen gave up Babe Ruth's 708th career home run, his last hit in the American league.
- In 1937 the Senators featured four infielders who all batted left-handed, the only team to ever have such an infield.

Joe Kubel	First base
Buddy Myer	Second base
Buddy Lewis	Third base
Cecil Travis	Shortstop

- In a game in 1933 fifty-seven-year-old Nick Altrock pinch-hit in a game for the Senators, becoming the oldest person to appear in a major league game.
- On April 16, 1940, in the opening-day game between Washington and the Boston Red Sox, President Franklin Roosevelt threw out the first ball, hitting photographer Irving Schlossenburg.
- On April. 17, 1951, the first opening-night game in American League history occurred, when Washington played Philadelphia.
- On August 27 and 28, 1963, two Senators–Minnesota Twins games were called on account of a civil rights march in Washington.
- Hector Maestri played for the original Senators in 1960, as well as for the expansion Senators franchise in 1961. He was a pitcher and appeared in just two games, one for each franchise.
- On April 23, 1966, in a game between the Washington Senators and the Cleveland Indians, Emmett Ashford became the first black umpire in the major leagues.
- Carl Bouldin is the only man to have played in an NCAA champion-

ship team (University of Cincinnati, in 1960–1961) and pitch in the major leagues (Senators, in 1961–1964).

- Tom Brown is the only man to have played in both a major-league baseball game and the Super Bowl. In 1963 he played for the Washington Senators in sixty-one games as a first baseman and an outfielder, and played in Super Bowls I and II with the Green Bay Packers.
- On July 30, 1968, Senators shortstop Ron Hansen made an unassisted triple play.
- Bobby Allison, on September 28, 1959, became the last of the original Washington Senators to hit a homerun.
- The Senators employed an outfielder named Benjamin Harrison in 1901, while President Benjamin Harrison was in office.

BASEBALL FACTS

- Washington's first baseball team was called the Olympics.
- President John Adams was the first President to play a form of baseball.
- Abraham Lincoln played an early version of baseball, but the sport at which he excelled was wrestling.

BASKETBALL

From 1946 to 1947, the Washington Capitols were members of the National Basketball Association.

- The Washington Bullets won the NBA championship in 1978.
- 5-foot, 9-inch guard Harold Hunter was the first black player signed by the NBA. He played for the Washington Capitols.

BICYCLING

Biking is a popular sport, as well as a popular means of transportation. The first bike commuter trail in the United States was created by the National Park Service in Washington. Approximately 7,000 commuters ride their bikes in Washington each working day.

BOXING

On May 23, 1941, Griffith Stadium became the site of the first world heavyweight boxing championship bout ever fought in Washington,

D.C., when champion Joe Louis defeated Buddy Baer in the seventh round after Baer was disqualified. Baer, who was one of the first to fight Louis in the "Bum of the Month Club," had knocked Louis out of the ring, early in the fight.

- Gerald Ford coached boxing at Yale University.

FOOTBALL
Redskins

The Washington Redskins were previously known as the Boston Redskins.

The Washington Redskins won Super Bowl XVII in 1983, defeating the Miami Dolphins 27 to 17. The Redskins are the only pro champions to have a losing record in the forty-two-year history of the College All Stars vs. the Pro Champs game. They lost twice, in 1938 and in 1943.

Sammy Baugh was the NFL's top passer for six seasons with the Redskins (1937, 1940, 1943, 1945, 1947, and 1949).

The team's most famous coach was Vince Lombardi, who coached the team in 1969 and 1970. He died of cancer, at age fifty-seven, on November 3, 1970. The Super Bowl trophy is named in his honor.

- The Washington Redskins are the first pro football team to feature a fight song, "Hail to the Redskins," which was written by Barnee Breeskin.
- In 1970 Larry Brown became the first Washington Redskin to rush for over 1,000 yards.
- The T-formation became a basic part of football in December 1940, after it was used in a game between the Redskins and the Chicago Bears in a championship game, which the Bears won 73 to 0.
- High school football coach Roy C. Baker invented the down marker in 1944. He later became an army colonel and after his military career went to work for the Washington Redskins as an usher.
- The Washington Redskins were the last team in the NFL to have an all-white lineup. In 1962 they drafted Heisman Trophy-winning running back Ernie Davis, only to trade him to Cleveland for black receiver Bobby Mitchell. Also joining the team that season were black players Ron Hatcher, John Nimsby, and Leroy Jackson.
- One-time Redskins player Ernest Pinchert is the brother of noted Washington psychic Jeanne Dixon.
- On December 8, 1940, in the championship game between the Washington Redskins and the Chicago Bears, the Bears were asked

by the referees not to kick any extra points, as too many footballs were getting lost. The Bears won anyway, 73 to 0.

- In Super Bowl XVII John Riggins (number 44) gained a record 166 yards in 38 carries. He also set a record by making the longest touchdown run from scrimmage, with 43 yards.

PRESIDENTIAL FOOTBALL FACTS

- President Theodore Roosevelt once attempted to outlaw football, because during his term of office too many young men were getting killed on the gridiron.
- Calvin Coolidge coached football at Amherst College.
- Woodrow Wilson coached football at Wesleyan and at Princeton.
- Herbert Hoover coached football at Stanford University.
- Franklin D. Roosevelt played football for Groton School.
- Dwight Eisenhower, playing for West Point, was injured when he attempted to tackle Jim Thorpe of Carlisle. Eisenhower was nicknamed the "Kansas Cyclone" when he played for West Point.
- Richard M. Nixon wore jersey number 12 for Whittier College.
- Ronald Reagan wore jersey number 33 for Eureka College. He portrayed Notre Dame's George Gipp in the 1940 movie *Knute Rockne, All American.*
- Gerald Ford played center for Michigan, where he became a College All-Star. He was offered a prop contract with the Green Bay Packers and with the Detroit Lions. Instead, he became an assistant football coach at Yale.
- John F. Kennedy played football at Dexter School.
- George Musso played football in college against both Ronald Reagan and Gerald Ford.
- President Richard Nixon telephoned Miami Dolphin coach Don Shula, suggesting he use Paul Warfield in a down-and-out play against the Dallas Cowboys in the Super Bowl, in January 1972. When the play was used it failed.

GOLF

The Congressional Country Club in Bethesda, Maryland, was the site of the 1964 U.S. Open (6,900 yards, par 72). Each year the Kemper Open is played at the course.

PRESIDENTIAL GOLF FACTS

- The first golf course ever built in the Soviet Union was constructed in 1959, when president Dwight Eisenhower was to have visited; his trip was called off because Gary F. Powers' U-2 aircraft was shot down over Russia. Eisenhower often practiced his putting on the White House lawn.
- Only two Presidents have shot a hole-in-one while playing golf: Dwight Eisenhower and Gerald Ford.

HOCKEY
Washington Capitals
(American Professional Hockey League)
The Capitals played their home games at the Capitol Center from October to April.

- During the 1974–75 season the Capitals won only eight of their eighty scheduled games, recording the worst record in hockey, 8–67–5.
- During their 1975–76 season the Capitals won only eleven of their eighty scheduled games.

Eagles
(Eastern Amateur Hockey League)
This team played its home games at Riverside Stadium.

HORSE RACING
The third running of the Washington, D.C., International, held at Laurel, Maryland, on November 3, 1954, featured the first American horse race in which British royal horses have participated. Willie Snaith rode the royal steed, Landau, to last place. Eddie Arcaro won on Fisherman.

JOGGING
Washington is a city for joggers, regardless of the weather. The many parks and trails make it ideal for jogging. The Rock Creek Park features a 1.5-mile-oval route for joggers.

SOCCER

The Washington Diplomats play the game in the 55,000-seat RFK Stadium from April through August.

TENNIS

Each January, the Virginia Slims Women's Tennis Tournament is played in Washington.

TRANSPORTATION

AUTOMOBILES

As in other American cities, there is no shortage of automobiles in Washington, which also means there is a shortage of parking spaces. Rush hour is hectic and frustrating, since most government employees get out of work at the same time. Many left turns are forbidden during the rush-hour period. If you park illegally you might get the Denver boot, a device that is locked onto your front wheel and makes it impossible to move your car. Unlike most U.S. cities, Washington, D.C., has a number of traffic circles for motorists to maneuver through. As in London and some other European cities, it takes a little planning ahead to master the art of circle driving.

- On August 22, 1902, Theodore Roosevelt became the first President to ride in a horseless carriage, when he rode through the streets of Hartford, Connecticut, in a Columbia Electric Victoria.
- William Howard Taft became the first President to use automobiles while residing in the White House, in 1909.
- Warren G. Harding, in 1921, became the first President to ride in an automobile during his inauguration parade.

AVIATION

In 1861, during the Civil War, Thaddeus S. C. Lowe launched the first balloon used for military purposes when his *Intrepid* was raised over Washington so that he could see any enemy movements across the Potomac River. Thaddeus Lowe later founded the Lowe Observatory in California.

Prior to Orville and Wilbur Wright's history-making flight in 1903, Washington inventor Samuel Langley had launched several aircraft off a barge on the Potomac River. On May 6, 1896, his model "No. 5" flew for a distance of 3,000 feet. The problem with Langley's experiments was that they were models. When he did attempt to fly a full-sized aircraft, it crashed into the Potomac. For many years the Smithsonian Institution recognized only Langley's invention of the airplane and credited him with the first motor-powered flight, ignoring any of the accomplishments of the Wright brothers. The reason for the bias is understandable: Samuel Langley was the Secretary of the Smithsonian Institution. Today the Wright brothers' Flyer and Langley's model aircraft can both be seen at the National Air and Space Museum on the Mall.

College Park is the world's oldest continuously operated airport. It first served as an airport in September 1909, when the Wright brothers, Wilbur and Orville, landed their aircraft there. On October 27, the same year, on a four-minute flight at College Park, the wife of Captain Ralph Van Deman of the U.S. Army became the first woman airplane passenger in history. Her pilot was Wilbur Wright.

The first regular airmail service, operated for the U.S. Post Office by the Department of the Army, flew between Washington, D.C., and New York City every day except Sundays. It began on May 15, 1918, when Lieutenant George Boyle became the first pilot to fly the route. To honor this historic flight the Post Office Department produced a C3A Curtis Jenny biplane 24-cent postage stamp. Some were printed upside down and are now extremely rare and valuable, a single stamp selling for over $40,000.

On December 31, 1934, twenty-five-year-old Helen Richey became the first woman to fly regularly scheduled airmail. She flew between Washington, D.C., and Detroit, Michigan, in a Ford Tri-Motor transport. The following year Miss Richey was forced to retire, due to pressure from the men in the Air Line Pilots Association. She died ten years later at the age of thirty-six.

PRESIDENTIAL AVIATION FACTS

- Theodore Roosevelt was the first President to fly in an airplane, when, as an Army colonel, he flew with pilot Arch Hoxsey in St. Louis on October 11, 1920.
- The first airplane to be used by a President in office was the *Dixie Clipper* flying boat. President Franklin D. Roosevelt flew in the aircraft, nicknamed "the Flying White House," to Casablanca (which means "white house"), in January 1943.
- President Dwight D. Eisenhower was the only President to hold a pilot's license. His wife, Mamie, had a fear of flying.
- The following is a list of presidential aircraft:

Franklin D. Roosevelt	*Sacred Cow*	DC-4
Harry S Truman	*Sacred Cow*	DC-4
	Independence	Constellation
Dwight D. Eisenhower	*Columbine II*	Constellation
	Columbine III	Super Constellation
John F. Kennedy through Ronald Reagan	*Air Force One*	Boeing 707 (2 planes)

- In 1988 two Boeing 747s will be put into service as Air Force One.
- The President's U.S. Marine helicopter is called *Marine One.*
- The Vice President's call sign on *Air Force One* is Air Force Two.
- The Vice President's call sign on *Marine One* is Marine Two.
- When the present two *Air Force One* Boeing 707s aren't carrying the President, Vice President, or First Lady—or their families, they use the call signs SAM (Special Air Mission) 26000 and 27000.
- President Richard Nixon nicknamed *Air Force One* the "Spirit of '76."
- President Eisenhower's presidential airplanes, *Columbine II* and *Columbine III,* were named by Mrs. Eisenhower after the state flower of Colorado.

National Airport

Washington National Airport was built by the WPA between 1938 and 1940, on landfill from the Potomac, as the first federal airport in the United States. The airport, located on the west side of the Potomac across the river from Bollings Air Force Base, serves over 15 million passengers a year, with over 560 landings and takeoffs during each weekday. National Airport is conveniently located just 3.5 miles from downtown Washington, with both taxis and the Metro available to take people there in a matter of minutes.

- President Dwight D. Eisenhower greeted Queen Elizabeth and Prince Philip at National Airport on October 17, 1957.

Dulles International Airport

The newer, more modern Dulles International Airport, located twenty-seven miles away at Chantilly, Virginia, opened in 1962.

- On May 24, 1976, both Air France and British Airways inaugurated regularly scheduled commercial SST flights from Washington.

THE METRO

On March 27, 1976, the first 4.6 miles of the projected 100-mile Washington, D.C., Metro subway system was opened to the public. As of 1987 the Metro runs 54.5 miles, with 53 stations, carrying over 400 cars on their Red, Blue, Orange, and Yellow lines. The Metro has some of the cleanest subway stations in the United States.

- The Woodly Park/Zoo station features one of the largest escalators in the world.

RAILROAD

The first railroad in Washington, D.C., was the Baltimore & Ohio. Their depot, which was built at Second Street and Pennsylvania Avenue, was the first in Washington and one of the first in the United States. In 1852 a second B & O station was built at C Street and New Jersey Avenue. Another railroad station, the Pennsylvania Railroad Station, was built on the Mall in 1872, where the National Gallery of Art is now situated. Because the station and tracks conflicted with Pierre L'Enfant's plans for a Mall, strong suggestions were made to the Pennsylvania Railroad to relocate their facilities. In 1901 the Pennsylvania Railroad volunteered to cease operations and their tracks were removed from the then-cluttered Mall area, and the station was torn down.

Union Station, located at Massachusetts Avenue and Delaware Avenue, N.E., was built in 1908 on a budget of $5 million. It was designed by Daniel H. Burnham, who took his inspiration for the facade from the

Arch of Constantine and the interior from the Baths of Diocletian. The massive train station was planned by the McMillan Commission as its first project. The concourse, 760 feet in length, was once the largest unobstructed room under a roof in the world. Six statues over the front entrance, called *The Progress of Railroading,* were sculpted by Louis Saint-Gaudens. They are Prometheus (fire), Thales (electricity), Themis (freedom), Apollo (imagination), Ceres (agriculture), and Archimedes (mechanics). Across the street from Union Station is the Columbus Memorial Fountain, which was sculpted by Lorado Taft from 1912 to 1914. It was designed by Daniel H. Burnham.

During World War II, every twenty-four hours, 200 trains from seven different railroads arrived and departed Union Station for destinations throughout the United States.

During Union Station's glory days, from the 1920s to the 1950s, such railroads as the C & O, Seaboard, Richmond, Fredericksburg and Potomac, the B & O, the Atlantic Coastline, and the Pennsylvania Railroad all had a terminus at the very busy Union Station. Today only about fifty trains a day arrive and depart the station, mostly Amtrak trains.

Union Station is now being renovated and will open in 1988 as the National Visitors Center, featuring a shopping mall with offices. Today, Union Station serves the rail lines of the Baltimore & Ohio, the Chesapeake and Ohio, the Penn Central, Richmond, Fredericksburg and Potomac, East Washington, and the Southern railroads.

- On August 24, 1835, President Andrew Jackson was present when the first train arrived in Washington, D.C. It was the Baltimore & Ohio Railroad.
- The B & O Railroad is one of four railroads featured in the board game of Monopoly.
- On April 29, 1851, on the Baltimore & Ohio Railroad, an electric locomotive was run for the first time in the world on a test run from Washington, D.C., to Bladensburg, Maryland.
- Amtrak's Metroliner, the country's fastest passenger train, runs between New York and Washington, covering 225 miles and three stops in only two hours and fifty-nine minutes.
- William Henry Harrison was the first President-elect to arrive in Washington by train.
- Andrew Jackson became the first President to depart Washington by train at the close of his term of office. At the end of President Harry S Truman's term, he, too, left Washington by train.

- During the 1949 inauguration of Harry S Truman, rooms at the city's hotels were so few that many visitors stayed in Pullman railroad cars in the railroad yard outside Union Station.
- The wife of the designer of the Pullman car was once the owner of the old Russian Embassy.
- It was A. Philip Randolph, president of the Union of Sleeping Car Porters, who—with a planned mass march on Washington to protest segregation—influenced President Franklin D. Roosevelt to sign the Fair Employment Practices Code, which desegregated all government workers.
- Scenes from the 1951 Alfred Hitchcock thriller *Strangers on a Train* were filmed at Union Station.

CITY TRANSPORT
Streetcars
Streetcars were a colorful part of Washington's past, until their demise in 1962.

The Eckington and Soldiers Home Railway was the first electric railway founded in the District of Columbia. The first horse-drawn streetcars were introduced in 1862, lasting until 1900. In 1886 the first electric cars were put into service. Cable cars lasted in Washington only from 1890 to 1899. On January 28, 1962, the last streetcar saw service within Washington, D.C.

- Overhead wires were banned from Washington by an act of Congress, so a third conduit rail, with the power underground, had to be constructed on all streetcar lines within the District.
- Just outside the District is located the National Capital Trolley Museum, where streetcars from Germany, Austria, and Washington can be seen.
- Many of Washington's streetcars can still be ridden on in such cities as Fort Worth, Texas; Barcelona, Spain; and Sarajevo, Yugoslavia, the cities that bought them when they were sold after 1962.

Taxicabs
Washington has more independent taxicabs than any other city in the United States, with many of the drivers owning the hack that they are driving or belonging to a corporation of only a handful of vehicles. Washington taxicabs have reasonable rates and are a bargain for those who hate to walk. The prices are limited by the various zones that a trip

will involve; there is no meter. If a rider stays within one zone, the cost will be lower than that for a trip through several zones. Many cab drivers are well versed on Washington's history, and often serve as tour guides.

- A law in Washington allows taxicabs to pick up several riders, as long as they are all going in the same direction. However, everyone still pays the full price.

Tourmobiles

The National Park Service runs daily tourist coaches to eighteen major attractions. Tourists can get on and off all day with only one ticket. A half-day tour takes visitors to Mt. Vernon.

VESSELS

There have been several presidential yachts used by the Presidents. President Dwight Eisenhower's yacht was called the *Barbara Anne*. Franklin D. Roosevelt's *Sequoia* had an annual upkeep of $800,000. The *Mayflower* was used by Presidents William McKinley, Theodore Roosevelt, Howard Taft, Woodrow Wilson, Calvin Coolidge, and Warren Harding.

- The clipper ship *Mediator* brought ten boxes of gold ($541,379.63) to the United States in 1838. This was the money that James Smithson gave to the United States to found the Smithsonian Institution.
- In 1873 the steamer *Wawaset* caught fire and sank in the Potomac River. The bodies of the victims were buried in the Congressional Cemetery in Washington.
- The floating lightship laboratory *Chesapeake* is moored on the Potomac. It is a fully operating weather station and aquarium.
- On February 28, 1844, the first propeller-driven warship, the U.S.S. *Princeton,* was anchored off Mt. Vernon on the Potomac River in order to test fire a new 12-inch gun called the Peacemaker. On one firing the gun exploded, killing Secretary of State Abel P. Upshur, Secretary of the Navy Thomas W. Gilmer, and six other government officials. Eleven spectators on the vessel were wounded. President John Tyler was below deck with his future wife, Julia Gardiner, whose father, David Gardiner, was one of the victims. Former First Lady Dolley Madison, who was on board, helped nurse the wounded. The victims were buried in a vault at the Congressional Cemetery.

- On July 1893, on board the 220-foot-long *Oneida,* President Grover Cleveland underwent a secret operation for a malignant growth in the top of his mouth. The operation took place on the private yacht on the Potomac in order to ensure secrecy. The story of the operation was kept secret until 1917. The *Oneida* again became a part of history when, on the night of November 19, 1924, Hollywood director Thomas Harper Ince died on board under mysterious circumstances. One story speculates that he was shot and killed by William Randolph Hearst, owner of the vessel, who thought he was shooting comic actor Charlie Chaplin, who had been dating Hearst's love interest, actress Marion Davies. The mystery has never officially been solved.
- At Franklin Street Pier in Alexandria is berthed the destroyer U.S.S. *Laffey,* which saw action in both World War II and the Korean conflict.

TELEVISION

The following are television series that were set in Washington, D.C.

"All's Fair" (1976–77) CBS.
Starred Richard Crenna and Bernadette Peters, with Michael Keaton

"Ball Four" (1976) CBS.
Starred Jim Bouton, Ben Davidson, and Jack Somack

"The Delphi Bureau" (1972–73) ABC.
Starred Laurence Luckinbill and Anne Jeffreys

"The Farmer's Daughter" (1963–66) ABC.
Starred Inger Stevens, William Windom, and Cathleen Nesbitt

"Get Smart" (1965–70) NBC and CBS.
Starred Don Adams, Barbara Feldon, and Edward Platt

"Goodtime Girls" (1980) ABC.
Starred Annie Potts, Lorna Patterson, and Georgia Engel

"Grandpa Goes to Washington" (1978–79) NBC.
Starred Jack Albertson, Larry Linville, and Sue Ane Langdon

"Hanging In" (1979) CBS.
Starred Bill Macy, Barbara Rhodes, and Dennis Burkley

"I'm a Big Girl Now" (1980–81) ABC.
Starred Diana Canova, Danny Thomas, and Rori King

"Karen" (1975) ABC.
Starred Karen Valentine, Denver Pyle, and Charles Lane

"Mr. Smith" (1983) NBC.
Starred Leonard Frey, Tim Dunigan, and C. J. (a chimpanzee)

"Pentagon U.S.A." (1953) CBS.
Starred Addison Richards

"Scarecrow and Mrs. King" (1983–1987) CBS.
Starred Bruce Boxleitner, Kate Jackson, and Beverly Garland

"The Senator" (1970–71) NBC.
Starred Hal Holbrook, Michael Tolan, and Sharon Acker

"Stop Susan Williams" (1979) NBC.
Starred Susan Anton, Ray Walston, and Michael Swan

"Temperatures Rising" (1972–75) ABC.
Starred James Whitmore, Paul Lynde, and Cleavon Little

"That's My Mama" (1974–75) ABC.
Starred Clifton Davis and Theresa Merritt

"227" (1985–) NBC.
Starred Marla Gibbs and Hal Williams

OTHER TELEVISION FACTS:

- A pilot episode of the TV series "D.C. Cop" aired in 1986. It starred Cotten Smith and Robert Hooks as members of the Metropolitan Police Department.
- Some background scenes for the TV series "The F.B.I." (1965–74), which starred Efrem Zimbalist, Jr., as Inspector Lewis Erskine, were filmed in Washington, D.C. FBI Chief J. Edgar Hoover made it common knowledge that he thought Efrem Zimbalist, Jr., best projected his image of how all FBI agents should look and act.
- There have been several TV miniseries that were set in Washington, D.C., such as "Backstairs at the White House" (1979, NBC) and "Blind Ambition" (1979).
- Two books written by U.S. Presidents have been made into TV series: Dwight D. Eisenhower's *Crusade in Europe* and John F. Kennedy's *Profiles in Courage*. "Crusade In Europe," narrated by Westbrook Van Voorhis and Maurice Joyce, ran on ABC-TV from May 5 to October 27, 1949. "Profiles in Courage" ran on NBC from November 8, 1964, until May 9, 1965.

- Franklin D. Roosevelt was the first President to appear on television, when he made an appearance on experimental television at the 1939 New York World's Fair in Flushing Meadows.
- The first successful long-distance demonstration of television occurred between New York City and Washington, D.C., in 1927.
- Willard Scott of NBC-TV's "Today" show played Bozo the Clown on local Washington, D.C., television from 1963 to 1966. He lost out as the national Ronald McDonald because he was overweight. He was a weatherman at WRC for twenty-nine years before joining "Today" in 1980.

TELEVISION SERIES THAT ORIGINATED FROM
WASHINGTON, D.C.

"America Forum of the Air" (1950–52) NBC.
Mediated by Theodore Granik

"Behind the News with Howard K. Smith" (1959) CBS.
Hosted by Howard K. Smith

"The Big Question" (1951) CBS.
Moderated by Charles Collingwood

"Capitol Capers" (1949) NBC.
Live musical program

"Capitol Cloak Room" (1949–50) CBS.

"Current Opinion" (1947) NBC.
Hosted by Robert McCormick

"Elder Michaux" (1948–49) Dumont.
Hosted by preacher Elder Solomon Lightfoot Michaux, the pastor of the Church of God

"The Eyes Have It" (1948–49) NBC.
Moderated by Ralph McNair

"Georgetown University Forum" (1951–53) Dumont.
Moderated by Frank Blair

"The Jimmy Dean Show" (1957–58) CBS.
Hosted by singer Jimmy Dean

"Keep Posted" (1951–53) Dumont.
Moderated by Martha Roundtree

"Meet the Press" (1947–present) NBC.
Moderated by Martha Roundtree (1947–63) and Ned Brooks
(1953–65)

"Meet Your Congress" (1949–54) NBC and Dumont.
Moderated by Blair Moody

"Meet the Veep" (1953) NBC.
Regulars were Alben W. Barkley and Earl Goodwin

"Walter Compton News" (1947) Dumont.
Hosted by Walter Compton

"Pentagon" (1951–52) Dumont.

"Ray Scherer's Sunday Report" (1963) NBC.
Hosted by Ray Scherer

"The Smithsonian" (1967) NBC.
Hosted by Bill Ryan

"The Starland Vocal Band Show" (1977) CBS.
Musical series

"Story of the Week" (1948–49) NBC.
Hosted by Richard Harkness

"U.S. Marine Band" (1949) NBC.
Under the direction of Major William Santelmann

"Washington Exclusive" (1953) Dumont.
Hosted by Frank McNaughton

"Washington Report" (1951) Dumont.
Moderated by Tris Coffin

"Youth Wants to Know" (1951–54) NBC.
Moderated by Theodore Granik

TELEVISION FACTS

- The Smithsonian Institution's National Gallery of Art was the subject of a 1967 TV documentary on the NBC series "America Profile."
- Television's longest-running series is NBC's "Meet the Press," first aired on November 20, 1947. Co-creator Martha Roundtree served as its first regular moderator. She and Lawrence Spivak created the

program. On November 9, 1975, Gerald Ford became the first incumbent President to appear on the program.

- The first network-news series to originate in Washington, D.C., was the 1947 Dumont series "Walter Compton News," which was hosted by Walter Compton.
- Speaker of the House Thomas P. "Tip" O'Neill made a cameo appearance on an 1983 episode of the TV series "Cheers."
- Kermit the Frog made his television debut in 1955 on a local Washington, D.C., five-minute program called "Sam and Friends."
- Fred Grundy, who played Gopher on TV's "Love Boat," was elected as a Representative from Iowa to the 100th Congress in 1987.

PRESIDENTS AND FIRST LADIES ON TELEVISION

- In a December 1983 episode of "Dynasty," former President and Mrs. Gerald Ford appeared at a party set at the Carousel Ball.
- First Lady Betty Ford once made a cameo appearance on "The Mary Tyler Moore Show."
- During his acting days, Ronald Reagan hosted two TV series, "Death Valley Days" and "The General Electric Theater."
- First Lady Jacqueline Kennedy won an Emmy Award for a TV special she hosted "A Tour of the White House," during the 1962–63 TV season.
- Richard M. Nixon appeared on TV's "Laugh-In" on September 16, 1968, in which he spoke one line, "Sock it to me?"—which took him six takes.
- Ronald Reagan was a mystery guest on "What's My Line" on July 19, 1953.
- Eleanor Roosevelt was the Mystery Guest on "What's My Line" on October 18, 1953.
- Gerald Ford was the Mystery Guest on "What's My Line" on August 28, 1969.

MOTION PICTURES

Thousands of movies have been produced about Washington—the politicians, the Presidents, the life-style, and the intrigue of the city fascinate people. Here are but a few movies set in Washington.

D.C. Cab (1983)

Mr. T made his major acting debut in this comedy about the exploits and frustrations of taxicab drivers in the nation's capital. Singer Irene Cara appeared in the film in an acting role.

The Exorcist (1973)

Directed by William Friedkin, this horror film, based on the best-selling novel by William Peter Blatty, takes place in a house in George-town. The actual house used during the filming is located at 3600 Prospect Street.

Mr. Smith Goes to Washington (1939)

This Frank Capra-directed movie starred James Stewart as young Senator Jefferson Smith, who vows to his constituents that "I'll do nothing to disgrace the office of the United States Senate." The real U.S. Senate gave Capra strong disapproval of the film. Actor Dustin Hoffman's brother, Ronald Hoffman, appeared in a bit role. The movie, which the *New York Times* listed as one of the year's top ten pictures, was remade in 1977 as *Billy Jack Goes to Washington.*

The Day the Earth Stood Still (1951)

Considered the best science-fiction movie ever produced, this film, starring Michael Rennie and Patricia Neal, is set entirely within Washington, D.C., with Klaatu's spacecraft landing on the Ellipse in front of the White House.

Babes in Arms (1939)

This Mickey Rooney–Judy Garland musical featured a mock-up of the Capitol in the "God's Country" segment.

First Monday in October (1981)

The release date of this Walter Matthau–Jill Clayburgh movie was pushed up when reality beat out fiction and President Ronald Reagan selected Sandra Day O'Connor as the first female on the Supreme Court, before Hollywood could put Jill Clayburgh there.

OTHER WASHINGTON-RELATED FILMS

Houseboat (1958), *The Man* (1972), *The Absent-Minded Professor* (1961), *How to Succeed in Business without Really Trying* (1967), *Seven Days in May* (1964), *The President's Analyst* (1967), *All the President's Men* (1976), and *Kisses for My President* (1967), about the first woman President, also have involved Washington. Who could forget the 1977 classic *The Happy Hooker Goes to Washington?*

The Oval Office is possibly the most often constructed room in Hollywood, having appeared in a great number of films.

MOVIE FACTS

- The names of the two main characters, George and Martha, in Edward Albee's play *Who's Afraid of Virginia Woolf?* (the 1966 movie version starred Elizabeth Taylor and Richard Burton) were taken from George and Martha Washington.
- Charlton Heston has portrayed Andrew Jackson in two movies, *The President's Lady* (1953) and *The Buccaneer* (1958).
- Actor Rip Torn has portrayed three Presidents on film: Richard M.

Nixon in *Blind Ambition* (1979 TV); Lyndon Johnson in *J. Edgar Hoover* (1987 TV); and Ulysses S. Grant in *The Blue and the Gray* (1982 TV).

PRESIDENTIAL MOVIE FACTS

- Theodore Roosevelt appeared as himself in a Matty Roubert one-reel comedy in 1908.
- D. W. Griffith's spectacular *Birth of a Nation* was the first movie to be shown at the White House, when Woodrow Wilson watched it on February 15, 1916.
- Both Theodore Roosevelt and Woodrow Wilson made guest appearances in the 1917 film *Womanhood: The Glory of a Nation*.
- John F. Kennedy's father, Joseph Kennedy, Sr., was a founder of RKO Pictures in the 1920s.
- President Franklin Delano Roosevelt created the story upon which the 1936 movie *The President's Mystery* was based.
- Franklin Roosevelt's son James was a motion picture executive in Hollywood in the 1950s.
- First Lady Pat Nixon had appeared in *The Great Ziegfeld,* winner of the 1936 Academy Award for Best Picture, only to have her scene edited out.
- The Quaker family featured in the 1956 movie *Friendly Persuasion* was actually based on the ancestors of Richard M. Nixon.
- During their movie careers, President Ronald Reagan and First Lady Nancy Davis Reagan appeared in one film together, *Hellcats of the Navy* (1957).
- Ronald Reagan's first wife, Jane Wyman, won the Academy Award for Best Actress for the 1948 movie *Johnny Belinda.*
- Ronald Reagan has referred to himself as "the Errol Flynn of the B movies."
- Ronald Reagan's brother Neil appeared in three Hollywood films.
- Jimmy Carter's brother Billy starred in the 1979 TV movie *Flatbed Annie and Sweetiepie: Lady Truckers.*
- Steven Ford, the son of former President Gerald Ford, played a deputy sheriff in the 1980 movie *Cattle Annie and Little Britches.*

FLAGS

There are more flags flying per building in Washington, D.C., than in any other city in the United States. Besides the prominent American flags, a variety of other colorful flags can be seen indoors and out. Each embassy flies its national flag; many states have flags flying; the Red Cross, the Post Office, churches, and organizations all fly flags in the city.

June 14, 1777, became the birthday of the Stars and Stripes as the official flag of the United States. The flag about which Francis Scott Key wrote when he penned "The Star Spangled Banner" during the War of 1812 had fifteen stripes instead of the usual thirteen, and today is on display at the National Museum of American History in Washington.

The Flag Office was created in 1955 to provide souvenir reproductions of flags that have flown over the nation's Capitol dome. Within the first year, 2,766 flags were requested. Two sizes of flags are raised over the Capitol—3 by 5 feet and 5 by 8 feet. As many as 300 flags are flown above the Capitol on any one day; each flag is officially flown, even if only for a second or two. Celebrities, such as Frank Sinatra and Boy George, have had flags flown over the Capitol in their honor.

Executive Order No. 2,390, on May 29, 1916, created the official presidential flag and, on February 7, 1936, by a congressional act, the official flag of the office of the Vice President of the United States was established.

In 1938 the District of Columbia was given its own flag. The D.C. flag consists of three red stars and two horizontal bars on a rectangular white background, patterned after George Washington's family coat of arms.

The most apparent display of the Stars and Stripes is at the Washington Monument, which has been surrounded by fifty flags flying since 1959, each representing a state of the Union.

FLAG FACTS

- Although the Stars and Stripes was accepted as the official flag of the United States in 1777, it wasn't until 1923 that the War Department finally established a set of rules for the display of the flag. The rules were adopted at a conference consisting of sixty-eight patriotic organizations in Washington.
- When the flag flies over the House or Senate chambers, night or day, it indicates that that body is in session.
- It was Francis Hopkinson, not Betsy Ross, who designed the American flag, which is based on the coat of arms of George Washington's family.
- The only day of the year on which flags are allowed to fly over the graves at Arlington National Cemetery is Memorial Day.
- The biggest flag in the world was unfurled on the Mall on Flag Day, June 14, 1980. At a cost of $850,000, the Great American Flag measured 411 feet by 211 feet and weighed 14,000 pounds.
- A flag flies both day and night over the White House, over the east and west fronts of the Capitol, at the grave of Francis Scott Key, over Fort McHenry in Baltimore, at the Little Big Horn, and on the moon.
- In New York State it is against the law to pawn a United States flag.
- It was Captain William Driver of Salem, Massachusetts, who first referred to the American flag as "Old Glory."
- "The Pledge of Allegiance," created in 1892, is credited to both Frances Bellamy and James B. Upham, an editor of *Youth's Companion*. The phrase "Under God" was added to the pledge on June 14, 1954. The Pledge of Allegiance was first introduced during the Columbus Day celebration in 1892.
- When George M. Cohan wrote the patriotic song "You're a Grand Old Flag" in 1906, he originally titled the song "You're a Grand Old Rag," from the expression that a Civil War veteran had used to describe the flag during General Pickett's charge at Gettysburg. Although Cohan meant no disrespect, he soon learned that several patriotic organizations protested calling the flag a rag, so he

changed the song's title. George M. Cohan himself sang the song in the 1932 movie *The Phantom President*.

- The fifteen-stripe flag about which Francis Scott Key wrote when he penned "The Star-Spangled Banner" was depicted on a U.S. 15-cent postage stamp.

WASHINGTON FIRSTS

No one could possibly document all of the original achievements that have sprung from the capital of the number-one country for introducing concepts, inventing machines, and creating the unusual. Listed are just a handful of some of Washington's firsts.

Agricultural journal	Agricultural Museum	1810
Airmail service	Between Washington and Philadelphia	1918
American Red Cross	Founded by Clara Barton	1881
Automatic push-button garage	Park-O-Mat	1951
Bank opened by blacks	Capital Savings Bank	1888
Boy Scouts of America	Chartered by Congress	1916
Drinking straw	Invented by Chester Stone	1886
Electric range	Invented by George B. Simpson	1859
Federally operated airport	Washington National	1941

Gramophone (disk-playing)	Emile Burliner	September 26, 1887
Miss America winner	Margaret Gorman	1921
Radio debate	WJH Radio (about Daylight Savings Time)	May 23, 1922
Toys Я Us	Founded by Charles Lazarus	1948

- In May 1844 the news that James Polk had been selected as the Democratic candidate was sent out over the telegraph from Baltimore to Washington, the first time that the telegraph had been used for political information.
- Elizabeth Cady Stanton became the first female to witness a U.S. congressional legislature in session. She had been a women's suffrage advocate.
- On July 7, 1948, six members of the Navy reserve were sworn into the regular Navy by Rear Admiral George Lucius Russell in Washington. These became the first six female members of the regular Navy.
- Benjamin Oliver Davis was the first black general in the U.S. military. His son, Benjamin Oliver Davis, Jr., became the first black general in the United States Air Force. Both were born in Washington.
- Robert C. Weaver was the first black to serve in the U.S. Cabinet, serving as the Secretary of Housing and Urban Development (HUD).

Many other "firsts" can be found throughout this book, including firsts pertaining to the Presidents, First Ladies, Congress, and Washington as a city.

TREES

The city of Washington has trees of many varieties. From the numerous trees on the Capitol grounds, complete with records of who planted each and every one and when, to the trees in the city's numerous parks, Washingtonians have an arboreal abundance. Some of the city's numerous varieties are: American holly, ginkgos, Campterdown elm, boxwood, black walnut, sassafras, spruce, bald cypress, cottonwood, magnolia, white ash, cherry, ash, basswood, redwood, fir, dogwood, bronze beech, yellowwood, English yew, Irish yew, American elm, sycamore, red oak, willow, acacia, hornbeam, locust, and ailanthus. At Lafayette Park alone, there are ninety-seven varieties of trees.

Japanese Cherry Trees

In 1912, as an act of good will, the mayor of Tokyo, Japan, sent 2,000 cherry trees to the City of Washington. Unfortunately, the first trees were infected with a disease and had to be destroyed. The good mayor then sent 2,000 newer, healthier trees to Washington, which were planted along the Tidal Basin and nearby areas. A bronze plaque commemorates the planting of the first two cherry trees on March 27, 1912, by First Lady Helen Taft and the Viscountess Chinda, wife of the Japanese Ambassador.

White House Trees

- In memory of his wife, Rachel, President Andrew Jackson had two southern magnolias planted on the White House grounds. The two trees are depicted on the back of the U.S. twenty-dollar bill.
- First Lady Grace Coolidge had a Vermont spruce planted on the White House grounds in memory of her son Calvin, Jr.
- The Carters, Jimmy and Rosalynn, planted four Georgia trees on the White House lawn, including a dogwood, a loblolly pine, and a red maple.

Capitol Trees

On the Capitol grounds are trees representing thirty-three states of the Union, nine varieties of elm and maple, and twelve varieties of oak, with California contributing a giant sequoia. On the Senate side of the Capitol grows a number of crab apple trees.

- On the Capitol grounds stands an elm tree called the Cameron elm. It was named for Senator Simon Cameron, who one morning in 1875 stopped a worker from chopping the tree down, raced back to the Senate Chamber, begged permission to speak to the Senate, and pleaded to save the elm tree.

Since the early 1900s ninety-four memorial and historic trees have been planted on the grounds. The following are a few of those memorial or historic trees:

- The first memorial tree, an American elm, was planted prior to 1800 in tribute to George Washington.
- Representative Richard Bartholdt planted the Peace Tree, a Pin oak, on April 21, 1913.
- The Mother's Tree, honoring mothers of America, a white birch, was planted on May 9, 1925.
- The Boy Scout Tree from Mt. Vernon, a white walnut, was planted on April 20, 1931.
- The War Memorial Tree, a white oak, was planted on May 30, 1946.
- The Arbor Day Tree, a Burr oak, commemorating the 75th anniversary of Arbor Day, was planted on April 10, 1947.
- In memory of the five Sullivan brothers killed on board the same ship, the *Juneau,* during World War II, five crab apple trees were planted on June 12, 1952.

- In memory of the 200th anniversary of Sequoya's birth, a redwood was planted on May 25, 1966.
- The Page School's class of 1977 planted a mountain ash on June 6, 1977, beginning a tradition for future graduation classes.

TREE FACTS

- The fictitious story of little George Washington chopping down a cherry tree and then confessing to his father, "I did it, I chopped down the cherry tree," first appeared in the fifth edition of *Life of Washington: with Curious Anecdotes, Equally Honourable to Himself and Exemplary to His Young Countrymen.* The book was by Parson Mason L. Weems, who added a few myths about the first President, the cherry tree confession being a prime example.

OUTDOOR STATUARY

In addition to the monuments, memorials, sculptures, statues, and graves already mentioned throughout this book, the majority of other outdoor statues, fountains, and memorials are listed below.

SUBJECT	SCULPTOR	LOCATION	YEAR
Acroterion Eagles	James Earle Fraser	National Archives	1935
American Farm Boy	Carl Mose	National 4-H Club	1959
American Farm Girl	Carl Mose	National 4-H Club	1961
American Legion Soldier	Adolph G. Wolters	American Legion Bldg.	1951
Alexandria Confederate Memorial	Casper Buberl	Alexandria	1889
Arlington Jaycees Creed	Una Hanbury	Wilson Boulevard	1969
Gen. José Gervasio Artigas	Juan M. Blanes	Constitution Avenue	1950
The Arts of War	Leo Friendlander	West Potomac Park	1951
The Arts of Peace	James Earle Fraser	West Potomac Park	1951

Subject	Sculptor	Location	Year
Francis Asbury	Henry Augustus Lukeman	16th Street	1924
Ascension	Rudolph A. Heintze	George Washington U.	1967
Commodore John Barry	John J. Boyle	Franklin Park	1914
Bartholdi Fountain	Frederic Auguste Bartholdi	1st Street	1876
Mary McLeod Bethune	Robert Burke	Lincoln Park	1974
William Blackstone	Paul Wayland Bartlett	Constitution Avenue	1943
Gen. Simon Bolivar	Felix W. de Weldon	18th & C Streets	1959
James Buchanan Memorial	Hans Schuler	Meridian Hill Park	1930
The Burghers of Calais	Francois Auguste Rodin	Hirshhorn Museum	1886
Edmund Burke	J. Harvard Thomas	Massachusetts Avenue	1922
Adm. Richard Byrd	Felix de Weldon	Avenue of Heroes	1961
Bishop John Carroll	Jerome Connor	Georgetown University	1912
Christ, the Light of the World	Eugene Kormendi	National Catholic Welfare Conference	1949
Cubi XV	David Smith	Universal North Bldg.	1964
Dante	Ettore Ximenes	Meridian Hill Park	1920
Joseph Darlington Fountain	Carl Paul Jennewein	Judiciary Park	1923
Jane A. Delano and Nurses	Robert Tait McKenzie	Red Cross	1933
Field Marshall John Dill	Herbert Haseltine	Arlington Cemetery	1950
Discus Thrower	replica of Greek statue by Myron	Kelly Park	1956

Subject	Sculptor	Location	Year
Adm. Samuel Dupont Memorial Fountain	Daniel Chester French	Dupont Circle	1921
Robert Emmet	Jerome Connor	Massachusetts Avenue	1917
John Ericsson Monument	James Earle Fraser	West Potomac Park	1926
The Expanding Universe Fountain	Marshall Maynard Fredericks	Department of State	1962
Adm. David Farragut	Vinnie Ream Hoxie	Farragut Square	1851
James Forrestal	Kalervo Kalio	Pentagon	1950
The Founders of the Daughters of the American Revolution	Gertrude Vanderbilt Whitney	D.A.R.	1929
Benjamin Franklin	Jacques Jouvenal	Pennsylvania Avenue	1889
James Garfield Memorial	John Quincy Adams Ward	1st Street	1887
Albert Gallatin	James Earle Fraser	Treasury Building	1947
Edward Gallaudet	Pietro Lazzari	Gallaudet College	1969
Thomas Gallaudet	Daniel Chester French	Gallaudet College	1889
Giant Anteater	Erwin French Springweiler	National Zoo	1938
James Cardinal Gibbons	Leo Lentelli	16th Street	1932
Samuel Gompers Memorial	Robert I. Aiken	Massachusetts Avenue	1933
Maj. Gen. Nathaniel Greene	Henry Kirke Brown	Stanton Square	1877
Capt. Nathan Hale	Bela Lyon Pratt	Dept. of Justice	ca. 1915
Alexander Hamilton	James Earle Fraser	Treasury Building	1923

SUBJECT	SCULPTOR	LOCATION	YEAR
Maj. Gen. Winfield Hancock	Henry Jackson Ellicott	Pennsylvania Avenue	1896
Dr. Samuel Hahnemann Memorial	Charles Henry Niehaus	Scott Circle	1900
Joseph Henry	William Wetmore Story	Smithsonian	1883
Heritage and Guardianship	James Earle Fraser	National Archives	1935
Hiawatha	Unknown	DeWitt Circle	ca. 1900
The Hiker	Theodora Alice Ruggles Kitson	Avenue of Heroes	1965
Cordell Hull	Bryant Baker	Pan American Union	1956
Queen Isabella of Spain	José Luis Sanchez	OAS Building	1966
Maj. Gen. Andrew Jackson	Clark Mills	Lafayette Park	1853
Joan of Arc	Paul Dubois	Meridian Hill Park	1922
Commodore John Paul Jones	Charles Niehaus	West Potomac Park	1912
Justice and History	Thomas Crawford	Capitol	1863
Maj. Gen. Philip Kearney	Edward Clark Potter	Arlington Cemetery	1914
Brig. Gen. Thaddeus Kosciuszko	Antoni Popiel	Lafayette Park	1910
Marquis Gilbert de Lafayette	Jean Alexandre Falguière and Marius Jean Mercié	Lafayette Park	1891
Abraham Lincoln	Lot Flannery	D Street	1868
Abraham Lincoln, Rail Joiner	Louis Slobodkin	Dept. of Interior	1940
Maj. Gen. John A. Logan	Franklin Simmons	Logan Circle	1901

SUBJECT	SCULPTOR	LOCATION	YEAR
Henry Wadsworth Longfellow	Thomas Ball and William Couper	Connecticut Avenue	1909
Martin Luther	Replica of statue by E. Reistschel	Thomas Circle	1884
The Madonna of the Trail	Auguste Leimbach	Wisconsin Avenue	1929
The Majesty of Law	Carl Paul Jennewein	Rayburn House Office	1964
Man Controlling Trade	Michael Lantz	Federal Trade Commission	1942
Guglielmo Marconi Memorial	Attilio Piccirilli	16th Street	1941
John Marshall	William Wetmore Story	Capitol Building	1884
Maj. Gen. George McClellan	Frederick MacMonnies	Connecticut Avenue	1907
Brig. Gen. James McPherson	Louis T. Rebisso	McPherson Square	1876
Andrew W. Mellon Memorial Fountain	Sidney Waugh	Constitution Avenue	1952
Minute Man	Felix de Weldon	National Guard Association	1966
Moroni	Thorlief Knapus	Mormon Church	1933
Negro Mother and Child	Maurice Glickman	Dept. of the Interior	1934
Pegasus and Bellerophon	Jacques Lipchitz	National Portrait Gallery	1967
Perry Lions	Roland Hinton Perry	Taft Bridge	1906
Brig. Gen. Albert Pike	Gaetano Trentanove	3rd and D Streets	1901
Proctor's Tigers	Alexander Proctor	16th Street	1910
Prodigal Son	Heinz Warneke	Washington Cathedral	1961

SUBJECT	SCULPTOR	LOCATION	YEAR
The Prophet	Harry Abend	Venezuelan Embassy	ca. 1960
The Prophet Daniel	Antonio Francisco Lisboa	Pan American Union	1962
Puck Fountain	Brenda Putnam	Folger Shakespeare	1932
Brig. Gen. Casimir Pulaski	Kasimiriez Chodzinski	Pennsylvania Avenue	1910
Queen Isabella	José Luis Sanchez	Pan American Union	1966
Benito Juarez	Enrique Alcaiti	Virginia Avenue	1969
Maj. Gen. John A. Rawlings	Joseph A. Bailey	Rawlins Park	1874
Maj. Walter Reed Memorial	Felix W. deWeldon	Walter Reed Hospital	1966
Maj. Gen. Comte Jean de Rochambeau	J. J. Fernand Hamar	Lafayette Park	1902
Theodore Roosevelt Memorial	Paul Manship	Roosevelt Island	1967
Dr. Benjamin Rush	Roland Hinton Perry	Naval Bureau	1904
St. Bernadette	Unknown	Franciscan Monastery	1958
St. Christopher	John J. Earley	Franciscan Monastery	1924
St. Dominic	Unknown	Dominican House	ca. 1905
St. Francis and the Turtledoves	Porfirio Rosignoli	Franciscan Monastery	ca. 1924
St. Jerome the Priest	Ivan Mestrovic	1359 Monroe Street	1954
St. Vincent De Paul	Unknown	Providence Hospital	ca. 1900
Father Godfrey Schilling	F. C. Shrady	Franciscan Monastery	1955
Lt. Gen. Winfield Scott	Henry Kirke Brown	Scott Circle	1874

SUBJECT	SCULPTOR	LOCATION	YEAR
Lt. Gen. Winfield Scott	Launt Thompson	Soldiers' Home	1873
St. Stephen	Felix W. deWeldon	St. Stephen's Church	1961
Serenity	José Clara	Meridian Hill Park	1925
The Spirit of Justice	Carl Paul Jennewein	Rayburn House Office	1964
Olive Risley Seward	John Cavanaugh	601 N. Carolina Avenue	1971
Alexander R. Shepherd	U.S. J. Dunbar	Pennsylvania Avenue	1909
Gen. Philip Sheridan	Gutzon Borglum	Sheridan Circle	1908
Maj. Gen. Friedrich Wilhelm von Steuben	Albert Jaegers	Lafayette Park	1910
Gen. William T. Sherman	Carl Rohl-Smith	15th & Pennsylvania	1903
Taras Shevchenko Memorial	Radoslav Zuk	P Street	1964
Stephenson Grand Army of the Republic Memorial	John Massey Rhind	7th and P Streets	1909
Oscar S. Straus Memorial Fountain	Adolph Weinman	14th Street	1947
Maj. Gen. George H. Thomas	John Quincy Adams Ward	Thomas Circle	1879
José Cecilio Del Valle	Juan José Sicre	Pan American Union	1967
War and Peace	Luigi Persico	Capitol	1835
Maj. Gen. Artemas Ward	Leonard Crunelle	Ward Circle	1938
Lt. Gen. George Washington	Clark Mills	Washington Circle	1860

SUBJECT	SCULPTOR	LOCATION	YEAR
Lt. Gen. George Washington	Herbert Hazeltine	Washington Cathedral	1959
Daniel Webster	Gaetano Trentanove	Scott Circle	1900
John Wesley	Arthur George Walker	Wesley Seminary	1961
John Witherspoon	William Couper	Connecticut Avenue	1909
Wrestling Bears	Heinz Warneke	National Zoo	ca. 1935

There is something magnificent about an equestrian statue that makes the rider appear larger than life. The following men and one woman have equestrian statues in Washington:

Francis Ashbury
General Simon Bolivar
Field Marshal Sir John Dill
Gen. Ulysses S. Grant
Maj. Gen. Nathanael Greene
Maj. Gen. Andrew Jackson
Joan of Arc
Maj. Gen. Philip Kearney
Maj. Gen. John Logan
Maj. Gen. George B. McClellan
Brig. Gen. James B. McPherson
Maj. Gen. Count Casimir Pulaski
Maj. Gen. Winfield Scott (two)
Gen. Philip H. Sheridan
Gen. William T. Sherman
Maj. Gen. George H. Thomas
Lt. Gen. George Washington (two)
John Wesley

Joan of Arc is the only female with an equestrian statue. Major General Winfield Scott and Lieutenant General George Washington both have two equestrian statues.

WHO'S WHO IN WASHINGTON HISTORY

Here is but a short list of men and women, in addition to those already mentioned throughout this book, who have contributed to the history of Washington, D.C.

Abbe, Cleveland

First director of the Mitchell Observatory in Cincinnati, who in 1869 organized the National Weather Service. He lived at 2017 I Street, N.W.

Abel, Joseph

Architect who designed the Shoreham Hotel (2500 Calvert Street, N.W.) in 1930.

Abel, Victor D.

Architect who designed the Government Printing Office warehouse (North Capitol Street and G Place, N.E.) in 1938.

Abend, Harry (1938–   )

Sculptor of *The Prophet* in the 1960s. The statue stands on the front lawn of the Venezuelan Embassy.

Adams, Henry (1838–1918)

Great-grandson of President John Adams, grandson of President John

Quincy Adams, and son of Charles Francis Adams, Minister to Great Britain. He wrote a nine-volume history of the United States. Augustus Saint-Gaudens sculpted the memorial *Grief* that stands at the grave of Henry Adams and his wife, Clover, at the Rock Creek Cemetery.

Addison, Reverend Walter Dulany

Founder in 1796 of St. John's, the first Episcopal parish in Georgetown.

Aitken, Robert Ingersoll

Architect who, with Cass Gilbert, sculpted the pediment of the front entrance to the Supreme Court Building.

Alexander, Archer

Last black to be recaptured under the Fugitive Slave Act. His photograph was used for the model of the man on the 1876 Emancipation Monument in Washington.

Anderson, Henry

Architect of the Walsh-McLean House (2020 Massachusetts Avenue, N.W.), which was built in 1903.

Anderson, Larz and Isabel

Married couple who built the Anderson House (2118 Massachusetts Ave., N.W.) and lived there from 1902 until 1905. The house is now the Society of the Cincinnati.

Anthony, Susan B. (1820–1906)

Social reformer whose bust is in the House of Representatives Chamber in the Capitol.

Asbury, Bishop Francis (1745–1810)

Pioneer Methodist bishop. In 1924 Augustus Lukemann sculpted his equestrian statue at 16th and Mount Pleasant Streets, N.W.

Babcock, General O. E.

Architect of the bronze statue of Brigadier General James B. McPherson in McPherson Square, of the equestrian statue of Lieutenant General

Winfield Scott in Scott Circle, and of the Emancipation Monument in Lincoln Park.

Bacon, Henry

Architect of the 10-foot-tall bronze statue of Alexander Hamilton that stands in front of the Department of the Treasury.

Baird, Spencer Fullerton

First Secretary of the Smithsonian Institution.

Baker, Bryant

Sculptor of the 3-foot-high bronze bust of Cordell Hull outside the Pan American Union building.

Ball, Thomas

Sculptor of the Emancipation Monument in Lincoln Park in 1876. With William Couper, in 1909, he sculpted the bronze statue of Henry Wadsworth Longfellow located at Connecticut Avenue and M Street, N.W.

Banneker, Benjamin (1731–1806)

Black mathematician who served on Pierre L'Enfant's commission to survey the Federal City. Banneker was personally chosen for the job by George Washington.

Balch, Stephen Bloomer

Founder of the Georgetown Presbyterian Church in 1782. He served as the church's first pastor for fifty-two years.

Bartlett, Paul Wayland

Sculptor of the statue of Sir William Blackstone located on Constitution Avenue and of the Apotheosis of Democracy in front of the House of Representatives.

Baruch, Bernard

U.S. financier who was an advisor to several Presidents of the United States. There is a bench in Lafayette Park labeled "Bernard Baruch Bench of Inspiration," because he spent so much time there talking to friends.

Belmont, Perry

Grandson of Commodore Matthew C. Perry; he built the Belmont Mansion in 1909, which in 1937 became the Eastern Star Temple.

Berks, Robert

Sculptor, in 1969, of the Memorial to Robert Francis Kennedy located in the courtyard of the Department of Justice, and in 1974 of the Mary McLeod Bethune Memorial in Lincoln Park.

Bethune, Mary McLeod (1875–1955)

Leading American black educator. In 1974 a 17-foot-high bronze statue of Mary Bethune next to two students was erected in Lincoln Park.

Blair, Francis Preston

Second owner of the Blair House, originally built by Dr. Joseph Lowell.

Boone, George

Landowner after whom Georgetown was named.

Borglum, Gutzon

Artist who in 1908 sculpted the equestrian statue of General Philip H. Sheridan, as well as several other Washington statues. Between the years 1927 and 1941 he sculpted the heads of four Presidents on Mount Rushmore.

Boyle, John J.

Artist who in 1914 sculpted the statue of Commodore John Barry in Franklin Park.

Bradlee, Ben

Managing editor of the Washington Post at the time of the Watergate break-in. He is the tenth cousin once-removed of Princess Diana. Ben Bradlee was portrayed by Jason Robards, Jr., in the 1976 movie All the President's Men.

Booth, John Wilkes (1838–1865)

Actor who on April 14, 1865, assassinated President Abraham Lincoln at Ford's Theatre in Washington. Future director Raoul Walsh portrayed Booth in the 1915 movie *Birth of a Nation* and John Derek portrayed him in the 1955 movie *Prince of Players.*

Brown, Henry Kirke

Sculptor of the equestrian statue of General Winfield Scott in Scott Circle.

Brown, Dr. William

Surgeon General of the Continental Army during the Revolutionary War. His Alexandria house is located at 212 South Fairfax Street.

Bulfinch, Charles

"First American Architect." In 1818 he succeeded Benjamin Latrobe as the first American-born architect to oversee construction of the Capitol.

Bunshaft, Gordon

Architect who designed the Hirshhorn Museum.

Burnett, Frances Hodgson

Author of the novel *Little Lord Fauntleroy.* She lived at 1770 Massachusetts Avenue, N.W.

Burnham, Daniel H.

Architect who, in 1908, designed Union Station, as well as the Columbus Fountain and the *Progress of Railroading* statues, near the station. He also designed the City Post Office and the Southern Building (H Street, N.W.)

Carpenter, Francis B.

Artist whose portrait of "First Reading of the Emancipation" is hung in the west staircase of the Senate wing of the Capitol.

Carroll, Daniel

One of the eighteen original landowners in the District of Columbia. He was the commissioner whose farmhouse architect Pierre L'Enfant dismantled because it was built on a proposed park site.

Carroll, John

Founder of Georgetown University in 1789. He was America's first archbishop.

Casey, Edward Pearce

Artist, who in 1893 sculpted the "Torch of Learning" atop the Library of Congress building and who, in 1914, designed the statue of Commodore John Park in Franklin Park. He is the architect of the equestrian statue of General Ulysses S. Grant on the Mall.

Christy, Howard Chandler

Artist whose painting of *The Scene at the Signing of the Constitution* hangs at the east stairway of the House wing of the Capitol.

Clara, José

Artist who sculpted the statue *Serenity* in Meridian Hill Park.

Clem, John (1851–1937)

Last Civil War veteran to serve on active duty, retiring from the U.S. Army in 1917. He had first served as a drummer boy at age twelve. John Clem is buried at Arlington National Cemetery.

Cleveland, Esther (1893–   )

Second Daughter of Grover and Frances Cleveland. She is the only President's child to be born in the White House.

Clinton, George

First Governor of New York. He was originally buried in the Congressional Cemetery, but his remains were later moved to New York.

Coffelt, Leslie

Guard who was shot and killed by two Puerto Rican nationalists in front of Blair House on November 1, 1950. Outside the House is a plaque commemorating Coffelt.

Cluss, Adolph

Architect of the Smithsonian's Arts and Industries Building, and the Department of Agriculture building.

Connor, Jerome

Architect and sculptor in 1912 of the statue of Bishop John Carroll on the Georgetown University campus. He is the sculptor of the 7-foot statue of Robert Emmet on Massachusetts Avenue at 24th Street, N.W.

Cook, John F.

Washington's first black Presbyterian minister (1843).

Corcoran, William Wilson

"Washington's First Philanthropist." Founder of the Corcoran Gallery of Art.

Craik, Dr. James

Physician General of the Continental Army during the Revolutionary War. His Alexandria house is located at 210 Duke Street.

Cranch, William

Federal District Circuit Court judge appointed by President John Adams. He was the nephew of First Lady Abigail Adams. William Cranch served on the Washington bench for fifty-four years.

Crawford, Thomas

Designer of the bronze doors depicting the life of George Washington to the East Portico entrance to the House wing of the Capitol.

Crunelle, Leonard

Artist who in 1938 sculpted the statue of Major General Artemas Ward in Ward's Circle.

Darlington, Joseph J. (1849–1920)

Washington attorney who was much respected by his colleagues. In Judiciary Square stands a bronze statue of a nude girl and a deer, which the Washington Bar Association had erected in his honor.

Dubois, Paul

Sculptor in 1922 of the equestrian statue of Joan of Arc in Meridian Hill Park.

Ellicott, Andrew

Surveyor who laid the boundary stones of the District of Columbia, with the Capitol as the exact center.

Ellicott, Henry

Sculptor of the equestrian statue of General Winfield Hancock at 7th Street and Pennsylvania Avenue, N.W.

Emmet, Robert (1778–1803)

Irish revolutionist who was hanged by the British. A 7-foot-tall bronze statue of Emmet stands at Massachusetts Avenue and 24th Street, N.W.

Evers, Medgar (1925–1963)

Civil Rights leader. He was the first black to be admitted to the University of Mississippi. He was buried in Arlington National Cemetery, in a grave facing the Lincoln Memorial.

Falguière, Jean Alexandre Joseph, and Marius Jean Antonin Mercié

Sculptors of the statue and monument of the Marquis de Lafayette in Lafayette Park.

Fraser, James Earle

Sculptor of the bronze statue of Albert Gallatin and of the bronze statue of Alexander Hamilton that stand in front of the Department of the Treasury Building. In 1926 he sculpted the John Ericsson Monument in West Potomac Park.

Freedlander, Joseph

Architect who, in 1941, designed the Guglielmo Marconi Memorial at 16th Street and Lamont Street, N.W.

Gales, Joseph (1786–1860)

Editor and publisher of the National Intelligencer, the first daily newspaper in Washington.

Gallaudet, Dr. Thomas Hopkins

World-famous teacher of the deaf. A bronze memorial to Gallaudet by Daniel Chester French is located in Chapel Hall of Gallaudet College.

Gardner, Alexander (1821–1882)

Civil War photographer who shot many pictures that were later credited to Mathew Brady. He took the last photograph of President Abraham Lincoln, five days before he was assassinated. Gardner was buried in Glenwood Cemetery.

Gibbons, James Cardinal (1834–1921)

Head of Baltimore's Roman Catholic archdiocese, and the second American cardinal in U.S. history. He was instrumental in the founding of Catholic University. A 6-foot bronze statue of Gibbons sitting in a chair is located in front of the Shrine of the Sacred Heart.

Greenough, Horatio

Sculptor who created the statue of Washington in the National Museum of History and Technology at the request of Congress in 1832. He finished the sculpture in 1841.

Hahnemann, Dr. Samuel (1755–1843)

Founder of the science of homeopathy. In 1900 a seated statue of Hahnemann was erected in Scott Circle.

Hallet, Stephen

Runner-up in the Capitol design competition in 1792.

Harden, Julius F.

Architect who, in 1900, designed the Dr. Samuel Hahnemann Memorial in Scott Circle.

Hardenburgh, Henry

Architect who, in 1901, designed the Willard Hotel on Pennsylvania Avenue.

Hastings, Thomas

Architect, in 1912, of the memorial to Commodore John Paul Jones in West Potomac Park.

Healy, Patrick J.

First black man to head a major white university, when he became the president of Georgetown University, from 1874 to 1882. He was also the first black person to earn a Ph.D.

Henry, Joseph

First Secretary of the Smithsonian Institution. There is a statue of him on the Mall, located outside the entrance of the Castle.

Hoban, James

Designer of the Executive Mansion (White House).

Hooker, General Joseph

Civil War general. Where the District Building is now situated on Pennsylvania Avenue, General Hooker set up a row of whorehouses for his troops. The girls became known as Hookers.

Hoxie, Vinnie Ream

Sculptor, in 1881, of the 10-foot-tall statue of Admiral David G. Farragut in Farragut Square. Also, first woman to receive a U.S. commission for a work of art, the sculpture of Abraham Lincoln in the Rotunda of the Capitol.

Hunt, Richard M.

Architect who, with Thomas U. Walker in 1851, designed the dome of the Capitol.

Johnson, Mordecai W.

Educator who became the first black president of Howard University.

Jones, Thomas Hudson

Sculptor of the 50-ton memorial at the Tomb of the Unknowns in Arlington National Cemetery.

Justement, Louis

Designer of the National Guard Memorial on Massachusetts Avenue, N.W.

Kayl, George

Architect in 1932 of the statue of James Cardinal Gibbons that stands in front of the Shrine of the Sacred Heart.

Kennedy, Eugene F. (1904–1986)

Designer of the National Shrine of the Immaculate Conception.

Kennedy, Robert Francis (1925–1968)

Attorney General of the United States (1961–1964). In the courtyard of the Department of Justice there stands a life-size memorial to Kennedy. RFK Stadium is named in his honor.

Kitson, Theodora Alice Ruggles

Sculptor of the 8-foot-tall statue of *The Hiker* on the Avenue of Heroes.

Kosciuszko, Thaddeus

Polish patriot Officer in Continental Army, who designed the fortress at West Point. A statue of Kosciuszko stands in Lafayette Park.

Lafayette, Marquis Gilbert de (1787–1834)

In December 1824 Lafayette became the first foreign visitor to speak before a joint session of Congress. His Alexandria house is located at 301 South St. Asaph Street. There is an 8-foot bronze statue of him on a 36-foot-high monument in Lafayette Park.

Latrobe, Benjamin Henry (1764–1820)

Surveyor of public offices in London who, in 1796, came to the United States and was assigned by Jefferson to design the south wing of the Capitol, alterations to the White House, and other Washington buildings.

Laws, Henry

Architect who, in 1885, designed Christ Church at 31st Street and O Street, N.W.

Lentelli, Leo

Artist who, in 1932, sculpted the statue of James Cardinal Gibbons in front of the Shrine of the Sacred Heart.

Lockwood, Mrs. Belva

First woman to practice law before the Supreme Court.

Lowell, Dr. Joseph

First Surgeon General of the United States Army. He built Blair House from 1824 to 1827.

Manning, J. F.

Architect of the statue of Benjamin Franklin at Pennsylvania Avenue and 10th Street, N.W.

McMillan, James

Senator who, in 1902, presented to Congress a plan for the future development of the Capitol. He headed the McMillan Commission (Senate Park Commission).

Meigs, Montgomery Cunningham

West Point graduate who, in 1852, was appointed to create a water supply for Washington. He also designed the Old Pension Building.

Mestrovic, Ivan

Sculptor, in 1954, of *St. Jerome the Priest* at 1359 Monroe Street, N.E.

Metcalf, Louis R.

Architect of the statue of Dr. Benjamin Ruth at the Naval Bureau of Medicine and Surgery.

Mills, Clark

Architect and sculptor, in 1860, of the equestrian statue of Lieutenant General George Washington in Washington Circle.

Mills, Robert

Architect of the Washington Monument and the Treasury Building. His plan for the 1850 expansion of the Capitol was rejected.

Morse, Samuel F. B. (1791–1872)

Artist and inventor. In 1822, prior to his invention of the telegraph, he had completed several paintings of the Congress.

Morris, Commander Charles

U.S. Naval hero at Tripoli. He lived in the corner house in Georgetown's Cox's Row (N and 34th Streets).

Morton, Levi Parsons (1824–1920)

Vice President under Benjamin Harrison. He is the only Vice President to die on his brithday, May 16, 1920.

Murphy, Richard

Architect of the 1917 statue of Robert Emmet at Massachusetts Avenue and 24th Street, N.W.

Myers, George Hewitt

Founder, in 1925, of Washington's Textile Museum.

Neratrov, Alexander

Architect who designed the St. Nicholas Cathedral (3500 Massachusetts Avenue, N.W.).

Niehaus, Charles Henry

Sculptor, in 1910, of the Dr. Samuel Hahnemann Memorial in Scott Circle and, in 1912, of the memorial to Commodore John Paul Jones in West Potomac Park.

Olmstead, Frederick Law

Designer in 1872 of the grounds of the Capitol.

Orr, Douglas W.

Architect in 1915 of the statue of Nathan Hale at the Department of Justice. He is also the architect of the Robert A. Taft Memorial.

Peale, Rembrandt

Artist whose portrait of George Washington hangs in the Old Senate Chamber.

Peets, Albert

Architect of the 8-foot statue of Admiral Richard Byrd, on the Avenue of Heroes.

Perry, Roland Hinton

Sculptor who designed *The Court of Neptune* in front of the main Library of Congress building. In 1904 he sculpted the statue of Dr. Benjamin Rush at the Naval Bureau of Medicine and Surgery.

Pershing, John J. (1860–1948)

Soldier who held the highest military rank in U.S. history, General of the Armies. After the death of his favorite mount, Kidron, on October 10, 1942, he had him stuffed and put on display in the Smithsonian Museum of Natural History.

Persico, Luigi

Sculptor of the statue *War and Peace* in the Capitol's main East Portico.

Peter, Robert

First mayor of Georgetown. He was appointed in 1790.

Peterson, William

Swedish tailor who owned the house at 516 10th Street, N.W., in which President Abraham Lincoln died on the morning of April 15, 1865, across the street from Ford's Theatre.

Piccirilli, Attilio

Artist who, in 1941, sculpted the Guglielmo Marconi Memorial at 16th Street and Lamont Street, N.W.

Pike, Albert

Civil War officer. A statue of Pike stands at 3rd Street and D Street, N.W., the only statue to a Confederate officer in Washington, D.C.

Platt, Charles A.

Architect of the Freer Gallery of Art.

Plumer, William

New Hampshire Senator who cast the lone electoral vote for John Quincy Adams. James Monroe thus received all but one of the 232 electoral votes in 1820.

Potter, Edward Clark

Sculptor of the equestrian statue of Major General Philip Kearney in Arlington National Cemetery.

Pratt, Bela Lyon

Sculptor, in 1915, of the statue of Nathan Hale at the Department of Justice.

Proctor, William, Jr.

Father of American pharmacy. A statue of Proctor by Richard Burge stands in the entrance to the American Institute of Pharmacy.

Protopappas, Archie

Architect, in 1956, of St. Sophia's Greek Orthodox Cathedral (Massachusetts Avenue and 36th Street, N.W.).

Pujol, Paul

Architect, in 1891, of the statue of Major General Marquis Gilbert de Lafayette located in Lafayette Park.

Push-ma-ta-ha (–1824)

Choctaw Indian chief and commissioned officer in the U.S. Army during the War of 1812. He was buried in the Congressional Cemetery.

Randolph, James Madison

Grandson of Thomas Jefferson who, in 1805, was the first baby born in the White House.

Rankin, Kellogg, and Crane

Architects who, in 1905, designed the Department of Agriculture building at 14th Street and Independence Avenue, S.W.

Rich, Lorimer

Architect of the 50-ton memorial at the Tomb of the Unknowns.

Richardson, H. H.

Architect who, in 1885, designed the Lutheran Church Center on 16th Street, N.W.

Robbins, Warren

Founder in 1964 of the Museum of African Art.

Rodin, Francois Auguste René

Sculptor, in 1886, of the *Burghers of Calais* statue located outside the Hirshhorn Museum.

Rogers, Randolph

Designer of the Bronze Doors that depict the life of Christopher Columbus, leading to the Capitol Rotunda.

Ross, Albert

Architect who, in 1926, designed the granite memorial to John Ericsson in West Potomac Park.

Ross, Edmund G.

Republican Senator from Kansas who saved President Andrew Johnson from being impeached at his impeachment trial, when Ross cast the one vote needed.

Rush, Dr. Benjamin

First psychiatrist in the United States. A statue of Rush stands across the street from the Old Naval Observatory.

Rush, Richard

The President dispatched Rush to Britain to bring back the $500,000 that James Smithson left to the United States to establish the Smithsonian Institution.

Ruth, Babe

In the Shrine of the Immaculate Conception there is a black marble plaque honoring baseball player Babe Ruth.

Saint-Gaudens, Augustus

Designer of *Victory*, kept in the Trophy Room at the Tomb of the Unknowns, and the sculptor of the *Progress of Railroading* statue at Union Station.

Satterlee, Henry Yates

First Episcopalian bishop of Washington.

Schevchenko, Taras (1814–1861)

Russian Ukrainian poet who was exiled to Siberia. A bronze statue of Schevchenko is located at 22nd and P Streets.

Seller, Kathryn

First woman judge in the federal government when she was appointed to the Juvenile Court in Washington, D.C., in 1918.

Seward, Olive Risley

Daughter of Secretary of State William H. Seward. A statue of Olive is located in the front yard of their house at 601 North Carolina Avenue, S.E.

Shepherd, Alexander Robey "Boss" (1835–1902)

Governor of the District of Columbia. Going into great debt, he installed a sewage system, sidewalks, paved roads, and parks, and had trees planted. A statue of Shepherd stands on Pennsylvania Avenue.

Shrady, Henry Merwin

Sculptor of the equestrian statue of General Ulysses S. Grant, which was dedicated on April 27, 1922.

Sickels, Daniel

Civil War officer who, at his trial for murder, became the first defendant in U.S. court history to plead "temporary insanity," after which he was acquitted.

Simmons, Franklin

Artist who in 1877 sculpted the Peace monument, which is located on the Mall. He is also the sculptor of the 12-foot-high equestrian statue of Major General John A. Logan in Logan Circle.

Smith, Captain John

Captain Smith is believed to have been the first European to set eyes on the area which is now Washington, D.C., in 1608. He sailed his ship up the Potomac. Henry Adams once researched the John Smith–Pocahontas legend, concluding that it was no more than a work of fiction.

Stewart, J. George

Architect who added onto the east front of the Capitol building.

Story, William Wetmore

Sculptor of the bronze statue of John Marshall on the Capitol's west terrace.

Stuart, Gilbert

Artist whose set of portraits of the first five U.S. Presidents can be seen in the National Gallery of Art.

Taft, Lorado

Sculptor of the Columbus Memorial Fountain at Union Station.

Tappan, Robert

Architect who, in 1928, designed the Church of St. Stephen and the Incarnation at 16th and Newton Streets, N.W.

Thompson, Launt

Sculptor of the statue of General Winfield Scott at the Soldiers' Home.

Thornton, Dr. William (1759–1828)

Commissioner of the Federal City and first superintendent of the Patent Office, as well as a member of the District's Medical Society. Thornton was the designer of the Capitol and the Octogon House.

Tracy, Evarts

Architect who designed the equestrian statue of Francis Asbury at 16th Street and Mt. Pleasant Street, N.W.

Trentanove, Gaetano

Sculptor, in 1900, of the 12-foot statue of Daniel Webster in Scott Circle.

Turner, Henry McNeal

Pastor of the Israel African Methodist Episcopal Church. In 1863 he became the first black chaplain in the U.S. Army.

Uphues, T.

Sculptor of the statue of Frederick the Great at the Army War College.

Vaughan, Henry

Boston architect who, with George F. Bodley, in 1907 designed the Washington National Cathedral located at Wisconsin Avenue and Massachusetts Avenue, N.W.

Vernon, Edward

British Admiral for whom Lewis Washington, the brother of George Washington, named Mt. Vernon.

Walter, Thomas U.

Architect appointed by President Millard Fillmore to enlarge the Capitol, which he did from 1851 to 1865. He is the architect of the *Apotheosis of Democracy* in front of the House of Representatives.

Ward, John Quincy Adams

Sculptor of the bronze statue of Maj. Gen. George H. Thomas located in Thomas Circle.

Warnecke, John Carl

Designer of the monument at the gravesite of John F. Kennedy.

Weir, Robert

Painter of the historic *Embarkation of the Pilgrims*, on display in the Capitol Rotunda.

Weldon, Felix de

Sculptor of the 20-foot-high Minute Man in front of the National Guard Memorial and of the 8-foot-tall statue of Admiral Richard Byrd on the Avenue of Heroes, among many of his works in Washington.

White, George M.

Architect who designed the James Madison Memorial Building of the Library of Congress and the Everett Dirksen Office Building.

White, Stanford

Member of the prestigious architectural firm of McKim, Mead, and White, which renovated the White House in 1902.

Whittington, Lieutenant Julon

Medal of Honor winner during World War II, who served as the model for the statue at the American Legion Building.

Willard, Henry

Steward who bought the City Hotel in 1850, renaming it the Willard Hotel.

Williams, George Washington

America's first black historian; he wrote about Washington, D.C.

Williams, Wheeler

Sculptor of the Robert A. Taft Memorial in 1959.

Zantizinger, Borie and Medary

Architects who, in 1934, designed the Department of Justice building at 9th Street and Constitution Avenue.

QUIZZES

THE DISTRICT OF COLUMBIA

1. What was the original size of the District of Columbia before land was returned to Virginia?
2. What is the meaning of the District's motto "Justitia Omnibus"?
3. In 1967, who became the Mayor of Washington, the first black Mayor of a major U.S. city?
4. Outside the District Building stands a statue of what former territorial governor of the District?
5. What President did D.C. police officer William West once arrest for speeding in his horse and buggy?
6. What tragic event involved D.C. policewoman Gail A. Cobb in September 1974?
7. Margaret Gorman of Washington was the first woman to win what contest in 1921?
8. If the District ever achieves statehood status, what name has been suggested for the fifty-first state?
9. The per capita income of Washington is second to what state?
10. In what year were Washingtonians given the right to vote in the national elections?

THE CAPITOL

1. By what name did architect Pierre L'Enfant refer to the Capitol?
2. What is the name of the physician who designed the Capitol?
3. Who laid the cornerstone of the Capitol on September 18, 1793?
4. What state capitol building is taller than the Capitol?
5. What is the name of the 19½-foot-tall statue on the top of the Capitol's dome?
6. On what hill is the Capitol located?
7. Who was the first Speaker of the House in Washington?
8. What famous message did Samuel Morse send out on telegraph from the basement of the Capitol in 1844?
9. Who painted most of the 300-foot frieze in the Rotunda?
10. Who was the only President to have been sworn in on the west side of the Capitol?

PRESIDENTIAL INAUGURATIONS

1. In 1817, what President became the first man to have his inauguration outdoors?
2. Who was the only President to have been inaugurated in two different cities?
3. In 1853, who became the first (and only) President to use the word "affirm" in his oath?
4. At what hotel was Vice President John Tyler sworn into office?
5. In what city was Theodore Roosevelt sworn into office upon the death of President William McKinley?
6. What President was sworn into office in the House Chambers twice, in 1809 and again in 1813?
7. Besides outside the Capitol, what other three places in Washington have been the site of inaugurations?
8. Who gave the shortest inaugural speech, at just 133 words?
9. Who gave the longest inaugural speech, of 8,443 words?
10. What President was sworn into office by his father?

THE WHITE HOUSE

1. Who was the first President to live in the White House?
2. During what war did the British burn the Capitol and the White House?

3. Who submitted a design for the White House under the initials A. Z.?
4. In what city was the first presidential mansion located, at 1 Cherry Street?
5. Where did the Trumans live while the White House was being renovated from 1948 to 1952?
6. In what room have the funeral services been held for six Presidents?
7. During whose administration was the second-story porch added onto the White House, causing the twenty-dollar bill to be redesigned?
8. During whose administration was a swimming pool added to the White House grounds?
9. What is so unusual about the Zip Code of the White House?
10. What is the address of the White House?

THE SUPREME COURT

1. Prior to moving to its present building in 1935, what building did the Supreme Court call home?
2. Who was the first Chief Justice of the Supreme Court?
3. What is the time limit for an attorney arguing a case before the Supreme Court?
4. What motto is engraved above the entrance to the Supreme Court?
5. Who designed the Supreme Court building?
6. The Liberty Bell cracked while it was ringing at the funeral of what Supreme Court Justice?
7. What President selected the most Supreme Court justices since George Washington?
8. Who was the only man to have served as both President of the United States and Chief Justice of the Supreme Court?
9. Who became the first woman to sit on the Supreme Court?
10. What percentage of cases submitted to the Supreme Court does the court choose to decide on?

GOVERNMENT DEPARTMENTS AND BUILDINGS

1. What is the site of twelve government buildings formed by Pennsylvania Avenue, Constitution Avenue, and 15th Street called?
2. What is the life expectancy of a one-dollar bill?
3. Which congressional office building, constructed in 1965, features a swimming pool?

4. A father and son, Henry C. Wallace and Henry A. Wallace, both headed what cabinet post?
5. The National Aquarium is located in the basement of what government building?
6. What is the largest government building ever constructed?
7. What is the official title of the head of the Government Printing Office?
8. The U.S. Coast Guard is a branch of what department of the government?
9. Frances Perkins was the first female to head what government department?
10. Who served as the first Secretary of State?

C & O CANAL

1. What organization oversees the C & O Canal?
2. For what do the initials C & O stand?
3. The C & O Canal connected Georgetown with what other town 184 miles away?
4. What was used to propel the original barges on the canal and is still being used today?
5. What eventually caused the downfall of the C & O Canal?
6. What President was an investor in the C & O Canal?
7. From what Georgetown site does the 90-foot-long Georgetown boat leave each day?
8. What was the main cargo that the canal boats brought into Washington?
9. Why were steam vessels banned from the canal?
10. What President turned over the first shovelful of dirt to begin the construction of the C & O Canal?

CEMETERIES

1. Who once owned the land that is today Arlington National Cemetery?
2. What Polish Prime Minister is buried in Arlington?
3. Where can the inscription by Chester W. Nimitz, "Uncommon Valor was a Common Virtue," be found?
4. What country gave the United States the 49-bell carillon located near the Marine memorial?

5. In what cemetery are buried many of the Congressmen who died between the years 1807 and 1876, including Henry Clay?
6. In what cemetery can be found the graves of poet John Howard Payne and of Secretary of State Dean Acheson?
7. In what cemetery is the famous statue *Grief* featured at the grave of Henry and Clover Adams?
8. Where were Helen Keller and her teacher Annie Sullivan both buried?
9. What famous football coach died in Washington, D.C., on September 3, 1970?
10. Where is President George Washington buried?

SCHOOLS

1. What is the name of the school where the pages from the Capitol and the Supreme Court attend classes?
2. What Washington university was founded in 1887 by Cardinal James Gibbons, as a school of theology?
3. In what school building did Alexander Graham Bell make his first wireless telephone call, on June 3, 1880?
4. What school is the world's only accredited liberal arts college for the deaf?
5. America's first bishop, John Carroll, founded what university in 1789?
6. What Washington school was founded in 1821 as Columbian College?
7. What black university was founded in 1867 by a Civil War general?
8. At what college did Dwight D. Eisenhower once serve as president?
9. Who is the only U.S. President to have earned a Ph.D.?
10. What President was taught to read and write by his wife?

PARKS AND GARDENS

1. What is the name of the greenhouse home of thousands of plants, located on Capitol Hill?
2. What new park was created on the Mall next to the Reflecting Pool in time for the U.S. Bicentennial?
3. What is the name of the oval park located just south of the White House, where softball games are often played?
4. What is the name of the park across from the White House, which was originally called President's Park?

5. What park was previously named Meridian Hill Park?
6. What is the name of the National Zoological Park's most famous bear?
7. In 1972 the People's Republic of China presented the National Zoo a pair of what rare animals?
8. Who was the first person to raise jackasses in America?
9. What was the original name of Theodore Roosevelt Island, located in the middle of the Potomac River?
10. Where was the site for the first bathing beauty contest ever held in the United States, in 1921?

THEATERS

1. What theater-in-the-round was founded by producer Zelda Fichandler and built in 1960?
2. What is the name of the 4,000-seat auditorium owned by the Daughters of the American Revolution?
3. In what 10th Street theater was President Abraham Lincoln fatally shot on the evening of April 14, 1865?
4. What play was President Lincoln watching when John Wilkes Booth shot him?
5. What is the name of the sixty-four-seat movie theater in the James Madison Building of the Library of Congress?
6. What is the name of the outdoor theater located near the Washington Monument?
7. What is the name of the $72 million National Cultural Center, on which construction began in 1958?
8. At what movie theater can tourists see such films as *To Fly* and *On the Wing?*
9. What is the name of the theater at 1321 Pennsylvania Avenue, one of the oldest in Washington?
10. What Academy Award-winning actor and actress have both worked at the National Theater?

MILITARY FACILITIES

1. What Air Force base is situated on the east side of the Potomac River?
2. What U.S. Army post is situated west of Arlington National Cemetery and oversees the cemetery?

3. At what military installation is the Vice President's house located?
4. What President selected the land for the Marine Barracks, the oldest Marine post in the United States?
5. At what Air Force base is the President's aircraft, *Air Force One,* kept?
6. Who was the most famous Marine bandmaster?
7. What World War II U.S. submarine is permanently moored at the Navy Yard?
8. Actress Elizabeth Taylor was once married to what former Secretary of the Navy?
9. Secretary of the Navy Frank Knox was the father-in-law of what football great?
10. What five Presidents have been Navy men?

ORGANIZATIONS

1. What "think tank" was founded by a man who made his fortune manufacturing clothes pins?
2. First Lady Caroline Scott Harrison served as the first president-general of what organization?
3. What 2.5 million-member women's organization is associated with the Masons?
4. At what club did Ronald Reagan announce his candidacy for President on November 20, 1975?
5. "The Right of the People to Keep Arms Should Not Be Infringed" is the motto of what organization?
6. What organization is located in the historic Sewall–Belmont House?
7. What organization is made up of twenty-seven member countries in both North and South America?
8. What Ohio city was named after a society founded in Washington?
9. President Calvin Coolidge made the first national radio broadcast to the West Coast at the dedication to what organization, in 1924?
10. World War II Medal of Honor winner Lieutenant Hulon Whittington served as the model for the statue on the facade of what building?

MUSEUMS AND ART GALLERIES

1. In what museum on Jefferson Drive is James Smithson buried?
2. What is the world's most visited museum?
3. Rodin's sculpture *The Burghers of Calais* stands in front of what museum?

4. The Peacock Room, designed by James Abbott Whistler, is located in what Smithsonian museum?
5. What museum has more memorabilia related to William Shakespeare than any other museum in the world?
6. A sculpture of a dinosaur nicknamed Uncle Beazley is located outside of what museum?
7. *Time* magazine has a display of its famous covers in what Smithsonian museum?
8. At what museum can Dorothy's ruby slippers and Howdy Doody be seen on display?
9. What branch of the Smithsonian was opened in 1972 across from the White House?
10. What Washington museum has the largest collection of Russian decorative art outside the Soviet Union?

MEMORIALS AND MONUMENTS

1. Rudolph Evans sculpted the 19-foot-tall statue in what memorial?
2. What monument was hit by shellfire during World War II?
3. The son of what President of the United States has a memorial on Capitol Hill?
4. What is the tallest monument in the world?
5. What monument in Alexandria was constructed in 1932 from the contributions of over 3 million Americans?
6. Who designed the U.S. Marine monument, as well as the National Guard Memorial?
7. In Washington's Channel Park there is a monument to what famous ship?
8. Where is the Boy Scout Memorial located?
9. What memorial was designed by Maya Ying Lin?
10. What memorial fountain is in front of Union Station?

LIBRARIES

1. What library has a million volumes relating to the life and works of William Shakespeare?
2. What is the name of the main library of the District of Columbia?
3. What President lent his personal library to begin the White House library?
4. What President sold his library to begin the Library of Congress?

5. What other job did the first Librarian of the Library of Congress also hold?
6. What university library features Mark Twain's handwritten manuscript of *The Adventures of Tom Sawyer*?
7. At what Washington location can be found the world's largest collection of Masonic literature?
8. What type of library can be found at the Kennedy Center of the Performing Arts?
9. What is considered to be the Library of Congress's most valuable possession?
10. What are the names of the three Library of Congress buildings?

EMBASSIES

1. What avenue is sometimes referred to as Embassy Row?
2. What is the largest embassy building in Washington?
3. What is the second-largest embassy building in Washington?
4. Why does one foot of the statue of Sir Winston Churchill stand on British embassy soil and the other on American soil?
5. What were the first four countries to have ministers in Washington?
6. Which was the only country to have a minister in Washington during the first six months of the city's existence?
7. What flower is named after a U.S. minister to Mexico?
8. Of the seven countries to establish a permanent mission in the United States, which one has never broken diplomatic relations with the United States?
9. Who was the first reigning European monarch to visit the United States?
10. In Washington the embassy refers to the Ambassador's residence. What name is given to his offices?

HOSPITALS AND MEDICAL FACILITIES

1. What Vice President was once employed as a pharmacist?
2. At what organization is there a World War I ambulance on display?
3. Who founded the American Red Cross in 1882?
4. To what facility was President Ronald Reagan taken after he was shot on March 30, 1981?
5. Where was John Hinckley incarcerated in 1982 after he shot President Ronald Reagan?

6. At what medical facility can a tourist see John Wilkes Booth's cervical vertebrae?
7. What organization was founded in 1913 to "elevate the standard of surgery to establish a standard of competency . . . . "?
8. What late Motown superstar was born in Washington, D.C., on April 2, 1939?
9. Who was the first President to be born in a hospital?
10. Who is the only President to have studied medicine?

HOTELS

1. What large hotel chain got its start in Washington, D.C.?
2. What apartment/hotel complex was the home of the Democratic Headquarters in 1972?
3. At what Connecticut Avenue hotel did FBI Director J. Edgar Hoover eat lunch every workday?
4. What exclusive hotel has the same name as the title of a 1981 Alan Alda movie?
5. What hotel was featured in the 1974 movie *The Godfather?*
6. What famous hotel reopened for business on August 19, 1986?
7. President Ronald Reagan was shot by John Hinckley in March 1981 after Reagan had departed what hotel, where he had just made a speech?
8. After the assassination of Abraham Lincoln, in what hotel was Vice President Andrew Johnson sworn into office?
9. What song did Julia Ward Howe compose at the Willard Hotel one day in 1861?
10. Cary Grant and Sophia Loren stayed at the fictitious Continental Hotel in what 1958 movie?

HISTORIC HOUSES

1. In what Massachusetts Avenue house is the Society of Cincinnati located?
2. What famous Washington house was built by Dr. Joseph Lowell, the Army's first Surgeon General?
3. Dwight F. Davis, who lent his name to tennis's Davis Cup, once owned what house on Decatur Place?
4. By what other name is the Custis-Lee Mansion known?
5. In what Georgetown house were the proposals for the United Nations Charter drawn up in 1944?

6. What Washington first did the Miller House, constructed in 1901, feature?
7. How many sides does the Octagon House have?
8. What is the name of the house in which President Abraham Lincoln died on April 15, 1865, across from Ford's Theatre?
9. In the Woodrow Wilson House is a replica of the bed of what President?
10. In what historic house did architect Pierre L'Enfant plan out the District of Columbia?

PUBLICATIONS

1. Next to the government, what is the largest industry in Washington, D.C.?
2. What popular book published in 1886 was written by Washingtonian Frances Hodgson Burnett?
3. Inventor Alexander Graham Bell's father-in-law, Gardner Hubbard, founded what magazine in 1888?
4. For what newspaper did Carl Bernstein and Bob Woodward work when they broke the Watergate scandal?
5. What newspaper published in Arlington is the biggest-selling daily newspaper in the United States?
6. What First Lady was once employed at the *Washington Times-Herald* newspaper as the Inquiry Camera Girl?
7. What Washington museum publishes a monthly magazine?
8. What President's daughter has authored a number of murder mysteries, including *Murder in the White House*?
9. What church owns the *Washington Times*?
10. The files of what former Washington newspaper are located at the Martin Luther King Library?

STREETS

1. What is the center of Washington's four quadrants?
2. In 1931 what new name was given to B Street?
3. Down what famous thoroughfare do presidential inauguration parades travel?
4. What is the only state that does not have a street named for it in Washington?
5. What was so unusual about the streetcars that ran on Washington streets?

6. What building obstructs the view of the Capitol from the White House?
7. What Washington Mayor was instrumental in having many Washington streets paved and sidewalks built?
8. On what street does the annual St. Patrick's Day parade take place?
9. What is the wackiest parade held annually in Washington?
10. What is the most popular street name in the United States?

BRIDGES

1. On what holiday in 1921 did a traffic jam occur that finally caused the building of Memorial Bridge across the Potomac?
2. On what bridge is there a plaque to the President of the Confederate States, Jefferson Davis?
3. By what other name is the Dumbarton Bridge called?
4. Into what bridge did Air Florida 90 crash after takeoff on January 13, 1982?
5. After whom was the Key Bridge named?
6. Where can a tourist find one of the world's largest displays of model bridges?
7. What bridge, named after a President, was called "the million dollar bridge"?
8. What bridge was named after the twenty-eighth President of the United States?
9. What one thing do all the bridges in Washington lack?
10. What was the name of the first bridge built in Washington, in 1797?

SPORTS

1. At what Washington stadium do the Redskins play their home games?
2. Prior to RFK Stadium, what stadium was the home of the Washington Senators baseball team?
3. In April 1910, in a game between the Senators and the Phillies, what tradition did President William Howard Taft begin?
4. President Taft is responsible for starting what other baseball tradition?
5. Who pitched for the Senators in seven of their opening-day games?
6. In 1960 the Senators left Washington to become what new baseball team?

7. In 1972 the Senators again left Washington to become what new baseball team?
8. In what year did the Capitol Bullets win the NBA championship?
9. Whom did Joe Louis defeat to defend his heavyweight boxing title at Griffith Stadium on May 23, 1941?
10. For what two seasons did Vince Lombardi coach the Washington Redskins?

TRANSPORTATION

1. Who was the first U.S. President to ride in an automobile during his inauguration parade?
2. What Secretary of the Smithsonian tested model airplanes on the Potomac River in the late 1800s?
3. Who was the first President to fly in an airplane?
4. What was the first federally built airport in the United States?
5. What is the name of the large railroad depot in Washington?
6. What is the name of the floating lightship laboratory moored on the Potomac River?
7. What was the last year that streetcars ran in Washington?
8. What government agency operates the Tourmobiles in Washington?
9. Who was the first President to arrive in Washington on a train?
10. Who was the first President to be honored with a funeral train, which took his body back to his home state?

OUTDOOR STATUARY

1. What President has two equestrian statues showing him as a soldier?
2. Who is the only actor to have a statue in the Capitol's Hall of Fame?
3. At the Mormon Church stands a statue of what prophet?
4. Where in Washington is the site of Alexander Hamilton's statue by James Earle Fraser?
5. What "Savior of the South" was the subject of the first statue to be placed in Statuary Hall at the Capitol?
6. What is the only female equestrian statue in Washington?
7. What religious person has a statue in Statuary Hall for the state of California?
8. Whose statue is located in the center of Lafayette Park?
9. What famous statue, sculpted by Augustus Saint-Gaudens, is located over the grave of Henry and Clover Adams?

10. What Mexican-American War hero has two equestrian statues in Washington?

WHO'S WHO IN WASHINGTON HISTORY

1. Who was the original architect of the Federal City?
2. Who was the black mathematician who helped to survey Washington?
3. What famous Civil War photographer is buried in Arlington National Cemetery?
4. What poet once worked in Washington as a clerk while he searched for his brother?
5. What popular author called the Smithsonian "America's attic"?
6. Who served as the first female cabinet member in 1933, appointed by President Franklin D. Roosevelt?
7. Who, in December 1824, became the first foreign visitor to speak before a joint session of Congress?
8. Buried in Arlington National Cemetery, who was the only astronaut to have an Air Force base named for him?
9. What former U.S. Ambassador to Britain and financier bequeathed large sums of money for the museums and art of Washington?
10. Ike Hoover was employed from 1891 to 1933 at what Washington establishment as its chief usher?

ANSWERS

Answers to the District of Columbia Quiz

1. 100 square miles; 2. "Justice for all"; 3. Walter Washington; 4. Alexander Shepherd; 5. Ulysses S. Grant; 6. She became the first police-woman in the U.S. to die in the line of duty; 7. Miss America Contest; 8. New Columbia; 9. Alaska; 10. 1961.

Answers to the Capital Quiz

1. The Congress House; 2. Dr. William Thornton; 3. George Washington; 4. Austin, Texas; 5. *Freedom;* 6. Capitoline Hill or "Capitol Hill"; 7. Theodore Sedgwick; 8. "What hath God wrought?"; 9. Constantino Brumidi; 10. Ronald Reagan.

Answers to Presidential Inaugurations Quiz

1. James Monroe; 2. George Washington in New York and Philadelphia; 3. Franklin Pierce; 4. Indian Queen Hotel; 5. Buffalo, New York; 6. James Madison; 7. White House, House Chambers, and Senate Chambers; 8. George Washington; 9. William Henry Harrison; 10. Calvin Coolidge.

Answers to the White House Quiz

1. John Adams; 2. War of 1812; 3. Thomas Jefferson; 4. New York City; 5. Blair House; 6. The East Room; 7. Harry S Truman; 8. Franklin D. Roosevelt; 9. It is the only Zip Code in the country that ends in a double "00": 25000; 10. 1600 Pennsylvania Avenue.

Answers to the Supreme Court Quiz

1. Capitol Building; 2. John Jay; 3. Thirty minutes; 4. "Equal Justice Under Law"; 5. Cass Gilbert; 6. John Marshall; 7. Franklin D. Roosevelt; 8. William Howard Taft; 9. Sandra Day O'Connor; 10. 4 percent.

Answers to Government Departments and Buildings Quiz

1. The Federal Triangle; 2. Eighteen months; 3. Rayburn House Office Building; 4. Secretary of Agriculture; 5. Department of Commerce; 6. The Pentagon; 7. Mr. Public Printer; 8. Transportation; 9. Labor; 10. Thomas Jefferson.

Answers to C & O Canal Quiz

1. The National Park Service; 2. Chesapeake and Ohio; 3. Cumberland; 4. Mules; 5. The B & O Railroad; 6. George Washington; 7. The Foundry; 8. Coal; 9. Their wake eroded the sides of the canal; 10. John Quincy Adams.

Answers to Cemeteries Quiz

1. Robert E. Lee; 2. Ignace Jan Paderewski; 3. On the base of the Marine Corps War Memorial; 4. The Netherlands; 5. Congressional Cemetery; 6. Oak Hill Cemetery; 7. Rock Creek Cemetery; 8. The Washington Cathedral; 9. Vince Lombardi; 10. Mount Vernon, Virginia.

Answers to Schools Quiz

1. Capitol Page School; 2. Catholic University; 3. Franklin School; 4. Gallaudet College; 5. Georgetown University; 6. George Washington University; 7. Howard University; 8. Columbia University; 9. Woodrow Wilson; 10. Andrew Johnson.

Answers to Parks and Gardens Quiz

1. United States Botanic Gardens; 2. Constitution Gardens; 3. The Ellipse; 4. Lafayette Park; 5. Malcolm X Park; 6. Smokey the Bear; 7. Panda bears; 8. George Washington; 9. Analostan Island; 10. Tidal Basin.

Answers to Theaters Quiz

1. Arena Stage; 2. Constitution Hall; 3. Ford's Theatre; 4. *Our American Cousin;* 5. The Mary Pickford Theatre; 6. National Sylvan Theatre; 7. John F. Kennedy Center; 8. Langley Theater, National Air and Space Museum; 9. National Theatre; 10. Shirley MacLaine and Warren Beatty.

Answers to Military Facilities Quiz

1. Bolling Air Force Base; 2. Fort Myer; 3. Naval Observatory; 4. Thomas Jefferson; 5. Andrews Air Force Base; 6. John Philip Sousa; 7.

U.S.S. *Drum;* 8. John Warner; 9. Tom Harmon; 10. John F. Kennedy, Lyndon B. Johnson, Richard Nixon, Gerald Ford, and Jimmy Carter.

Answers to Organizations Quiz

1. Brookings Institute; 2. Daughters of the American Revolution; 3. Eastern Star Temple; 4. National Press Club; 5. National Rifle Association of America; 6. National Women's Party; 7. Organization of American States; 8. Cincinnati; 9. Chamber of Commerce; 10. American Legion.

Answers to Museums and Art Galleries Quiz

1. The Castle (Smithsonian); 2. National Air and Space Museum; 3. Hirshhorn Museum; 4. Freer Gallery of Art; 5. Folger Shakespeare Library; 6. National Museum of Natural History; 7. National Gallery of Art; 8. National Museum of American History; 9. Renwick Gallery; 10. Hillwood Museum.

Answers to Memorials and Monuments Quiz

1. Jefferson Memorial; 2. Lincoln Memorial; 3. William Howard Taft; 4. Washington Monument; 5. George Washington Masonic Memorial Temple; 6. Felix de Weldon; 7. *Titanic;* 8. On the Ellipse; 9. Vietnam Veteran's Memorial; 10. Columbus Memorial Fountain.

Answers to Libraries Quiz

1. Folger Shakespeare Library; 2. Martin Luther King, Jr., Memorial; 3. Millard Fillmore; 4. Thomas Jefferson; 5. Clerk of the House of Representatives; 6. Georgetown University Library; 7. Masonic Eastern Star Temple; 8. Film and theater arts; 9. The Declaration of Independence; 10. Thomas Jefferson Building, John Adams Building, and James Madison Building.

Answers to Embassies Quiz

1. Massachusetts Avenue; 2. The Soviet Union's; 3. Great Britain's; 4. His father was British and his mother was American; 5. Great Britain, France, the Netherlands, and Spain; 6. Spain; 7. Poinsettia (after Joel Poinsett); 8. Denmark; 9. King Albert of Belgium; 10. Chancery.

Answers to Hospitals and Medical Facilities Quiz

1. Hubert Humphrey; 2. American Red Cross; 3. Clara Barton; 4. George Washington University Hospital; 5. St. Elizabeth's Hospital; 6. Walter Reed General Hospital; 7. American College of Surgeons; 8. Marvin Gaye; 9. Jimmy Carter; 10. William Henry Harrison.

Answers to Hotel Quiz

1. Marriott Hotels; 2. Watergate; 3. The Mayflower Hotel; 4. The Four Seasons; 5. Hotel Washington; 6. The Willard; 7. Capital Hilton; 8. Kirkwood Hotel; 9. "The Battle Hymn of the Republic"; 10. *Houseboat.*

Answers to Historic Houses Quiz

1. Anderson House; 2. Blair-Lee House; 3. Codman House; 4. Arlington House; 5. Dumbarton Oaks; 6. A garage; 7. Six (it was misnamed); 8. Petersen House; 9. Abraham Lincoln; 10. Old Stone House.

Answers to Publications Quiz

1. Publishing; 2. *Little Lord Fauntleroy;* 3. *National Geographic Society;* 4. *Washington Post;* 5. *U.S.A. Today;* 6. Jacqueline Kennedy; 7. Smithsonian Institution; 8. Margaret Truman; 9. Reverend Sun Myung Moon's Unification Church; 10. *Washington Star.*

Answers to Streets Quiz

1. The Capitol; 2. Constitution Avenue; 3. Pennsylvania Avenue; 4. Washington; 5. They had no overhead wires; 6. Treasury Department; 7. Alexander Shepherd; 8. Constitution Avenue; 9. The Annual Gross National Parade; 10. Park.

Answers to Bridges Quiz

1. Armistice Day; 2. Cabin John Bridge; 3. Buffalo Bridge; 4. 14th Street Bridge; 5. Francis Scott Key; 6. National Museum of American History: 7. Taft Bridge; 8. Woodrow Wilson Bridge; 9. Overhead structure; 10. Chain Bridge.

Answers to Sports Quiz

1. RFK Stadium; 2. Griffith Stadium; 3. The "seventh inning stretch"; 4. Making the opening-day pitch; 5. Walter Johnson; 6. Minnesota Twins; 7. Texas Rangers; 8. 1978; 9. Buddy Baer; 10. 1969 and 1970.

Answers to Transportation Quiz

1. Warren G. Harding; 2. Samuel Langley; 3. Theodore Roosevelt; 4. National Airport, Washington; 5. Union Station; 6. *Chesapeake;* 7. 1962; 8. The National Park Service; 9. William Henry Harrison; 10. Abraham Lincoln.

Answers to Outdoor Statuary Quiz

1. George Washington; 2. Will Rogers of Oklahoma; 3. Moroni; 4. The

Treasury Department Building;   5. Nathanael Greene;   6. Joan of Arc; 7. Junipero Serra;   8. Andrew Jackson;   9. *Grief;*   10. Winfield Scott.

Answers to Who's Who in Washington History Quiz

1. Pierre L'Enfant; 2. Benjamin Banneker; 3. Mathew Brady; 4. Walt Whitman; 5. Mark Twain; 6. Frances Perkins; 7. Marquis de Lafayette; 8. Virgil Grissom (Grissom A.F.B.); 9. Andrew Mellon; 10. The White House.